T0272649

MACARTHUR RECONSIDERED

General Douglas MacArthur as a Wartime Commander

James Ellman

STACKPOLE BOOKS

Essex, Connecticut
Blue Ridge Summit, Pennsylvania

STACKPOLE BOOKS

An imprint of Globe Pequot, the trade division of
The Rowman & Littlefield Publishing Group, Inc.
4501 Forbes Blvd., Ste. 200
Lanham, MD 20706
www.rowman.com

Distributed by NATIONAL BOOK NETWORK

British Library Cataloguing in Publication Information available

Library of Congress Cataloging-in-Publication Data

978-0-8117-7158-0 (cloth)
978-0-8117-7159-7 (electronic)

♾™ The paper used in this publication meets the minimum requirements of American
National Standard for Information Sciences—Permanence of Paper for Printed Library
Materials, ANSI/NISO Z39.48-1992.

To my great uncle, Captain Alfred (Fred) Glattauer (1915–1986)

- Born in Vienna under Hapsburg rule in the early days of World War I.
- Sent into exile after the Anschluss by his parents who were forced to remain and await the grim fate of all Jews living under Nazi rule.
- Finished medical school at the University of Zurich, Switzerland, before emigrating to the United States.
- Joined the U.S. Army in 1942 and became a captain assigned to the 92nd Evacuation Hospital. He served in Hollandia, New Guinea (1944), and Luzon and Cebu in the Philippines (1945) in General MacArthur's Southwest Pacific Area.
- Married Judy Phillips, a nurse with the 92nd, on April 8, 1945, to whom he was devoted for the rest of his years.
- Returned to the United States and built a thriving medical practice in Miami and raised four children.
- A Great American.

CONTENTS

LIST OF ABBREVIATIONS

ABC-1	American-British Conversations
ABDA	American-British-Dutch-Australian
AIF	Australian Imperial Force
DPRK	Democratic People's Republic of Korea (North Korea)
FDR	Franklin Delano Roosevelt
FEAF	Far East Air Force
GI	General infantryman (U.S. Army)
GOP	Grand Old Party (U.S. Republican Party)
IJA	Imperial Japanese Army
IJN	Imperial Japanese Navy
JANPC	Joint Army and Navy Planning Committee
JCS	Joint Chiefs of Staff
KMT	Kuomintang (Chinese Nationalist Party)
KMAG	Korean Military Advisory Group
KPA	Korean People's Army (North Korea)
LVT	Landing Vehicle Tracked
PA	Philippine Army
PLA	People's Liberation Army (Communist China)
POA	Pacific Ocean Areas
PRC	People's Republic of China (Communist China)
PVA	People's Volunteer Army (Communist China)
RCT	Regimental Combat Team
ROK	Republic of Korea (South Korea)
SCAP	Supreme commander for the Allied Powers
SWPA	Southwest Pacific Area
USAAF	U.S. Army Air Force
USAF	U.S. Air Force
USAFFE	U.S. Army Forces in the Far East
USMC	United States Marine Corps
VFW	Veterans of Foreign Wars
WPO	War Plan Orange

INTRODUCTION

Douglas MacArthur is one of America's most famous and idolized generals. He is remembered for the great arc of history through which he led his armies, the soaring heights of his oratory, and his appearance, complete with an erect bearing, dark sunglasses, campaign hat, and made-to-order prop pipe. He reconquered the Philippines, was America's shogun in Japan, engineered the miraculous victory at Inchon, and openly defied a president. His renown seems well earned, and his legacy continues to generate great passion in his supporters and detractors alike.

While many remember his costume, his speeches, his swagger, and his oversight of the occupation of Japan, most can agree that the General's fame derives from his leadership in time of war. *MacArthur Reconsidered* attempts to strip away the posturing, the spin, and the peacetime administrative roles so as to evaluate the record of Douglas MacArthur as a wartime commander.

Was he a great leader of men in World War II and Korea, as his promoters attest, or, as others argue, was he a dangerous egotist who willfully led his men into some of the greatest defeats in U.S. military history? Was he the architect of nearly miraculous victories such as at Hollandia in New Guinea and at Inchon in Korea, or was he a reckless gambler who could not admit any error and whose failures drenched Asian soil with the blood of tens of thousands of American men, devastated the Philippines, and nearly triggered World War III? Was he a towering genius who, through character, bravery and integrity, inspired men to follow him into battle, or was he a man of poor judgement and an inflamed sense of self-importance that overwhelmed his intellect? This volume will attempt to answer these questions.

America certainly loves its generals. Consider that almost 25 percent of our presidents (eleven out of forty-six) previously held that military rank.

Not one admiral has been elected to our highest office, so there is something about boldly commanding men on a solid field of battle that appeals to our electorate. Victory through quiet competence is rewarded but not adored in this nation. After all, Nathaniel Greene, George Meade, Winfield Hancock, Philip Sheridan, John Pershing, Mark Clark, Omar Bradley, Norman Schwarzkopf, Matthew Ridgway, Walter Krueger, David Petraeus, and Robert Eichelberger are not exactly household names. Many even remember Dwight D. Eisenhower more for being an overseer of a wartime coalition and a friendly, avuncular president rather than a battlefield general. Political, risk-taking, image-conscious generals are the ones most loved by Americans such as George Washington, Andrew Jackson, Ulysses Grant, Robert Lee, George Custer, George Patton . . . and MacArthur. It is a riddle that, as President Harry S Truman put it, "I do not see how a country that can give people like Robert E. Lee, John Pershing, Eisenhower, Bradley, can, at the same time, produce people like Custer, Patton and McArthur [sic]."[1]

The literature on MacArthur generally falls into two groups: overall biographies that range from complementary to idolatrous and a few volumes that conclude that he was a brilliant but flawed leader. This book is less than a full accounting of his life as it focuses more narrowly on an evaluation of his career in World War II and the Korean conflict. As MacArthur's reputation is primarily derived from this period (1941 to 1945 and 1950 to 1951), such a retrospective is important. Was he a genius and master strategist as so many declare? Or was he an egomaniacal blunderer who failed upward due to domestic political calculations? Eisenhower, who served for years as MacArthur's aide in both Washington, DC, and Manila, made two very different observations about his former superior. He gushed that MacArthur "did have a hell of an intellect! My god but he was smart!"[2] But he also concluded, "I just can't understand how such a damn fool could have gotten to be a general."[3] Which was the true MacArthur . . . or could it have been both?

MacArthur's career as a wartime leader is separated in this book into three great advances and three distinct retreats for which his performance is evaluated:

- First Retreat: The Fall of the Philippines—December 1941 to May 1942
- First Advance: The Hard Way Back—Milne Bay to Morotai, June 1942 to October 1944
- Second Advance: Honolulu to Tokyo—October 1944 to August 1945.
- Second Retreat: Seoul to the Naktong—July to September 1950
- Last Advance: Inchon to the Yalu—September to November 1950
- Last Retreat: From the Yalu to the Potomac—December 1950 to April 1951

The analysis of MacArthur's battlefield command for each period focuses on examining the following seven questions:

1. In the peacetime immediately prior to armed conflict, did he ensure that rigorous training and proper motivation yielded a military force with a high level of readiness to fight and win on the battlefield?
2. Were plans prepared that took into account the capabilities both his command and that of the enemy being confronted to maximize the odds of American victory?
3. Did MacArthur identify, promote, and support competent subordinates who were best able to execute his orders?
4. Were military efforts concentrated where the enemy was weakest and his forces' capabilities the strongest?
5. Did he risk the lives of men under his command on the battlefield in an appropriate manner, where the likelihood of casualties was commensurate with the advantages to be won?
6. Was MacArthur able to exhibit adaptability and take initiative in the field balanced with a willingness to accept subordination to the chain of command?
7. Did MacArthur provide accurate appraisals of the situation on the ground to his superiors even if such reports reflected poorly on his leadership?

Unfortunately for those who lionize the General, this volume concludes that MacArthur's record as a wartime general is a poor one. It is true that he was comfortable commanding and coordinating large numbers of men on the offensive. He also adapted well to utilizing the new weapons that technological change brought to the battlefield over his lifetime. Nevertheless, his victories were often bought more dearly than necessary and trumpeted as much more consequential than they were in reality. Even worse, his defeats were attributable to poor planning, willful disregard of military intelligence, and a refusal to consider probable enemy actions. His strength was on the attack when he had a preponderance of force and mobility against an opponent that had lost the initiative. In such situations he could be counted upon to act as an aggressive risk taker. He knew how to choose excellent field commanders but had terrible judgment in selecting staff officers. He understood the importance of broadcasting positive public relations in an age when the power of propaganda rose to new levels. However, at the same time MacArthur repeatedly falsified the historical record presented to the American people in a dishonest effort to burnish his reputation.

Compared to his strengths, MacArthur's weaknesses were manifestly greater on balance. His failings were most evident at the start of three separate

conflicts when he repeatedly underestimated the capabilities of his opponent
and incorrectly assessed those of his own forces. While MacArthur readily incorporated the increased firepower and speed that technology brought to war
after 1918, he never seemed to accept the commensurate magnification in the
importance of proper logistics and supply. When evaluating MacArthur's tenure in wartime command, one is often reminded of a remark attributed to U.S.
Army general Omar Bradley: "Amateurs talk strategy. Professionals talk logistics." MacArthur repeated the error of not ensuring that his men were properly
supplied and supported time and again: at Bataan in 1941, Buna in 1942, and
Leyte in 1944, as well as in several battles in Korea at Pyongtaek, Chonan,
Unsan, and Pakchon in 1950.

MacArthur failed most spectacularly at the commencement and conclusion of his wartime leadership due to an inability to understand enemy capabilities and intentions. When attacked by an inferior force, he tended to
convince himself that he was outnumbered by the enemy and concluded that
the situation was helpless without massive reinforcements. When these were
not forthcoming, MacArthur withdrew physically from the situation at the
front and delegated authority so as to absolve himself from any resulting defeat. The record clearly shows a repetition of multiple faults over his career,
which included repeatedly being caught by surprise by enemy forces, surrounding himself with sycophants of questionable competency, and refusing to follow
lawful and clear orders that did not suit him. Most importantly for a man in a
military leadership role in a democracy, he was guilty of consistently lying to
his men, the American public, and his direct superiors, including successive
presidents of the United States. If one follows the historical record rather than
MacArthur's propaganda, the clear conclusion is that the General's deficiencies
were many and significant.

Such conclusions will sit poorly with those who revere MacArthur as one
of the greatest Americans—a towering genius, a man of honor, and one of the
world's exemplary military leaders. Proponents will claim that the criticisms
on the following pages should be leveled not at MacArthur but rather at his
subordinates, Washington bureaucrats, or even Presidents Franklin Roosevelt
or Harry Truman. However, an honest assessment of the past, utilizing MacArthur's own words, those of his most accomplished contemporaries and leading
historians, is not kind to the General. This book attempts to make the case,
with facts and logic, for removing the laurel crown from the brow of the American Caesar.

A Note on Sources

A massive amount of scholarship is in existence regarding World War II and
the Korean War in general and the life of Douglas MacArthur in particular.

Thus, any review of the General's military record will invariably omit sources thought to be of primary importance by individual readers. The analysis in this book rests on a foundation of several specific troves of documents. First there are the writings of General MacArthur himself and those issued by his command. These include his letters, cables sent to superiors, his memoir *Reminiscences*, the daily communiqués issued by his headquarters, and the multivolume *Reports of General MacArthur*, compiled by his staff and published by the Department of the Army in 1950.

Next, there are the letters, transcriptions of radio messages, diary entries, and memoirs from MacArthur's contemporaries in the U.S. Army. While these senior officers did not always agree with MacArthur, he would have likely acknowledged that men such as generals Eisenhower, Bradley, Eichelberger, Krueger, Ridgway, George Marshall, Henry "Hap" Arnold, Lawton Collins, and George Kenney, were generally on his side in the great crusade against the Axis and, later, the menace of global communism. This book also relies on similar sources from senior American politicians and commanding officers from the U.S. Navy and U.S. Marines. MacArthur often accused these men of shortsightedness, cowardice, defeatism, and appeasement. However, even he would have agreed that these were influential decision makers who were well informed regarding America's foreign policy and military choices. Thus, while MacArthur would not have wanted them included, the voices of Presidents Roosevelt and Truman, Admirals Ernest King, Chester Nimitz, William Halsey, Thomas Hart, and James Doyle, and U.S. Marine Corps generals Lemuel Shepherd, Charles Krulak, and Oliver Smith are included in this book. U.S. government documents from the National Archives, U.S. Department of State, and so forth, are also heavily cited. When possible, internet links have been provided at the end of citations so that readers can easily verify sources and their context.

Secondary sources relied upon fall into a few major categories. Emphasis is given to the most influential biographies of the General, including ones that are extremely complimentary toward MacArthur, such as those by William Manchester and D. Clayton James, as well as more critical volumes by Richard Frank, Gavin Long, and Michael Schaller. Military histories of the Pacific and Korean wars published by the U.S. Army's Center of Military History are also heavily cited, as are the *New York Times* and other national news publications. Finally, major histories of the period by well-respected authors who are considered authoritative are used as additional references.

FIRST RETREAT

The Fall of the Philippines

"Arthur MacArthur was the most flamboyantly egotistical man I had ever seen, until I met his son."[1]

—Maj. Gen. Enoch Crowder, 1859–1923

CHAPTER 1

An Appointment
with Destiny

Who was Douglas MacArthur? While this volume is not a biography, at least some portrait of his life prior to World War II must be sketched here to understand the man and his towering reputation. His experience prior to senior wartime military command commencing December 8, 1941, was extensive and varied. MacArthur and his fervent admirers would have you believe that his career could be summed up as follows:

> He was born to a famous American general and followed in his footsteps before achieving even greater military glory. The son's genius and courage were obvious from a young age in an early career that took him from West Point to the Philippines to fighting on the western front in World War I. Through the interwar period he successfully reformed West Point, before leading the U.S. team to success and fifty-six medals in the 1928 Olympics. Later he served as army chief of staff in which he squashed a budding Communist uprising in Washington, DC, when he dispersed the Bonus Army. As the first commander of the nascent Philippine Republic's armed forces, he sounded the alarm about Japanese aggression and worked against time to prepare the new nation's army for war.
>
> After the Japanese attack on Pearl Harbor, MacArthur and his men were abandoned in the Philippines by a defeatist navy and Franklin Roosevelt's administration. A vastly larger Japanese force besieged the General's heroic American and Filipino defenders of Bataan and Corregidor, who fought stoutly while so many others were rapidly defeated by Tokyo's initial offensive. At the last minute, as the enemy closed in for the killing blow, FDR ordered the General to attempt a daring escape to Australia as his talents would be needed to lead the inevitable American counteroffensive. After assuming his new command, MacArthur chose to blunt the Japanese advance in New

9

Guinea while the U.S. Navy and Marines covered his right flank in Guadalcanal. A rapid advance across the north coast of New Guinea bewildered the enemy and allowed for a triumphant armed return to the Philippines, where the lives of so many fallen Americans and Filipinos were redeemed.

With the dropping of the atomic bomb and the end of the war, MacArthur became the American military governor of Japan, in which role he achieved his greatest triumph of miraculously resurrecting a prostrate and previously militaristic society as a peaceful, democratic, and prosperous one. Then, in 1950, the North Koreans invaded the South, and MacArthur was called to battle one last time. After he heroically stemmed the tide around Pusan, his amphibious landing at Inchon was a victory of great brilliance that would have ended the war were it not for the intervention of Mao Zedong and his hordes of communist Chinese. Rather than accept a prolonged stalemate where American soldiers would die by the thousands in a no-man's-land along the 38th parallel, MacArthur pushed for a broader war to defeat the enemy. This defied President Harry Truman's policy of containment, for which the General was relieved of command. After a triumphant return to the United States, MacArthur gracefully faded away, leaving behind a legacy to be revered.

Some of these details are true; however, this hagiography glosses over a bloody trail of costly U.S. military defeats of forces under MacArthur's command and questions regarding whether the General intentionally and repeatedly distorted the facts around his conduct to elevate his standing with the American public. Divisions in the United States over his career, heated in the 1940s and 1950s, still reverberate today as Americans seek to grapple with the true weight of his legacy on the scale of history. Nevertheless, despite significant evidence pointing to repeated instances of insubordination, gross errors in command, and blatant prevarication, most histories present a strongly positive view of the General. There are scores of Douglas MacArthur biographies, but the two most popular books on his life are the idolatrous *American Caesar* and the General's own memoir, *Reminiscences*. The best-selling book on the subject aimed at younger readers is an entry from the Heroes of History series titled *Douglas MacArthur: What Greater Honor*.[1]

What can we say with confidence about the early life of Douglas MacArthur that had bearing on his mind-set when he finally became a commander of large formations of men in time of war? He was born in 1880, the son of Gen. Arthur MacArthur, who had won the Medal of Honor in the Civil War. Arthur held many important posts but never obtained the army's highest rank, chief of staff, for which he nursed a grudge against powerful bureaucrats who he believed had conspired to hold him back. Douglas grew up on a succession of army posts, and it was always assumed that he would enter the military in due course.

His mother, Mary "Pinky" MacArthur was a true "helicopter mom" decades before the invention of such flying machines. Each night when she tucked her son into bed, she told him, "You must grow up to be a great man like your father."[2] When he was accepted to the United States Military Academy at West Point, she moved to an apartment across the street from his dormitory, where she could ascertain that his bedroom light was on and that he was regularly studying late into the night. His grades were excellent, and he graduated first in his class. Douglas spent much of his early years after graduation from West Point acting as an aide to his father, at that time the military commander of the U.S. colony of the Philippines. Arthur believed that America's future lay in Asia, and he inculcated this thinking in his son. Douglas also absorbed some of his father's paranoia and was always quick to believe that desk generals and bureaucrats were holding him back from the glory that was rightfully his.

Along with his significant intellect and steadfast commitment to a career in the U.S. Army, the most important thing to understand about Douglas MacArthur was his great ego and sense of self-importance. This remained a constant throughout his life. Col. (later Maj. Gen.) Enoch Crowder, Arthur's aide in the Philippines, remarked, "Arthur MacArthur was the most flamboyantly egotistical man I had ever seen, until I met his son."[3] Forty years later little had changed. Prominent New York Times journalists Turner Catledge and Arthur Sulzberger spent time with the General soon after his triumphant return to the Philippines. Catledge remarked, "He was variously the military expert, the political figure, the man of destiny. Sulzberger and I later agreed that we had never met a more egotistical man, nor one more aware of his egotism."[4] Such an outsized sense of self-worth is not necessarily an impediment to success as a military commander. However, as we will see, it consistently interfered with MacArthur's ability to motivate his troops, communicate truthfully in his reporting, choose proper subordinates, and follow orders from superiors.

The younger MacArthur's first days of glory came after his father's death in 1912. Douglas was clearly on a path to high achievement in the army, but it was World War I that catapulted him into the limelight. He was rapidly promoted from major to colonel and shipped out with the American Expeditionary Force's new 42nd "Rainbow" Division as its chief of staff. Once at the front in France in February 1918, MacArthur repeatedly led men into no-man's-land, showed great courage under fire, and distinguished himself on the field of battle. He often declared that he was destined for great things in the future. As if to verify this prediction, bullets passed through his uniform without harm to his body on multiple occasions during his early career. In contravention of regulations, he refused to wear a steel helmet or carry a gas mask at the front. Instead he opted for accoutrements such as long scarves, riding crops, and distinctive hats. While he was lightly wounded and gassed twice over the next few months, he was never seriously incapacitated or forced to leave his division.

U.S. forces were instrumental in halting the German offensive, which was strengthened as the Central Powers redeployed divisions from the east after Russia was knocked out of the war. As American formations stiffened the faltering British and French lines, MacArthur received several commendations and honors for his exploits at the front. Soon the Allies were the ones on the attack and pushing back the Germans who were suffering from a dearth of supplies and wracked by waves of Spanish influenza. Behind the scenes, Pinky engaged in a sustained letter-writing campaign to the secretary of war and senior generals in the army who had been colleagues of her late husband. She lobbied for her son to be promoted and constantly reminded these men of MacArthur's bravery and successes.

Pinky's efforts paid off when MacArthur was promoted to brigadier general at the end of June 1918. Only thirty-eight years of age, he was the youngest man of that rank in the American army at the time. U.S. reinforcements continued to stream across the Atlantic to the front and joined the British and French in a counteroffensive that drove the enemy back toward the German frontier. MacArthur was placed in command of the 84th Infantry Brigade at the start of August and was then appointed commander of the entire 42nd Division on November 10, 1918. However, a day later an armistice was announced, and the fighting was over. Germany's loss of will to fight denied the young general a chance to lead a large force on the field of battle. That opportunity would not come for more than another two decades.

Back in the United States, MacArthur's reputation as a military hero was established, and his career thrived. He was assigned to several positions of authority, including superintendent of West Point, commander of the military district of Manila, president of the American Olympic Committee for the 1928 Summer games in Amsterdam, and one of a panel of judges overseeing the sensational court-martial of Army Air Force general Billy Mitchell. Pinky continued to work her magic, and her son was promoted in rank to become the nation's youngest major general in 1925. In addition to his successful career, MacArthur was often prominently featured in the American press, especially after he courted and then married the fabulously rich socialite Louise Cromwell Brooks.

Pinky never approved of her son's choice, and the couple became estranged after only a few years. Louise did not accompany Pinky and MacArthur back to Manila in 1929 when he was made military commander of the Philippines and she divorced him soon after. Through his many postings in the colony, MacArthur came to love the Philippines as his second home and cultivated strong ties with many of the local elites. He believed the islands to be the most strategic point in the Pacific and the door through which U.S. influence in Asia would be maintained and enlarged. Once in his new post, the General turned fifty and secretly took as his mistress the sixteen-year-old Filipina movie starlet Isabel Rosario Cooper.

In 1930, President Herbert Hoover recalled MacArthur to Washington, DC, where he was sworn in as chief of staff of the army. He had succeeded where his father had failed. Unfortunately for MacArthur, his tenure in this post corresponded with the onset of the Great Depression, and he had to manage a force that suffered consistent reductions in funding and personnel size. The nation was also wracked by political unrest as the economy and society seemed to be coming apart. This marked the start for MacArthur of what became an ongoing dalliance with right-wing elements in the Republican Party, and he began exhibiting a strong anti-communist mind-set. He employed a public relations staff, was frequently quoted in the press, and began to refer to himself in the third person.

When a "Bonus Army" of the General's fellow World War I veterans descended on Washington, DC, the chief of staff was initially sympathetic to their plight. These men were destitute and demanded that the retirement bonus promised to them by the Congress be paid out immediately. However, MacArthur increasingly became concerned that Communists were leading the men living in the makeshift camps along the south bank of the Anacostia River. In June 1932, President Hoover ordered Secretary of War Patrick Hurley to use the army to evict the Bonus marchers from some vacant buildings earmarked for demolition that lay on the north side of the Anacostia. MacArthur accompanied a formation of infantry, cavalry, and tanks to the river. Two senior military staff officers arrived to deliver messages from the president directing that the troops not cross the bridge and enter the main Bonus Army encampment. MacArthur refused to accept receipt of these orders, saying that he was "too busy."[5] The soldiers then fixed bayonets, the calvary drew their sabers, and the force proceeded to cross the Anacostia and clear out the encampments. The Bonus marchers responded with a hail of rocks and bricks in what devolved into a riot. Sparks from army tear gas cannisters were supposedly the source of fires that soon engulfed the veterans' encampments, and the protesters were ejected from the city.

MacArthur gave a press conference at the end of the day in which he grandly announced that he had likely saved the republic. Right-wing elements of the GOP approved, but most Americans did not, and the General's actions were a public relations disaster for President Hoover. When the Democratic Party nominee for president, Franklin Delano Roosevelt, saw photos of the burning Bonus Army camps, he stated confidently, "This will elect me."[6] The birth of MacArthur's legacy as a controversial figure in American history can be traced to this event. Hoover chose not to dispute MacArthur's version of the riot and kept him on as chief of staff. If MacArthur learned a lesson from his actions, it was that he could safely disobey or ignore orders from superiors as long as he could produce a "victory" and retain the support of a large portion of the GOP. It was a path he would turn to repeatedly over his career.

The riot in Anacostia also emphasized to him the importance of managing and safeguarding his public image. Prominent newsmen Drew Pearson and Robert Allen decried the General's heavy-handed and insubordinate actions against the Bonus marchers in the press. MacArthur was incensed and sued for defamation, demanding the then extremely large sum of $1.75 million. Unfortunately for him, the journalists soon found the General's mistress, now all of nineteen years of age. She had been transported from Manila to Washington, DC, to live in rented rooms, where MacArthur had stated her job was "to lie in bed." She had fallen out with her paramour and shared with the journalists not only a trove of love letters but that he had called Hoover "a weakling" and the recently elected FDR "that cripple in the White House."[7] When MacArthur found out that Rosario Cooper would be the first witness called by Pearson and Allen's defense at trial, he immediately settled the lawsuit. In addition, he soon negotiated a hush-money settlement with his former mistress, who moved away from DC. MacArthur's aide, Maj. Dwight D. Eisenhower, noted that during this time the General developed "an obsession that a high commander must protect his public image at all costs and must never admit his wrongs."[8]

In 1932, FDR labeled MacArthur one of the two most dangerous men in America (the other was demagogue Huey Long of Louisiana).[9] He saw the General as a potential "man on horseback" who right-wing politicians and their supporters would attempt to elevate to command a military government in the face of a breakdown of law and order during America's ongoing economic distress. The new president, hoping to "tame" MacArthur and make him useful, retained him as chief of staff after his election. The relationship between the two men was often fraught. Most notably, one meeting concerning funding for the army degenerated into a shouting match, with the General harshly insulting FDR and the politician yelling back, "You must not speak that way to the president!" MacArthur offered his resignation, which was refused. The General's nerves got the better of him, and he vomited on the outer steps of the White House as he took his leave.[10]

FDR did not want MacArthur to retire from the army and go out on the campaign trail with GOP candidates in the 1934 midterm elections. Thus, he extended the chief of staff's term by an extra year. However, as 1935 moved toward its close, it became increasingly clear that MacArthur needed a new job, and FDR wanted him away from American politics. The General's extremely rapid record of promotion had caught up to him: at only fifty-five and in vigorous health, he had already held the highest rank in the U.S. Army. A solution was found in America's recent creation of the Commonwealth of the Philippines, which was granted a decade of self-rule prior to gaining full independence. The first president of the commonwealth, Manuel Quezon, asked MacArthur to supervise the establishment and training of the new Philippine Army (PA) with the august rank of field marshal. FDR agreed to the new post, and MacArthur sailed from San Francisco for Manila in October. He took Eisenhower along, as well as the now ailing Pinky. On board his ship to the Philippines, MacArthur met the thirty-seven-year-old Jean Faircloth, who was soon to become his wife and constant companion until his death.

The General who left the U.S. mainland was one of the most decorated and respected military officers in American history. MacArthur was a hero of the battlefield and a successful peacetime leader who had intimate knowledge of the inner workings of both the military and the Washington political establishment. He seemed a perfect fit to build the PA and potentially lead that force in case of a threatened war with Japan. MacArthur was confident that he was sailing off to an appointment with destiny, and he did not return to the U.S. mainland for more than fifteen years.

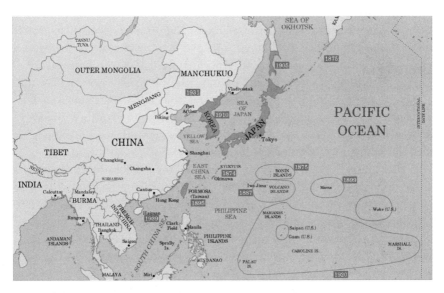

The Growth of the Japanese Empire in 1939.

Wikimedia: https://commons.wikimedia.org/wiki/File:Imperial_Japan_map_1939.svg.

TO DEFEND THE PHILIPPINES

The colony to which the General returned had been conquered by the United States from Spain in 1898. The acquisition of the Philippines effectively happened by accident. The strategic imperative driving America's declaration of war on Spain was to seize control of its island colonies of Cuba and Puerto Rico, which lay astride the vital shipping lanes between New Orleans, U.S. East Coast ports, and the soon-to-be-completed Panama Canal. The U.S. Asiatic Squadron only sailed into Manila Bay to eliminate the threat posed by the Spanish naval forces based there. However, once the United States had taken control of Manila, relinquishing it became difficult. With the destruction of its navy, Spain had been eliminated as an overseas power. If U.S. forces were withdrawn, the Philippines would clearly fall into the hands of another imperial nation such as Germany or Japan. Thus, despite significant political resistance at home and a lengthy and bloody insurrection by Philippine nationalists, the United States began its half century of control of the islands.

From the start of the occupation, the American military was unsure as to how it could hold on to the new colony if it faced a concerted attack from a foreign power. Manila was terribly distant from California. The colony was also further from the U.S. territory of Hawaii than it was from British, French, and German possessions in the region. Most worryingly for American defense planning, Luzon was very close to the expanding Japanese Empire, particularly its naval bases on the island of Formosa (now Taiwan).[11] The U.S. military was quite small in the early years of the twentieth century, and its ability to project power across the oceans was limited. The plan in case of a war in the Pacific, particularly one with Japan, was for the garrison in Luzon to hold out for as long as possible until a force could be sent across the ocean to save it. The military accepted that the Philippines might fall prior to relief arriving from California or via the Panama Canal. In fact, U.S. wargames prior to World War I regularly predicted a successful Japanese seizure of not only the Philippines but also Hawaii in any armed conflict.[12]

This strategy of the Philippine garrison taking a defensive stance around the entrance to Manila Bay was codified by the Joint Army and Navy Planning Committee (JANPC) in 1919 when it compiled its War Plan Orange (WPO) for a conflict against Japan. Both the army and the navy recognized the strategic position of the Philippines and its value to the United States in projecting power into East Asia. However, at the same time they concluded that it was too close to an increasingly powerful Japan and too far from the West Coast and even Hawaii to be supported in time of war. The U.S. military assumed correctly that in the event of a conflict, the Japanese strategy would be to strike quickly and without warning to seize territory across the western Pacific. Tokyo would then establish a fortified perimeter and fight a grinding war of attrition in the hope that American concerns about high casualties would lead to a negotiated peace, allowing Japan to keep its new conquests.[13] In such a scenario, WPO assumed that U.S. Army forces in the Philippines would retreat to the Bataan Peninsula and fortified islands in Manila Bay and hold out against Japanese opposition for as long as possible.[14]

In the best case, the garrison would be rescued by the U.S. Navy fighting its way across the Pacific. In the worst, the men under siege in the Philippines would "force the Japanese to make the capture of this bay a major operation, and might offer sufficient prospect of resistance to deter an enemy from undertaking the capture of Manila and Manila Bay."[15] The United States was under no illusions that the men stationed on its islands in the Western Pacific had much chance against Tokyo's rising military power. In 1922 JANPC concluded, "It seems probable that a Japanese major effort could succeed in taking both the Philippines and Guam before our Fleet could arrive in the Western Pacific, but it is believed that the sacrifice of all our forces, both naval and military, would be justified by the damage done to the enemy."[16]

When MacArthur became army chief of staff, his attachment to the U.S. project in the Philippines led to an immediate change in U.S. strategy. He believed not only that the islands were too important and strategic to lose but that the United States had a moral obligation to defend them. In 1931 he told Secretary of War Hurley, "The Philippines can be successfully defended by the employment of native manpower against any probable attack."[17] Of course, at the time there was no large pool of trained native manpower to protect the islands. In the interim, MacArthur's plan was that in the event of war with Japan, two U.S. infantry divisions would be dispatched to assist Luzon's garrison from the U.S. East Coast by way of the Suez Canal. While this plan may have been committed to paper, it was not clear how long America would need to mobilize these divisions in the event of war and how long transporting them the more than 11,000 nautical miles from the U.S. East Coast to Manila would take.

During his tenure as chief of staff, the General was never able to convince the planning staff of the viability of a robust Philippine defense. This strategy became increasingly untenable as the U.S. Army suffered major cutbacks in both funding and manpower at the same time that the Japanese Empire significantly expanded its military. The Five-Power Naval Limitation Treaty of 1922 was designed to eliminate a naval arms race by limiting the size of the Japanese and American fleets to a certain tonnage and a 3:5 ratio among capital ships. In addition, the treaty restricted construction or improvement of existing fortifications and military bases in the Pacific for thirteen years. However, while America retreated into isolationism and reduced the U.S. Army's budget, there was no restriction on the growth of Japanese ground and air forces. The Imperial Japanese Army was in the midst of a significant expansion and modernization period, growing from seventeen to thirty-four divisions between 1931 and 1937. Military aircraft design and production was similarly rapid.[18] Subsequent to MacArthur's term as army chief of staff, the Japanese withdrew from the terms of the Five-Power Naval Limitation Treaty upon its expiration in 1936.

After MacArthur left to take up his post in Manila as commander of the new Philippine Army, war planners in Washington, DC, reverted to an assumption that in time of war with Japan, the Luzon garrison would retreat to the island of Corregidor and the Bataan Peninsula while the United States initially focused on defending a line from Alaska to Hawaii to Panama. However, once in the Philippines, MacArthur set to work to change the strategy to one that would allow the Philippines to resist a Japanese invasion. As he told Philippine president Quezon, "I don't *think* the Philippines can defend themselves, I *know* they can."[19] The problem was how to build a Philippine Army that, combined with the U.S. garrison, could accomplish such a mission. Unfortunately, a lack of funding and political will in Washington and Manila created a yawning gulf between MacArthur's vision and reality.

Most military planners in Washington were not particularly impressed with the field marshal's plans. In 1938 Gen. Walter Krueger, then head of the War Plans Division and later MacArthur's commander of the 6th Army in World War II, concluded,

> The idea of a definite period of self-sustained defense is no longer a part of our present concept of the defense of the Philippines in an Orange war, nor is it authorized under any approved Joint Board action now in force. Whatever form the new Joint Army and Navy Basic War Plan-Orange may take, it is highly improbable, as matters now stand, that expeditionary forces will be sent to the Philippines in the early stages of an Orange war. Even if the dispatch of such forces were contemplated, it would be impossible to predict, with any degree of accuracy, when they would arrive.[20]

In other words, in a war with Japan, the Philippines could not be saved.

CHAPTER 2

The Southern Road to War

Douglas MacArthur's return to Manila in 1935 came at a fraught time. Armed conflict between Japan and the United States over control of the Western Pacific had long been predicted, and tensions were rising. Both nations had begun expanding their empires in the region in the late nineteenth century and were unwilling to accept the status quo. After the U.S. ejection of Spain from the Philippines and Guam and Japan's wresting of Korea and Formosa from China, Germany was stripped of its Pacific colonies in World War I, which were primarily awarded to Japan. Both the United States and Japan sent armed contingents into Siberia via the port of Vladivostok from 1918 to 1922 to support the Whites during the Russian Civil War. The two nations' forces were suspicious of each other, and these tensions resulted in the Evgenevka Incident in which Japanese and American soldiers came to blows and the fighting threatened to expand into general warfare before cooler heads prevailed.

While the United States retreated into isolationism during the Depression, Japan engaged in a brutal war of conquest in China to expand its access to raw materials and obtain new markets for the output of its industrializing economy. In 1931 the Japanese invaded Manchuria and then in 1937 pushed into the heartland of China, which led to a large-scale war with the Nationalist Chinese (Kuomintang, or KMT) government. Japanese atrocities following the capture of Shanghai and Nanking were repugnant to the American public and damaging to U.S. business interests in China. While Franklin Roosevelt's administration pushed the long-standing policy of calling for open and equal access to China's markets and opposed Japan's war of aggression, the irony was that Japan was dependent upon imports of American steel, oil, aluminum, and other industrial inputs to wage the conflict. Thus, the planes, tanks, and ships driving Japan's offensives were fueled by U.S. petroleum, and the bullets, bayonets, and swords used to massacre Chinese soldiers and civilians alike were forged from American steel. Relations between Tokyo and Washington deteriorated steadily, driven by the war in China and as Japan formally allied itself with the European fascist nations of Germany and Italy: the three Axis countries entered into the Anti-Comintern Pact in 1937 and 1938 and the Tripartite Pact in 1940. Clauses in the latter agreement were specifically aimed at threatening the United States with a two-ocean war if it attacked one of the Axis powers.

Japan's militarism and anti-communist policies also brought it into conflict with the Soviet Union. Memories of the 1904–1905 Russo-Japanese War and the intervention in Siberia against the Reds after World War I drove mutual antipathy. Skirmishes broke out often in the 1930s along the Japanese-controlled Manchurian border with the USSR, which occasionally escalated into full-scale battles. Moscow sent aid to the Kuomintang, and Joseph Stalin's naval fleet and air force based in Vladivostok threatened the Japanese Home Islands. The Japanese military desired to eliminate the nearby Red Army threat and coveted the resources of the Soviet Far East, especially the oil fields of Sakhalin Island.

With Japan's military victories over KMT armies and seizure of great swaths of China's territory, the military and political elites in Tokyo contemplated the next move toward the goal of becoming a world power of the first rank. The Chinese Nationalists continued to fight on from their new capital of Kunming in the southwest of the country, and their ability to tie down a large portion of Japan's forces was supported by aid received from the Soviets, British, and Americans. In addition to winning the war in China, the Imperial Japanese Army (IJA) was most interested in defeating its primary land enemy, the USSR, with an attack into the Soviet Far East. This was known as *Hokushin-ron* ("Northern Road"). Such a course of action would eliminate Soviet aid to the Chinese government. The Imperial Japanese Navy (IJN) was most anxious to seize the European imperial colonies in the Western Pacific. This was known as *Nashin-ran* ("Southern Road"). Multiple factors eventually pulled the Japanese south rather than north.

First, the border conflict between the Japanese and Soviets intensified. In two battles at Lake Khasan (1938) and Khalkhin Gol (1939), the Japanese inflicted lopsided casualties and destroyed hundreds of advancing tanks but were outnumbered by significant Soviet reinforcements and driven back by waves of Red Army assaults. The IJA lagged behind the Red Army in armored vehicles and heavy artillery. It was insufficiently mechanized for success against a USSR able to focus its efforts in the Far East.

Second, the outbreak of World War II in Europe offered Japan significant opportunities for Japan to its south. France's defeat left the colonial government in French Indochina (today's Vietnam, Laos, and Cambodia) without hope of significant military reinforcement. The conquest of the Netherlands left the Dutch East Indies (today's Indonesia) in a similar state. British authorities in Malaya (now Malaysia), Singapore, and Burma (now Myanmar) could still hope for support from London, but with England at risk of invasion and hard-pressed in the Mediterranean, there was little military force to spare for the defense of the Far East. Vast territories rich in oil, coal, iron ore, rubber, and rice production suddenly seemed easy targets for Japanese conquest. Germany urged Tokyo to enter the war and seize Britain's colonies in Asia. In Japan, many talked of moving fast and not "missing the bus" before the fighting in Europe ended and France and Britain could strengthen the defense of their Far Eastern possessions.

Tokyo wasted little time after the German victory over France and, in June 1940, demanded of the French Indochinese government that supplies of aid to China transiting Haiphong harbor be halted and that a Japanese inspection team be admitted to the colony to ensure compliance. The Japanese soon increased their demands to include the use of several air bases in the north of Indochina and the right to transit troops to attack the Chinese. The French stalled for time, but in late September, Japanese forces invaded northern Indochina. After brief fighting, the local French forces surrendered, and the Japanese took control of Haiphong and the desired airbases. This not only allowed Japan to increase pressure on China but also brought its forces further south toward British Malaya, the Dutch East Indies, and the American Philippines. Washington and London were alarmed, and FDR retaliated by embargoing certain metal sales to Japan and closing the Panama Canal to Japanese shipping.

In November 1940 the German auxiliary cruiser *Atlantis* shelled and boarded the British *Automedon* off the coast of Sumatra. The captured cargo ship carried a treasure trove of top-secret mail from London bound for Britain's Far Eastern Command in Singapore; it contained both detailed notes on Singapore's defenses and Winston Churchill's War Cabinet's conclusion that Britain was so weak in the Pacific that it expected a rapid victory by the Japanese if war were to break out. The Germans immediately shipped this intelligence to Yokohama.[1] To the Japanese military the Southern Road increasingly looked to be wide open.

With the Axis nations on the march, the U.S. military began developing plans for a war in alliance with Britain against both Germany and Japan. In the Pacific, the Dutch and Australians were included to form the American-British-Dutch-Australian (ABDA) Command. Joint planning between the United States and Britain in early 1941 yielded American-British Conversations–ABC-1, which called for a "Germany First" strategy in a war with the Axis: the Allies would remain on the strategic defensive in the Pacific and focus first on victory in Europe. For U.S. forces this was incorporated into the "Rainbow 5" war plan.

FDR approved of this strategy and was later quoted as saying, "Defeat of Germany means the defeat of Japan probably without firing a shot or losing a life."[2] ABC-1 called for the U.S. Navy to withdraw its Manila squadron south to the Dutch East Indies and send no significant army reinforcements to the Philippines.[3] This was followed by joint U.S.-British military staff talks in Singapore in April 1941 to formulate specific defensive plans for the Western Pacific. A revised War Plan Orange (WPO) released in Washington, DC, that same month assumed that it could take up to two years from the start of a conflict with Japan before the U.S. Navy would be able to fight its way back to the Philippines.[4] While MacArthur was informed of these plans, he argued against them and continued to lobby for an active defense of the colony.[5]

A CHANGE OF PLAN IN MANILA

MacArthur was certainly aware of the gathering war clouds but remained confident that no conflict would break out for at least a year. This optimism was in contrast to the outlook of the army and the navy, which both ordered all family members of active personnel in the Philippines to return to the United States in April due to the imminent threat of an outbreak of hostilities. As MacArthur was not officially on active duty in the army at that time, his wife and infant son Arthur remained with him in Manila. In May 1941 MacArthur granted an interview to journalist John Hersey and stated, "If Japan entered the war, the Americans, the British and the Dutch could handle her with about half the forces they now have deployed in the Far East," and "the Philippine situation looks sound: twelve Filipino divisions are already trained." He also stated that half of the Japanese army was degraded due to fighting in China and that Japan wouldn't attack anyway as the ABDA united front was too strong to crack and "the Germans ha[d] told Japan not to stir up any trouble in the Pacific."[6] It is not clear from what sources MacArthur gleaned these "facts."

As war looked increasingly likely, MacArthur lobbied to rejoin the U.S. Army in active duty to oversee both the Philippine Army and the local U.S. garrison. FDR agreed, and on July 26, 1941, MacArthur became commander of all U.S. Army Forces in the Far East and was soon promoted back to his former rank of four-star general. In addition to Philippine Army (PA) forces, he was now in charge of the 22,000-strong U.S. Army garrison; half of these troops were well-trained Filipinos known as Philippine Scouts. While he was once again under the authority of the War Department, the General chose to ignore the standing order to send his family back to the United States.

MacArthur continued to push for a change in WPO, as well as for reinforcements to his command. He claimed that the local conscript force he had raised and trained would soon be able to defend the islands. He argued that he only needed until the middle of 1942 to finish preparing the Philippine Army as long as he received additional equipment from the United States and some squadrons of aircraft to provide air cover. He promised Washington that by April 1942 he would have 125,000 trained troops and could repel a landing of up to 100,000 Japanese on the beaches of Luzon.[7] On paper he certainly had many men under arms, but were they really the effective soldiers MacArthur claimed? In a time of war, would they stand and fight the Japanese or flee the frontlines and return to their homes?

Army Chief of Staff George Marshall had an uneasy relationship with the commander of the Philippine garrison, as the former had been only a lieutenant colonel when the latter ascended to the chief of staff position in 1930 despite the two men having been born in the same year. MacArthur found it increasingly difficult to take orders from anyone as he aged, and it was quite galling to receive instructions from a man like Marshall, who had only held staff positions in World War I, who had not attended West Point, and whose quiet demeanor had resulted in promotions at a more sedate pace. Nevertheless, for more than a decade through 1951, Marshall generally supported MacArthur's positions and went to great lengths to massage MacArthur's easily bruised ego. While the War Department did not immediately accept MacArthur's change of plan, Marshall did adopt a policy of increasing the military strength of the Philippine garrison. With FDR's acquiescence, significant equipment and in excess of 8,000 reinforcements sailed to Manila. These included 25 self-propelled artillery guns, 36 antiaircraft guns, and two armored battalions with 108 tanks.[8] MacArthur remained extremely optimistic regarding the fighting prowess of the Philippine Army. In fact, when Marshall proposed rushing an additional American infantry division to the Philippines in September, MacArthur turned down the offer as unnecessary for the defense of the colony.[9]

The U.S. Army Air Force (USAAF) also rapidly expanded its presence in the islands. By December 1941, there were more heavy American bombers in Luzon than anywhere else in the world. MacArthur had under his command 74 bombers, 175 fighters, and 58 miscellaneous aircraft. That was 76 more military planes than were based in Hawaii. Of America's most modern planes, the Philippines had 35 B-17 bombers compared to Hawaii's 12, and the Philippines had 107 P-40E fighter aircraft compared to 39 in Hawaii.[10] However, these planes were concentrated at a small number of airfields, and there seemed to be no rush to establish dispersal landing strips to utilize in time of war.

In addition, despite the expiration of the Five-Power Naval Limitation Treaty and its provisions against improvement of military installations on the islands, MacArthur did not utilize the reservoir of PA manpower to construct revetments to help protect his aircraft from attack. The most important air base, Luzon's Clark Field, held all the B-17s in one place and had limited radar and antiaircraft protection. Del Monte Field in Mindanao, which could also accommodate B-17s, only opened at the start of December. In addition, more planes, guns, and soldiers were on their way to the Philippines. At the time of the attack on Pearl Harbor, ships already at sea or soon to leave West Coast ports "were scheduled to bring MacArthur two bombardment groups, one pursuit group, a reconnaissance squadron, an infantry regiment, a field artillery brigade, two light artillery battalions and several service units."[11]

The best explanation for why such large resources were rushed to the Philippines in the last days of peace is that MacArthur was a convincing and believable source, and he told decision makers in Washington what they wanted to hear: that the colony could be defended successfully. Naysayers such as Gen. Leonard Gerow, head of the U.S. Army War Plans Division, attempted to warn Marshall against MacArthur's plan and argued that the Philippine Army "is of doubtful combat efficiency."[12] However, the thought of losing the Philippines at the start of a war with Japan was a painful one for FDR, Marshall, and the rest of the political and military establishment. How convenient that the dynamic and charismatic former army chief of staff, deeply experienced in the defense of the colony, proclaimed with great confidence that he and his PA forces could hold the islands as long as they received shipments of weapons and a few U.S. Army units. In contrast, more conspiratorially minded historians believe that FDR was attempting to goad the Japanese and Germans into attacking and thereby pull the United States into the war before the British and Soviets were defeated by the Axis powers. Lend-Lease aid was a serious provocation in German eyes. Similarly, the metal embargo and basing of long-range offensive bombers in the Philippines drove the Japanese closer to war with the United States.

No matter why reinforcements were rushed to the Philippines, a question is whether the United States had the right commander for the garrison. Historian Alan Schom has pointed out,

What Washington failed to take into account was that the MacArthur of 1918 was no longer the same man. The youthful general who had spent every day of that first war at the front with his men, personifying drive, extraordinary leadership, and sound split-second judgement, all based on meticulous staff planning, seemed no longer capable of any of these things. Since 1935 he had been excessively lax in executing his duties of preparing a new Filipino army. . . . Described now as "extremely aloof," he rarely met with many of his officers any more, even men in key positions. Instead he bastioned himself in an office, no longer in a trench or field headquarters and was protected by a relatively new staff headed by Richard Sutherland, a frequently unsound, secretive chief of staff, full of his own personal superiority.[13]

Relations between Japan and the Western powers continued to deteriorate. Tokyo was able to secure a neutrality pact with Moscow in April 1941, which opened up the Southern Road by ensuring peace along the Soviet frontier. Even though the ink on this agreement had barely dried by the time the Germans attacked the USSR in June, the government of Prime Minister Fumimaro Konoe still considered appeals from its Axis allies to join the war and attack the Soviets in the Far East. For a time, the IJA was authorized to engage in a major buildup, and more than 800,000 men were soon massed along the Soviet border ready to invade in September if the Red Army showed signs of collapse. However, Hirohito personally intervened at the end of July and "suggested" to the IJA that the buildup in Manchuria and Korea be reversed. The emperor knew the Soviets would notice a large reduction of Japanese forces along its Far Eastern border, and this would allow Stalin to withdraw troops to fight the Nazis—troops that could then not threaten Japan's rear in the event of a war with the British and Americans.[14] As the IJA pulled back its troops in Manchuria, more than twenty-eight Red Army divisions traveled west to defend Moscow, Leningrad, and Kiev in the second half of 1941, along with tens of thousands of sailors stripped from Soviet naval ships based at Vladivostok and absorbed into Red Army infantry formations.

With the world focused on the fighting in Europe and the USSR no longer an immediate threat to Japanese-occupied Manchuria and Korea, Tokyo increased pressure on the Vichy French colonial government in Hanoi. With begrudging acceptance by the French, the Japanese occupied the southern half of French Indochina in late July 1941. This gave Tokyo control of more rubber, tin, and rice production. It also tightened the noose around the Philippines and brought Japanese forces perilously close to the oil fields of British Malaya and the Dutch East Indies. FDR retaliated by freezing Japanese assets in the United States and embargoing the sale of petroleum products. The British, Dutch, and Canadian governments soon followed suit. As Japan imported more than 80 percent of its oil from the United States and the British and Dutch refused to make up the shortfall, Tokyo faced a difficult choice: go to war before its reserves of fuel were used up or enter into a negotiated settlement with Washington.

The Konoe government authorized a dual-track strategy with the United States: a diplomatic understanding was the preferred solution, but military preparations for war commenced as well. Konoe hoped that the Americans would accept Japanese dominance of the Western Pacific in return for peace. However, FDR and Secretary of State Cordell Hull threatened armed intervention if the Japanese moved on the British and Dutch colonies. The U.S. terms were unacceptable to nationalists in Tokyo: in exchange for a normalization of trade relations, Japan would have to pull its forces out of both Indochina and

China. While the Japanese were willing to consider a withdrawal from Indo-china, too much blood had been spilled and too much prestige was at risk to surrender territory seized from the KMT. Konoe's offer of a face-to-face meeting with the American president to work out a compromise was turned down, and negotiations increasingly became deadlocked.

Hawkish members of the government, led by War Minister Hideki Tojo, pushed for action as Japan's oil reserves dwindled and the IJN's relative strength in the Pacific increased as both the British and the Americans shifted warships to the Atlantic to fight Germany's U-boats. On the ground, the force imbalance was even more tilted in favor of the Japanese. Not only were the infantry forces defending the Dutch, British, and American colonies in the Western Pacific outnumbered by the IJA, but the great majority of the Western powers' soldiers in the region were made up of Philippine, Malay, Javanese, and Indian troops. It was not clear how hard these Asians would fight for their white-dominated colonial governments in what Japanese propaganda would portray as a crusade to expel Europeans from the region.

While Tokyo prepared to seize the Dutch East Indies and Malaya, the Konoe government watched events in the Western Hemisphere closely as the Americans' undeclared naval war against Germany ramped up in intensity. The Lend-Lease Act, passed into law in March 1941, effectively offered unlimited U.S. supplies and armaments to Britain and the USSR. On September 11, after U-boats torpedoed several American merchant ships and a naval tanker, FDR ordered the U.S. Navy to attack German and Italian ships on sight. Ten days later he went before Congress to urge the repeal of the Neutrality Acts, which restricted American vessels from sailing to ports of nations at war. Thus, the United States was clearly moving toward entering the European conflict, which meant it would soon be in a military alliance with Britain. It was unlikely that the Americans would remain neutral in a war between Japan and Britain in the Far East if the two Anglo-American nations were at the same time fighting side by side against Germany.

Senior IJN leaders feared a war with the United States. At the same time, they did not see how Malaya and the East Indies could be seized while leaving the increasingly well-armed American forces in the Philippines astride their crucial supply lines. The B-17 was a long-range offensive weapon of great provocation to the Japanese. A large fleet of them on Luzon was perfectly positioned to interdict the economic lifeline of shipments of raw materials and food heading north to the Japanese Home Islands. As historian Richard Connaughton concludes, "The belated arrival of the U.S. Army Air Corps in strength in the Philippines with all its attendant, exaggerated hope, meant that Japan's invasion of the Philippines was no longer a probability. It became a certainty. The establishment of a long-range American air force based in the

Philippines was a threat to Japanese aspirations in southeast Asia which the Japanese felt obliged to remove."[15]

Despite his reservations, Japan's commander in chief of the combined fleet, Adm. Isoroku Yamamoto, planned his surprise attack on Pearl Harbor, which would be immediately followed by raids on Hong Kong, Luzon, Guam, and Malaya. The Harvard-educated military leader was exceedingly negative about his nation's chances in an extended war against America. In September 1941 he wrote, "It is evident that a U.S.-Japanese war is bound to be protracted. The United States will not give up fighting as long as Japan has the upper hand. The war will last for several years. In the meantime, Japan's resources will be depleted, battleships and weaponry will be damaged, replenishing materials will be impossible. . . . Japan will be impoverished."[16] Adm. Mineichi Koga, who commanded the Second Fleet at the time, was even more emphatically against a war with America when he exclaimed, "We won't win!"[17]

Such opinions were supported by war games Konoe had the Total War Research Institute in Tokyo organize, which concluded, "Should Japan go to war with the United States and its allies, Japan would *necessarily* lose. If such a war occurred, Japan might very well prevail in a few initial battles, but it would then be forced into a prolonged war that would see its resources dwindle and eventually run out."[18] In contrast, the IJA generals were ready for war. They believed that if the IJN could drive back the outnumbered British and American navies in the Western Pacific, their troops would quickly conquer the fragmented garrisons in the Philippines, Malaya, Singapore, the East Indies, Burma, Guam, and Wake Island. Japan would then be able to set up a strong defensive perimeter protecting its newly expanded empire, which possessed all the oil, rubber, rice, and iron ore it required to become a self-sufficient great power on the world stage.

Yamamoto agreed that setting up the envisioned plan of initial conquests was viable. In late September he made his famous and accurate prophesy: "In the first six to twelve months of a war with the United States and Great Britain I will run wild and win victory upon victory. But then, if the war continues after that, I have no expectation of success."[19] Many in the government and military in Tokyo believed that Americans would flinch from suffering the casualties necessary in a war of attrition to breach Japan's planned string of outer defenses. Under increasing pressure, Konoe resigned on October 16 and was replaced as prime minister by Tojo. That same day, U.S. High Commissioner to the Philippines Francis Sayre gave a speech in Manila and was quoted by the *New York Times* as stating, "Gradually the United States is moving closer toward the brink of war," and characterizing the embargo on Japan as "a sword to carry on economic warfare."[20]

Then, on October 23, the destroyer USS *Reuben James* was torpedoed and sunk by a German submarine off the coast of Iceland while in the act of depth-charging another U-boat. Congress responded by repealing the Neutrality Acts on November 17. U.S. warships, under U.S. air cover when available, could now escort American merchant vessels carrying armaments and supplies right into the ports of Liverpool and Murmansk. Adolf Hitler could not allow such unrestricted aid to flow to its British and Soviet enemies as German offensives ground to a halt in front of Moscow and Cairo. However, U-boat sinkings of American ships could only lead to a rapid U.S. entry into the European war, as had taken place in 1917.

This news helped solidify the plans of Japan's military. Its generals and admirals may have wished they could bypass the Philippines and leave the large U.S. fleet at Pearl Harbor undisturbed in their plans for conquests to the south. However, a glance at the map of the Pacific, in which the British and Americans would soon be allies at war, made such a strategy foolhardy. Tojo and his government prepared to strike first, and Yamamoto's fleet prepared to sail for Hawaii. The war hawks in Tokyo must have been heartened when, only a few days prior to the attack on Pearl Harbor, the isolationist *Chicago Tribune* and its sister paper in Washington, DC, leaked the administration's "Victory Program" for a simultaneous conflict against both Japan and Germany based on Rainbow 5. A banner headline, "FDR'S WAR PLANS!," announced that America and Britain would focus on defeating Germany while remaining on the defensive in the Pacific.[21] Even better for the Japanese was the admission in the leaked strategy that the United States would need upward of eighteen months before it would be ready to go on the offensive in Europe. This was exactly what Japan's war planners had hoped for: time to seize territory across the Pacific and then more time to fortify a perimeter bristling with a string of air and naval bases protected by large army garrisons. Then Tokyo could negotiate acceptance of its newly expanded empire with a United States unwilling to suffer massive casualties.

As MacArthur continued to boast of the PA's competence and ability to resist an attack, Washington granted a change in Rainbow 5. On November 21 he was authorized, in a war with Japan, to defend the entire colony of the Philippines rather than concentrate his forces to hold only Bataan and Corregidor.[22] This change set the United States on the road to a great defeat and the surrender of the largest American-commanded military force in U.S. history. Sadly, MacArthur's assessment of his Filipino troops did not conform to reality. Most of these men were poorly trained and armed and often could not even understand the language spoken by their superior officers.[23]

The readiness of U.S. Army forces in the Philippines was not that much better. A great deal of carelessness pervaded MacArthur's command, with little hard training taking place. Even the garrison's chief field commander, Gen. Jonathan Wainwright, "reported in 1941 that his typical workday included an hour of horseback riding in the morning, followed by breakfast, observing the troops, a visit to his office, luncheon at one, and afternoons devoted to golf or, occasionally, office work."[24] Discipline in the U.S. garrison was similarly lax. This lack of focus on training and preparing for potential hostilities by a force commanded by a MacArthur who isolated himself from the men in the field would repeat itself with similarly dire consequences a decade later on the eve of the Korean War.

It was not MacArthur's fault that the Philippine Army and the U.S. garrison were poorly funded and equipped. However, as the senior commander on the scene, the General had a responsibility to do the best he could with what he had, maximize readiness, and accurately evaluate the ability of the forces under his command. Only honest reports should have been transmitted to his superiors, not those based on hopes of where the colony's defenses might be in several months' time. It is unclear why MacArthur believed his green Filipino conscripts would act with such competence in a shooting war against seasoned Japanese divisions. Perhaps it was simply the wishful thinking of a man who loved the people of his second home. It is also uncertain why the General incorrectly disparaged the fighting prowess of the Japanese. In this he was not alone, as many American and British military professionals thought little of the capabilities of the IJA and IJN due to a belief in Asian racial inferiority. However, MacArthur claimed to be an expert on the Far East, its people, and their worldview. He somehow dismissed the success the Japanese military had demonstrated defeating large Chinese army formations trained by German and Soviet experts, as well as the skill with which Japanese aviation and naval forces accomplished their wartime missions in the late 1930s.

While MacArthur was tasked with the defense of the Philippines, his duty demanded that he provide the best possible advice to Washington. The General refused to consider that positioning a significant American offensive force, such as a large fleet of long-range B-17 bombers, in Luzon might do the opposite of deterring an attack. In addition, with the imbalance of naval strength in the Western Pacific, what was the risk that his garrison would be cut off and forced to surrender in case of a war with Japan? Would America's limited armament and manpower have been better deployed defending the more easterly line of Alaska–Hawaii–Panama Canal prior to launching a counteroffensive? MacArthur seems never to have considered such questions.

Once his plan to defend all of the Philippines was approved, the General issued new orders:

> He told his officers that the beaches "must be held at all costs." They were ordered "to prevent a landing." Should the enemy reach the shore, their troops were "to attack and destroy the landing force." The implications of this were enormous. Under the Orange and revised Rainbow plans, quartermasters were to have stored supplies on Bataan. Now their depots were established at four points on the central plain. It was an audacious strategy, and typical of MacArthur, but its drawback was obvious.[25]

When MacArthur's supply officer, Col. Jim Collier, asked if he could still maintain substantial supplies in Bataan, MacArthur's reply was an immediate "Oh no!"[26]

In addition, the peninsula had not been properly prepared to act as a defensive position: anti-mosquito spraying did not take place, defense fortifications were not built, and so forth. While the General fervently believed in defending his second homeland, the plan he had championed was out of step with the facts on the ground. He overestimated the competence of the forces under his command and underestimated that of the Japanese. The time to adopt a new plan is when the capability is in place to put it into effect and not before. It is marginally possible that MacArthur would have had the Philippine Army ready as promised to carry out his new mission orders by his promised date of April 1942. However, preparations were far from complete in late 1941. If the Japanese refused to wait for his timetable, the General's choices would have terrible costs for those who served under him.

Nevertheless, MacArthur chose to believe the Japanese would do what he wanted them to do rather than plan for what they could do. He argued that the Japanese would likely bypass the Philippines in any move south to seize Malaya and the Dutch East Indies, and in any event a war in the Pacific was not imminent. On November 27, he met with High Commissioner Sayre and Adm. Thomas Hart, who commanded the U.S. Navy's Asiatic Squadron based in Manila. MacArthur was not worried and stated that "the existing alignment and movement of Japanese troops convinced him that there would be no attack before the spring."[27] Hart had been friends with the General for many years but believed war was imminent. The constant stream of positive pronouncements from the General led Hart to fear that his counterpart had become increasingly disconnected from reality. Hart wrote in his diary, to his wife, and to his superiors in Washington that he believed MacArthur was no longer sane.[28]

Despite his concerns, the admiral hoped to keep his squadron in the area if the Japanese attacked. While the U.S. Navy's plan for years had been for the Asiatic Fleet to pull back from the Philippines in time of war, Hart had asked to retain his squadron in the area under cover of the increasingly strong USAAF presence.[29] This was a brave move as he did not have much to take on Japan's battleships and aircraft carriers: his flotilla consisted of three cruisers, thirteen destroyers, twenty-nine submarines, and several smaller ships. What he had was old and outdated as well. Hart joked, "I used to say that all my ships were old enough to vote" and admitted that they were "both weaker and slower" than those of the Japanese.[30] MacArthur's relationship with Hart deteriorated as war grew closer. MacArthur crowed about the reinforcements he was receiving and cruelly joked to the admiral, "Get yourself a real fleet, Tommy, then you will belong."[31] On other occasions he described his counterpart's situation as "small fleet, big admiral."[32]

MacArthur was unwilling to accept how outnumbered U.S. forces were in the Far East and discounted the importance of guarding the modern planes of his air force if he wanted to keep the navy squadron in Philippine waters in time of war. Without them, Admiral Hart's ships would be exposed to attack from the air and would not be able to sortie from Manila Bay to interdict any approaching Japanese amphibious landing force. MacArthur also refused to coordinate reconnaissance flights between planes of the Army Air Force and those of the navy. MacArthur opined, "The Navy has its plans, the Army has its plans and we each have our own fields."[33] This lack of concern for doing everything possible to maintain local air power is difficult to understand. MacArthur himself had written while army chief of staff in the 1930s, "The next war is certain to be one of maneuver and movement. . . . The nation that does not command the air will face deadly odds. Armies and navies to operate successfully must have air cover."[34] The General was soon to find out how right he had been.

Major General Lewis Brereton, MacArthur's chosen commander for his newly enlarged air arm, arrived in the Philippines in early November to take command of the Far East Air Force (FEAF). He hand-delivered updated orders to MacArthur modifying Rainbow 5 to authorize offensive air strikes on Japanese bases in the event of war.[35] The newly arrived general was shocked to find that the FEAF was still operating on relaxed peacetime schedules under MacArthur's assumption that hostilities would not commence prior to the middle of 1942. Brereton instituted a war footing and on November 21 urged MacArthur to move the B-17 fleet south from Clark Field to Del Monte in Mindanao to place it out of range of Japanese planes based in Formosa. MacArthur issued the order, but only half the bombers were moved south. After the war, MacArthur wrote, "I never learned why those orders were not promptly implemented." Biographer William Manchester, fawning admirer of MacArthur, still concluded, "It was, of course, his job to know, and he must be faulted for his ignorance."[36]

As we conclude the chapter on MacArthur's efforts in the Philippines prior to the attack on Pearl Harbor, what can be said of his military leadership in the months leading up to the war? It is clear that the General deluded himself and his superiors about the fighting ability of the army he had raised, while at the same time he denigrated the competence of his likely opponent. MacArthur neglected defensive preparations and unit training prior to the Japanese attack despite repeated warnings that war was imminent. Finally, he abandoned a long-standing conservative strategy and implemented an overbroad defense plan that would disperse his unprepared forces across the Philippine archipelago in the face of an enemy invasion.

Of course, the General and his supporters would vehemently disagree with such an assessment. In *Reminiscences*, MacArthur summarized the prewar situation as follows:

> We began an eleventh-hour struggle to build up enough force to repel an enemy. The ten-year period so essential for the successful completion of my basic plan was evidently going to be cut in half. Too late, Washington had come to realize the danger. Men and munitions were finally being shipped to the Pacific, but the crucial question was, would they arrive in time and in sufficient strength? In the meantime, all possible use was being made of available resources. . . . As the signs of impending conflict became unmistakably clear, I prepared my meager forces, to counter as best I might, the attack that I knew would come from the north, swiftly, fiercely, and without warning. . . . Whatever might come, we were as ready as we possibly could be in our inadequate defenses, on the night of December 7th. Every disposition had been made, every man, gun and plane was on the alert.[37]

Sadly this passage deviates significantly from the truth. But it was written long after the war, when the General was near the end of his life. Most are guilty of playing a bit fast and loose with the truth in their memoirs. However, MacArthur took such liberties to far extremes. He was an inveterate prevaricator throughout his time as a wartime commander. In writing, in conversation, and in oration, the General lied to his superiors, to the American people, and to the men who fought and died for him. Historian Richard Frank relates this in the most delicate manner: "So the first rule of writing about Douglas MacArthur is that he is a tempting resource for color, but for facts one should often look elsewhere."[38]

In addition to *Reminiscences*, we also have a more detailed source supporting the General's actions throughout the Pacific War: the multivolume *Reports of General MacArthur: The Campaigns of MacArthur in the Pacific*, complied by his staff under his supervision in Tokyo soon after the end of World War II. Many passages are reused verbatim in *Reminiscences*, so we can assume that they met with the General's approval. These extremely detailed, beautiful, in-depth books of maneuvers, battles, advances, and retreats, produced at taxpayer expense, are ensconced in thousands of libraries across the United States. While a useful reference, they may be the most outrageous piece of sycophancy ever released by an arm of the American government. Volume 1 narrates the operations of forces under MacArthur's command from preparations for war to the surrender of Japan. In its 333 pages of text (there are an additional 134 pages of maps and illustrations), MacArthur's name is mentioned 459 times, or more than 1.4 times per page. In this same volume, Adm. Thomas Kinkaid, MacArthur's chief naval subordinate in charge of the 7th Fleet, is mentioned 26 times; Gen. Walter Krueger, commander of the 6th Army, and Gen. Robert Eichelberger, commander of the 8th Army, MacArthur's premier field generals, are mentioned 17 and 25 times, respectively. General George Kenney, the innovative head of MacArthur's 5th Air Force, gets a de minimis 10 mentions. All in all, the name MacArthur is printed almost six times more often than the combined total of his four primary subordinates in World War II. With that in mind, *Reports of General MacArthur* summarizes the General's efforts in the Philippines in the years leading up to December 7, 1941, as follows:

> Among the few, General MacArthur had clearly recognized the danger signals. His long and close association with the Philippines and the Orient had given him a rich background of knowledge and experience with which to judge the situation in the Far East. His grasp of the Japanese character and psychology and his understanding of Japanese military policy and aggressive intentions had induced him to voice repeated warnings of the shape of things to come. In a desperate race against time, he had attempted to stem the tide by initiating preparations for the defense of the Philippines. Working against almost insuperable political and administrative obstacles, he had commenced in 1935 to create a modern Philippine Army of ten divisions to counter the Japanese attack that he knew would soon come from the north, swiftly, fiercely, and without warning.[39]

In other words, in the face of evidence to the contrary, *The Reports of General MacArthur* claims that the commander of the Philippine garrison had a keen appreciation of Japanese capabilities, readied his force for a surprise attack, and did everything humanly possible in what was ultimately a tragic and losing cause. Events would prove otherwise.

CHAPTER 3

Air Raid on Pearl Harbor

This Is Not a Drill

B y December 1941 it was clear that the United States would soon be at war with Japan. Less than two weeks before the outbreak of hostilities, Franklin Delano Roosevelt approved a "final alert" to be sent out to commanders across the Pacific. Douglas MacArthur received a cable from the War Department which read, in part,

> Japanese future action unpredictable but hostile action possible at any moment period If hostilities cannot repeat cannot be avoided the United States desires that Japan commit the first overt act period This policy should not repeat not be construed as restricting you to a course of action that might jeopardize your defense period Prior to hostile Japanese action you are directed to undertake such reconnaissance and other measures as you deem necessary. . . . Should hostilities occur you will carry out the tasks assigned in revised rainbow five which was delivered to you by General Brereton period.[1]

These were clear orders: prepare for an attack the Japanese might launch at any time on U.S. forces. After such an attack, a state of war would exist, and the U.S. Army Forces in the Far East (USAFFE) in the Philippines would be authorized to attack Japanese bases in the region.

However, MacArthur interpreted his instructions differently. As he related later, "My orders from Washington were not to initiate hostilities against the Japanese under any circumstances. The first overt move in the Philippine area must come from the enemy. There was apparently some hope that the somewhat indeterminate international position of the commonwealth might eliminate it from attack."[2] Of course this is not factual. Nowhere in the war warning do the orders indicate that the first overt act needed to come in the

Philippines, and nowhere did the instructions indicate that the United States had decided to grant the Commonwealth of the Philippines an independent foreign policy. Under this interpretation, even if the Japanese navy sailed under the Golden Gate Bridge and seized San Francisco, MacArthur's orders would preclude him from launching an air attack on Japan's military bases on Formosa. More likely, the General understood his orders clearly enough but hoped that his adopted home might avoid becoming a battlefield. If the Philippines were bypassed by the Japanese, he might also avoid personal defeat. This would not be the last time the General chose to twist his interpretation of orders in ways beneficial to his goals.

While MacArthur claimed later that he had done everything possible to prepare for war with the resources at hand, many things clearly were not done in the final months leading up to the war. In addition to not moving his B-17s south, he did not do the following:

- Prepare defenses and obstacles at the most likely points along the Lingayen Gulf beaches where MacArthur and army planners had long expected a Japanese landing would take place
- Have the men of his Philippine Army (PA) dig revetments and additional dispersal areas at Clark and other airfields
- Prepare defensive lines in Bataan and pre-position supplies there in case a fighting withdrawal to the peninsula became necessary as per war plans that had been in place for decades
- Work out details with the civilian government as to the military's requisition of food, supplies, fuel, and transportation (such as commercial buses) in time of war
- Initiate planning for air strikes on Japanese airfields and ports in Formosa
- Consider the use of volunteer civilian labor to clear emergency airfields, dig trenches, and so forth, after the start of any hostilities
- Contemplate scenarios for action in the event the enemy staged significant landings both north and south of Manila
- Prioritize what necessary supplies should be removed from Manila in the event of a Japanese attack so as to spare the population and infrastructure hub of the commonwealth but not jeopardize the Luzon garrison's defense

FIRST BATTLE, FIRST DEFEAT

The phone rang at MacArthur's headquarters at 3:30 a.m. on December 8. It was still December 7 in Hawaii on the other side of the international date line, and Pearl Harbor had been attacked. At 5:30 a.m. official orders were delivered to the General, and his long-awaited appointment with destiny had arrived: a state of war existed with the Empire of Japan, and Rainbow 5 was to be implemented. MacArthur was finally a field commander in time of war. However, from the General's office came only silence. William Manchester notes, "Those who were around him would recall afterward that he looked gray, ill and exhausted, and we know little about his actions and nothing of his thoughts that terrible morning. He was the commanding officer and therefore he was answerable for what happened."[3]

Brereton wanted to immediately launch an attack on Japanese targets on Formosa. He tried to see MacArthur personally around 5 a.m. and again at 7:15 a.m. but was blocked by Sutherland, who said that his boss was "too busy." A second visit a couple of hours later had the same result. A phone call from the U.S. Army Air Force (USAAF) general around 10 a.m. was also intercepted by the chief of staff, and Brereton reported that he warned Sutherland that if Clark Field was successfully attacked, the Far East Air Force (FEAF) would lose the ability to use its B-17s in an offensive role. Sutherland's records show that his order was to "hold off on bombing of Formosa for present."[4]

Unable to obtain access to MacArthur and worried about an incoming airstrike on his planes, Brereton had his bombers and many of his fighters take off and circle Clark Field so that they would not be caught on the ground. The Japanese plan to attack Luzon at sunrise had been delayed by heavy fog in Formosa, so all the American planes took off without incident. After hours of flying, they landed for refueling, and their crews relaxed over lunch. While this was taking place, MacArthur finally called Brereton and authorized a few B-17s to fly over southern Formosa in a photo reconnaissance mission. However, time had run out: the one working radar station in central Luzon picked up a large incoming flight of planes approaching from the north. Three squadrons of fighters scrambled, but they were unsuccessful in finding and intercepting the Japanese attack of close to 200 planes.

Communication failures among the American forces were significant, and air raid warnings were not communicated to Clark Field, where the B-17s for the reconnaissance mission were preparing to take off. Many of the P-40s at the base remained on the ground along with all but a couple of the large U.S. bombers. At 12:40 p.m., more than ten hours after the raid on Pearl Harbor, the fog-delayed Japanese aerial force from Formosa finally arrived over Clark and began its attack. Only 4 P-40s were able to take off during the raid; 12 of the 19 B-17s on Luzon were destroyed on the airstrip, 4 were damaged, and many P-40s were hit on the ground. A simultaneous attack on the nearby fighter base at Iba Airfield was also quite successful. In total, of the 91 P-40s on Luzon, 55 were destroyed. Losses were also high among the older 71 aircraft of the FEAF in Luzon, and around 30 of these miscellaneous craft were bombed, strafed, shot down, or otherwise rendered inoperable. The Japanese flew away leaving scores of broken American planes and bodies in their wake. Nearly 100 U.S. planes were lost on December 8. More than half of the FEAF was wiped out, with losses especially heavy among its most modern equipment.[5] In his first battle as a wartime commander, MacArthur had been handed a devastating defeat, and the Japanese, at a stroke, had achieved air superiority over the Philippines.

MacArthur never accepted any blame for the disaster and defended himself vigorously against any implication that he had been at fault. A year after the war's end, Brereton published his memoirs, in which he related his repeated attempts to see his commander and obtain authorization for an air attack on Formosa on the first day of the war.[6] This led MacArthur to release a 400-word statement the following month in which he called the USAAF general a liar: "General Brereton never recommended an attack on Formosa to me and I know nothing of such a recommendation having been made. . . . [I]t must have been of a most nebulous and superficial character, as no official record exists of it at headquarters."[7]

There are multiple falsehoods in this statement. MacArthur certainly did know that Brereton had asked to attack Formosa. After all, he approved a reconnaissance mission over the island that day to prepare for such a mission. Also, "contrary to MacArthur's assertion, an official record of Brereton's attack request *did* exist at USAFFE headquarters in Sutherland's office diary."[8] The real question is not why MacArthur refused to see Brereton, but why MacArthur didn't follow his orders and personally reach out to his air force commander to order an attack. Manchester writes, "But he should have *insisted* on seeing him, brushing aside Sutherland's zeal to act as his surrogate when major decisions loomed."[9] Alan Schom concluded in *The Eagle and the Rising Sun*, "Instead of taking action according to the plans he himself had earlier prepared, the stunned general had sealed himself off from everyone except his chief of staff, Major General Richard Sutherland."[10]

MacArthur repeated his case in his memoirs:

A number of statements have been made criticizing General Brereton, the implication being that through neglect or faulty judgement he failed to take proper security measures, resulting in the destruction of part of his air force on the ground. While it is true that the tactical handling of his command, including all necessaries for its protection against air attack of his planes on the ground, was entirely in his own hands, such statements do an injustice to this officer. His fighters were in the air to protect Clark Field, but were outmaneuvered and failed to intercept the enemy. Our air force in the Philippines contained many antiquated models, and were hardly more than a token force with insufficient equipment, incompleted fields, and inadequate maintenance.[11]

Once again, much in the above quote is simply not true. First, Brereton did not have true tactical control of his bombers, as he could only launch a raid on Japanese airfields or harbors in Formosa with MacArthur's permission—permission that was sought but never granted. Second, the B-17 "Flying Fortress" bombers were by no means antiquated as they were the most advanced model in the U.S. fleet. Similarly, the ninety-one P-40s based in Luzon were also the newest American fighter aircraft. The P-40 came into service in 1939 and achieved significant success against Japanese opponents in China as part of the famous "Flying Tigers." In any event, even if more of the fighters had taken off from Clark at the onset of the air raid, it was already too late: while it was an effective fighter, the P-40's greatest weakness was its poor climbing ability, as it needed a full five minutes of flying time to get up to 15,000 feet of altitude.[12] Thus, to be of use, the U.S. fighters needed to be over the airfield prior to any attack. Also, had the B-17s been relocated to Del Monte, they would not have been in range of Japanese land aviation in the first place.

In addition to absolving himself of blame for what happened at Clark Field, MacArthur also claimed in 1946 that Brereton's B-17s would have been ineffective even if they had not been surprised and destroyed on the ground and that the Japanese used carrier aircraft in their attacks on Clark in the first day of the war: "An attack on Formosa with its heavy air concentrations by his small bomber force without fighter support, which because of the great distance involved, was impossible, would have had no chance of success. . . . [T]he enemy's bombers from Formosa had fighter protection from their air carriers, an entirely different condition from our own."[13] Finally, he also stated that the B-17s were not at Clark to take on an offensive role: "The over-all strategic mission of the Philippine command was to defend the Philippines, not to initiate an outside attack."[14] He repeated this again in his memoirs fifteen years later.[15]

These statements by MacArthur are quite incendiary. Of what use were the B-17s if not to attack Japanese bases on Formosa or enemy shipping preparing an invasion force to land on Luzon? Why else had they been deployed to the Philippines? Also, was it true that the "Flying Fortress" could not engage in bombing missions without fighter escort? In fact, B-17s were sent on many unescorted bombing missions over Europe in World War II. As one of the craft's pilots commented regarding a mission to strike Berlin, "It is here that the ability of the B-17 to absorb such terrific battle damage and still fly is apparent. The plane can be cut and slashed almost to pieces by enemy fire and bring its crew home. It is the brilliant interlocking of its main structural members that keeps the B-17 flying."[16]

Next, the Japanese bombers on December 8 were escorted not by carrier aircraft but rather by land-based A6M "Zeros" operating from Formosa, which happened to have a range greater than MacArthur's expectations. It was one thing for the General to claim that Luzon was attacked by carrier aircraft in 1941. However, he stuck with this story even though he had access to contrary Japanese records after the war. MacArthur's statement was also false in asserting that the planes assigned to his command were in the Philippines only in a defensive role. The orders in Rainbow 5 were that, in the event of war, the FEAF was to engage in air strikes against "Japanese forces and installations within tactical operating radius of available bases."[17]

Finally, the General argued that the fate of the FEAF was already sealed before the last Japanese plane flew away from Oahu on December 7: "The stroke at Pearl Harbor not only damaged our Pacific Fleet but destroyed any possibility of future Philippine air power. Our sky defense died with our battleships in the waves off Ford Island. It cancelled Rainbow 5, and sealed our doom."[18] In this, MacArthur undermined his entire multiyear argument that the Philippines could be defended from the Japanese. The Five-Power Naval Limitation Treaty of 1922 ensured that the U.S. Navy would likely be outnumbered by its Japanese counterpart in the Pacific, and military planners in Washington had assumed for years that it would be a lengthy period before sufficient maritime force could be assembled to relieve the Philippines. Thus, if the FEAF was only viable if continuously open sea lanes were maintained to Hawaii, MacArthur should never have lobbied for additional aircraft to be positioned in the Philippines. After all, using this logic, his air force's "doom" would have been sealed as soon as fighting commenced. Japanese bases were already established to the north, east, and south of Manila on the islands of Formosa, Saipan and Truk, respectively. This fact, combined with the presence of the dominant size of the Imperial Japanese Navy (IJN) in 1941, meant that Luzon was sure to be cut off from U.S. resupply for at least a time at the start of any conflict.

Some MacArthur supporters have suggested that the General was caught in a bind as he remained the commander of the Philippine Army and military advisor to the commonwealth president Manuel Quezon, who hoped the Philippines could remain neutral in a U.S.-Japanese war. Under this theory, if the garrison on Luzon did nothing to threaten the Japanese, there was hope the islands would be spared in any conflict. While Quezon was free to hold such hopes and desires, MacArthur had asked for and accepted a recall to active duty in the U.S. Army. Thus, he was legally bound to follow his orders as communicated to him from President Roosevelt's War Department in Washington rather than the desires of President Quezon in Manila. MacArthur had been ordered to launch air raids on Japanese bases in the event of a war, and he was formally notified that a state of war existed early in the morning of December 8, 1941. Yet his most powerful offensive planes never left Luzon.

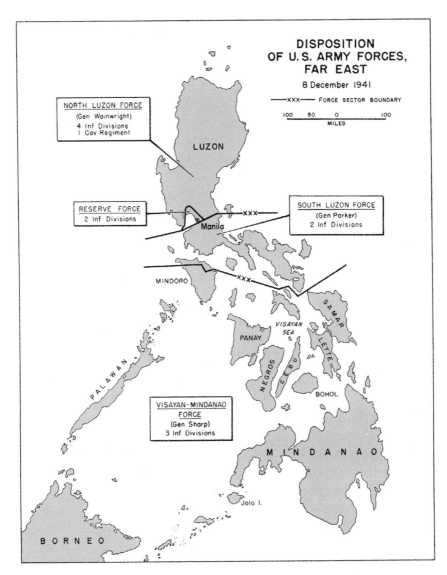

DISPOSITION
OF U.S. ARMY FORCES,
FAR EAST

8 December 1941

—XXX— FORCE SECTOR BOUNDARY

100   50   0   100
        MILES

NORTH LUZON FORCE
(Gen Wainwright)
4 Inf Divisions
1 Cav Regiment

LUZON

RESERVE FORCE
2 Inf Divisions

SOUTH LUZON FORCE
(Gen Parker)
2 Inf Divisions

Manila

MINDORO

SAMAR

VISAYAN
SEA

PANAY

LEYTE

NEGROS

CEBU

PALAWAN

BOHOL

VISAYAN-MINDANAO
FORCE
(Gen Sharp)
3 Inf Divisions

M I N D A N A O

Jolo I.

B O R N E O

Courtesy of the U.S. Army Center of Military History.

Many questions remain about the events of the first day of the war in the Philippines. Richard Frank goes as far as to title an entire chapter of his history of the war in the Asia-Pacific "8 December 1941, a Date That Will Live in Controversy."[19] While the commanders of the army and navy forces in Oahu were fired, MacArthur blocked all attempts to conduct a review of what happened that day in Luzon or prepare a report.[20] MacArthur's superiors in DC also shied away from investigating the debacle. Marshall certainly grasped the error of his Philippine commander's actions. The chief of staff told retired general John Pershing, "I just don't know how MacArthur happened to let his planes get caught on the ground."[21]

The commanding general of the USAAF, Harry "Hap" Arnold, angrily called Brereton after the attack to demand, "How in the hell could an experienced airman like you get caught with your planes on the ground? That's what we sent you out there for, to avoid just what happened. What in the hell is going on there?"[22] Certainly FDR also knew that MacArthur had suffered a great failure. The same evening as the attack on Clark Field, the president met with the journalist Edward R. Murrow. FDR pounded his fist on a table in frustration and exclaimed of the ravaged FEAF, "On the ground, by God, on the ground!"[23] He later commented that MacArthur's performance was similar to that of Adm. Husband Kimmel and Gen. Walter Short, who had been court-martialed for their laxity in command of the naval and army forces at Pearl Harbor.[24]

The president and the JCS likely concluded that the defeat in Hawaii could be blamed on the two local commanders. Investigating a second massive failure of ground and air forces in Luzon would not only tarnish MacArthur's reputation but also lead the American public to question the leadership of Marshall, Arnold, and FDR as well. Such a conclusion helps explain why both MacArthur and Brereton were allowed to continue in their jobs and even received subsequent promotions. A recall of MacArthur would have also had a political element in FDR's calculations. The president certainly did not need an aggrieved and popular general back in the United States working with the GOP and complaining about the ongoing conduct of the war. Thus, MacArthur remained in charge in the Philippines to prepare for the inevitable Japanese invasion of the colony.

HE WHO DEFENDS EVERYTHING DEFENDS NOTHING

The news that flowed to MacArthur's headquarters in Manila over the next few days was unrelentingly bad. First the great toll of loss at Pearl Harbor became clear. On December 9, enemy aircraft returned to Luzon and attacked the fighter base at Nichols Field, destroying additional U.S. planes and ground installations. The next day the Japanese bombed the naval base of Cavite on Manila Bay, igniting a massive fire that burned out of control. Upward of 500 men were killed, and large quantities of supplies and ammunition were destroyed. That evening Adm. Hart decided to evacuate his surface ships south to the Dutch East Indies, as remaining in Manila Bay had become untenable due to Japanese local air supremacy. Scores of merchant ships left Manila Bay as well.

Air raids continued daily on Luzon's defenses, reducing the FEAF to a handful of planes. News was also received that the Japanese had landed a large army in Malaya and that their aircraft had sunk the British battleship *Price of Wales* along with the battlecruiser *Repulse*. The Japanese now had the only battleships in the region and overwhelming naval superiority in the Western Pacific.

While MacArthur complained bitterly about the navy's withdrawal and demanded that immediate reinforcements be sent to his command, the Japanese captured Guam to his east on December 10, then landed in Borneo to the southwest on December 16 and on the large southern Philippine island of Mindanao on December 19. The invaders soon overwhelmed local opposition and captured Mindanao's main port city of Davao. The garrison on Luzon was now surrounded on all sides. MacArthur refused to accept this fact and argued that the Philippines were only isolated by a "paper blockade."[25] However, the truth was that a noose of Japanese air and naval power was tightening around Manila by the day. Any aid to MacArthur's forces would have to sail through hundreds of miles of enemy-controlled ocean patrolled by Japanese scout planes and IJN warships.

The question for MacArthur now was how to proceed in the face of rapid Japanese victories across the Pacific. Because his plan was to defend the entire archipelago, approximately one-third of the PA was based outside Luzon, and no effort was made to ship them north for a concentrated defense around Manila. This Visayan-Mindanao Force consisted of the 61st, 81st, and 101st PA infantry divisions along a with regiment of the PA's 1st Regular Division and a battalion of U.S. troops.[26] Of his forces in Luzon, MacArthur placed two PA divisions south of Manila and put Gen. Wainwright to the north with four PA divisions (the 11th, 21st, 31st, and 71st) along with a regiment of U.S. Army cavalry. A reserve composed of the 91st PA Division, the tank battalions, and the rest of the U.S. Army units remained near the capital under MacArthur's personal command.[27] In addition, the veteran 4th Marine Regiment had arrived in Manila from Shanghai soon before the outbreak of hostilities. It absorbed additional marine detachments based in Luzon, which enlarged the force to 1,500 men. However, this elite unit was deployed to garrison duty on the fortress island of Corregidor and remained there, involved in little more than enduring months of aerial and artillery bombardment until the very final days of the entire campaign.

MacArthur could have reverted back to War Plan Orange (WPO) and a strategy focused on preparing the Manila Bay area to withstand a lengthy siege with a gradual retreat to Bataan and Corregidor. It is difficult to see how such a decision would have been questioned in Washington, considering how the situation had deteriorated: the Pacific Fleet had taken grievous losses in Hawaii, the FEAF had been virtually wiped out, the navy had withdrawn all its major surface ships from the area, the arrival of significant reinforcement was doubtful, and the Philippine Army had not had time to complete its training. Few would have criticized MacArthur had he chosen to fall back to Bataan. In such a scenario, he would have had time to concentrate his forces, stockpile supplies, prepare fortifications, and plan for a counteroffensive if the Japanese overcommitted themselves. However, MacArthur had opposed WPO before the war and refused to make any changes to his scheme of forward defense. Harold Johnson, who served under MacArthur in 1942 in the Philippines and later rose to become JCS chairman, opined that the decision to defend the Philippines on the beaches was "a tragic error in judgement that should have been corrected much earlier."[28]

This was tragic as there was still time to prepare Bataan for a lengthy siege. Supplies of fuel, ammunition, medicine, and food were certainly available to be stockpiled. Despite his great admiration for MacArthur, Manchester writes of this decision,

> One depot alone, at Cabanatuan on the central Luzon plain, held fifty million bushels of rice—enough to feed U.S. and Filipino troops for over four years. The failure to move it was a major blunder, one which must be charged to MacArthur's vanity. Having scorned the Orange plan (WPO-3) as "stereotyped" and "defeatist," he could not bring himself to invoke it until he had no other choice. As long as the slimmest chance remained of hurling the invaders into the sea, he would station his men on the Lingayen coast a hundred miles north of Manila, keeping vigil on the low, sloping beaches. The capital and the General lived in a world of fantasy for two crucial weeks, rejoicing in the absence of enemy troops and feeding on vague rumors of Japanese defeats.[29]

This recalcitrance can be partially explained by MacArthur's belief that he could convince the president, the War Department, and the American public at large that national strategy should be shifted to a focus on the defense of the Philippines. Despite sending members of his staff to join American-British planning meetings in Singapore earlier in 1941, receiving multiple orders concerning Rainbow 5, and reading the details of the Victory Program in the newspapers, the General claimed to have been ignorant of FDR's "Germany First" strategy.[30] In his memoirs, he argued that the precious few U.S. carriers in the Pacific could have safely sailed past a string of enemy bases and launched reinforcement aircraft to land in the Philippines.[31] With this in mind, he ordered the emergency round-the-clock construction of thirteen new airfields across Luzon and Mindanao. Sadly, this work had not taken place before December 8, when it might have been of some use in promoting aircraft dispersal. Instead, the only planes to use those fields in 1942 were Japanese.

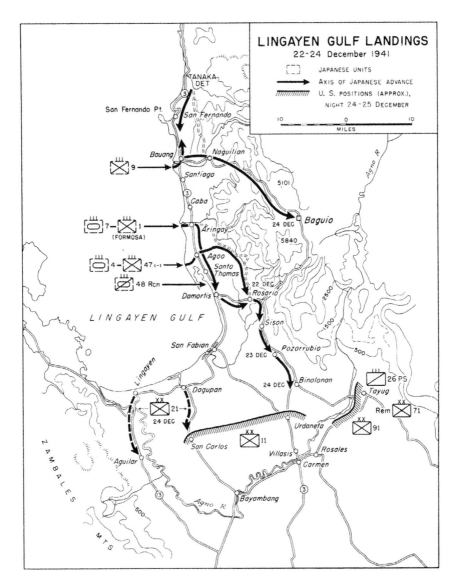

LINGAYEN GULF LANDINGS
22-24 December 1941

COURTESY OF THE U.S. ARMY CENTER OF MILITARY HISTORY.

With hope of reinforcement in mind, he lobbied the press and his superiors in Washington for a shift away from the president's "Germany First" strategy to rush aid to the Philippines. He called Hart a fearmonger, accused the navy of defeatism and wired the War Department messages such as "If the Western Pacific is to be saved it will have to be saved here and now" and "The Philippines theater of operations is the locus of victory or defeat."[32] He also sent fawning messages to Joseph Stalin and urged Washington to induce the Soviet Union to attack Japanese territory from Vladivostok. MacArthur clearly overstepped his bounds as a commander of military forces in a single U.S. colony as he actively opposed FDR's declared strategy for winning the war. Rather than receiving a reprimand, he was promised what aid was possible and complimented for his "magnificent defense" of the islands. Thus, it should come as no surprise that the General's behavior of undermining official U.S. foreign policy when it did not suit him became a pattern throughout his career.

Even more than a decade after the successful conclusion of World War II. MacArthur continued to argue that FDR had embarked on the wrong course in 1941 and 1942 and that "there was a great reservoir of Allied naval power in the Atlantic Ocean and Mediterranean Sea. A serious effort might well have saved the Philippines and stopped the Japanese drive to the south and east. One will never know."[33] Repositioning of these forces and the resulting loss of the Suez Canal, the starvation of Britain by the U-boats, and a reduction of aid to the USSR seem to have been an acceptable trade in MacArthur's mind when weighed against the pressing urgency of providing relief to his Philippine garrison.

On December 22, the main Japanese invasion force of eighty-five transport ships carrying the 14th Army under Gen. Masaharu Homma arrived in Lingayen Gulf. The enemy began landing 43,000 men from the 16th and 48th divisions of the IJA along with supporting artillery, tank, and engineer units along the region's beaches.[34] Inclement weather and high seas allowed some tanks to be landed, but most of the Japanese heavy equipment and artillery remained at sea. It took five days for the Japanese to finish the unloading process.

This should have been MacArthur's moment as the enemy had landed exactly where he was expected. To oppose the invasion, there were more than 75,000 men under arms in Luzon: 25,000 from the U.S. Army, USAAF, and U.S. Marine units, with the rest assembled in eight PA divisions.[35] MacArthur's most mobile offensive formations—his tank battalions, cavalry regiment, and self-propelled guns—were within striking range of the landing beaches. Half of his men in Luzon were already deployed along the Lingayen Gulf, and the rest were easily transportable to the battle area via paved highways that ran from Manila up the Central Luzon Plain. The garrison's artillery was outdated, as, of course, was the regiment of horse cavalry, but both would still be effective against infantry coming ashore and unloading equipment on open beaches. MacArthur also could have utilized his modern self-propelled guns and tanks to break up concentrations of the enemy as they landed. While the Japanese had achieved air superiority, the FEAF on Luzon retained a diminished force of aircraft that could be used for reconnaissance and hit-and-run attacks.[36]

Despite his significant numerical advantage and the inability of the Japanese to land much of their heavy equipment, MacArthur radioed Marshall that the actual numbers were exactly reversed, with the Japanese having landed 80,000 to 100,000 men, which was much greater than the 40,000 MacArthur claimed to have on hand on Luzon.[37] This discrepancy between total Japanese forces landed, and the number of the Luzon defenders in MacArthur's reports to Washington has never been properly explained. MacArthur doubled down on this 1941 falsehood when he wrote his memoirs in the 1950s: "A huge invasion force entered Lingayen Gulf in three transport echelons. . . . The troops convoyed were the 14th Army, commanded by Lieutenant General Masaharu Homma, comprising the 4th, 5th, 16th, 48th and 65th Divisions of the Japanese line, a total strength of approximately 80,000 combat troops. This was about twice my own strength on Luzon."[38] This quote is shockingly incorrect for someone who had extensive access to IJA records after the war. The 4th Division did not arrive in the Philippines from China until April 1942. The 5th Division was fighting its way south through Malaya on its way to Singapore in December 1941, and the 65th Division was not even formed until the middle of 1943. This unit was likely confused with the smaller 65th Independent Mixed Infantry Brigade, which was indeed assigned to the 14th Army but did not land in Luzon until January 1, 1942.[39]

In reality, General Homma came ashore on the Lingayen Gulf beaches with the 48th Division, a regiment of the 16th Division, three attached artillery units, and around 100 tanks. The total number of men landed between December 22 and 28 totaled 43,110, of which 34,856 were from the 14th Army, 3,621 were air unit support personal, and 4,633 were in logistics formations.[40] The force size of two divisions along with smaller specialist units assigned to the 14th Army was consistent with Japanese nomenclature of the time: An Imperial Japanese area army was approximately equivalent in size to a U.S. army composed of two corps of two divisions each. A Japanese army, the 14th in this instance, was generally equivalent to a U.S. corps of two divisions. An individual Japanese division had an approximate strength of 20,000 men, and an infantry regiment had around 3,900 men.[41] There are many honest reasons that could explain MacArthur's 1941 overestimation of the size of the enemy force that landed and defeated his command. There are few for repeating that mistake many years later when in possession of the IJA's records. MacArthur's undercounting of his own forces in reports to Marshall in 1941 and repetition of that obviously incorrect number many years later has only one logical explanation: he wished to cover up the fact that he was defeated by a Japanese force that was significantly inferior in size to his own.

Despite the defenders' larger numbers, intimate knowledge of the terrain, and correct deduction of the landing area, Homma's forces quickly overwhelmed resistance by the 11th and 21st PA divisions and moved inland. How do we explain the rapid defeat of MacArthur's forces and his subsequent order to withdraw? After all, the Philippine Army and the American garrison had trained for this exact scenario for years, and high seas on the landing date should have given the more numerous defenders a significant advantage to round up the Japanese on the beaches. While dominance of the sea and command of the air aided the invaders, there were two primary reasons for the debacle along the Lingayen Gulf.

First was MacArthur's failure to bring a preponderance of strength to bear when the enemy force was most vulnerable along the beachheads. This was especially true for his armored battalions of more than 100 tanks, which could have wreaked havoc among the enemy infantry. Wainwright urged the use of the garrison's tanks, but none were released from MacArthur's reserve to attack the Japanese along the shore in the first days of the invasion. The Japanese were surprised that MacArthur did not position his most mobile and hard-hitting units close to the expected landing beaches on Lingayen Gulf. After the war, Lt. Gen. Masami Maeda, chief of staff of the 14th Division, said he thought that MacArthur should have had his cavalry and armor ready to hit his forces as they came ashore.[42]

In addition to units in the area, a multitude of civilian buses, trucks, and cars were available in the greater Manila area, which could have been requisitioned to rapidly transport the defenders' reserve forces northward to Lingayen Gulf before the Japanese could finish landing their heavy equipment. This is especially true for many U.S. units of the garrison that were never deployed to oppose the main enemy landing. The most notable of these was the recently arrived 4th Marine Regiment. The marines were arguably the best shock forces the United States possessed in World War I. Throughout World War II they consistently fought aggressively, regardless of casualties taken. However, as already mentioned, MacArthur chose to use these men as garrison troops who slowly starved on Corregidor. In the end, they only fought for a few brief hours before being ordered to surrender. Historian Richard Connaughton called MacArthur's holding action in the Lingayen Gulf area "among the most lackluster, uninspiring defenses conducted throughout the duration of World War II."[43] Harsh words indeed, given the record of the French in 1940, the Soviets in the first months of the German invasion in 1941, the Italians in Libya, and the British in Singapore and Burma in 1942.

Second, and perhaps of even greater import, was the poor showing of the Philippine Army. After training for five years, and despite repeated enthusiastic messages to Washington by MacArthur regarding the high morale and competence of his new units, many of these green PA soldiers failed to fight, dropping their weapons at the first sound of gunfire and fleeing back to their homes.

Louis Morton, author of the U.S. Army's history of the campaign, writes politely, "The chief reason for the withdrawal order was the failure of the troops to hold the enemy. Up to this time General MacArthur seems to have had the greatest confidence in the fighting qualities of the Philippine Army reservists and in the ability of his forces to hold the central Luzon plain. The events of the 22nd and 23rd forced a revision of this view."[44] As Manchester concluded, "Though he would go to his grave insisting that he had been hopelessly outnumbered, on paper MacArthur had almost twice as many soldiers as Homma. The difficulty was that so many of them were melting into the hills."[45] The defense of the Lingayen Gulf area was also unhinged by a second Japanese landing along Lamon Bay to the east of Manila. This force, consisting primarily of the rest of the 16th Division with about 7,000 men, also had little difficulty driving back elements of a PA division defending the shoreline and achieved its initial objectives with the loss of only 84 dead and 184 wounded.[46]

Possibly believing he was outnumbered, unwilling to commit his force to a decisive battle against the enemy beachhead, having lost confidence in his Philippine Army, and worried about the new force driving on Manila from the east, MacArthur reported to Washington on December 22 that he would now "operate in delaying action on successive lines through the Central Luzon Plain to final defensive positions on Bataan."[47] All hope of defeating the Japanese on the beaches had been abandoned. Wainwright's 26th Cavalry Regiment fought stoutly to defend the crossroads town of Rosario, but as MacArthur chose not to commit reinforcements to the battle, the Japanese soon broke through southward toward Manila. If the forward defense strategy was to be abandoned, the obvious option was to switch to the older WPO. Yet "still MacArthur vacillated. It took him forty more terrible hours to overcome his aversion to the Orange plan."[48] Finally, he sent the order to all his commanders: "WPO is in effect," and the General's scheme to defend all of the Philippines along the beaches was officially dead.

Over the course of a week, MacArthur's forces pulled back in generally good order to Bataan. A retreat from a pursuing enemy can easily become a rout. That this did not happen was due to several reasons. First, the main Japanese force was focused on taking Manila to the south, while the American forces in front of them were retreating to the southwest. Initially, Homma did not realize that this was the U.S. plan and missed a chance to use his air force to bomb the bridges over the Calumpit River and nearby road junctions, which would have slowed the retreat to Bataan. Second, WPO had envisioned retreats to successive pre-established defensive lines, and this prior planning was invaluable in the execution of the withdrawal. The movement of the American forces was also aided through the use of buses, taxis, trucks, and private cars, which the military had finally commandeered.

Of course, these planned withdrawals of WPO were timed for a force retreating to a citadel that was already well provisioned. This meant that American and PA units did not have the opportunity to load and transport stores of supplies, which had to be left behind all across Manila and the Central Luzon Plain. Some of these were destroyed by demolition teams, but most fell into the hands of the Japanese. MacArthur also finally made use of his tank force, most of which had not been committed earlier in the fighting. The American armor was particularly successful in counterattacking the advancing Japanese north of the Calumpit and slowing the enemy's pursuit.

Once MacArthur reverted to WPO, he must have realized that his orders not to stockpile supplies in Bataan had been a terrible mistake. Every effort should have been made to make up for this deficiency. The easiest way to move large bulky items has always been by water, and huge stores of food, fuel, ammunition, and other supplies were stacked in warehouses and on the docks in Manila ready to be transported across the bay to Bataan. The vast majority of these supplies never made it, not because of enemy efforts but due to MacArthur's own orders that all military personnel immediately leave the capital.

MacArthur claims he declared Manila an "open city" on December 26 to convert it to a neutral site and save it from Japanese bombing attacks. While that may be true, what he wrote in his memoirs certainly was not: "Manila, because of the previous evacuation of our forces, no longer had any practical military value."[49] The city itself may not have had any further military value, but the supplies there, which his army needed to sustain an extended siege in Bataan, certainly had great worth. MacArthur's headquarters staff, and large contingents of the garrison were still in Manila on December 26. Thus, American forces did not evacuate until *after* MacArthur's declaration of Manila as an open city. Had Bataan been stockpiled for a siege before the outbreak of war or even in the two weeks of relative calm afterward, his decision would have been appropriate. However, WPO and MacArthur's orders from Washington were not to spare Manila from attack but to ensure that his men had the supplies required to maximize the amount of time they could hold out in Bataan. In this he failed his nation, the army, and the men under his command.

In retrospect, once MacArthur lost the ability to seriously contest Japanese airpower over Luzon on December 8 to 10, he must have realized that Manila could come under bombardment at any time. He believed the moral action in such an eventuality was to declare the capital an open city and continue to fight the enemy from other points on the island. As soon as he considered this option, his imperative and his duty was to order that as many items of military value as possible be moved out of the city to dispersed locations as soon as possible. Sadly, from December 11 to 26, this did not take place. MacArthur never explained this error in command judgement; nor was he questioned about it later by his superiors.

Finally, in addition to abandoning military-owned supplies, MacArthur chose not to argue with Philippine president Quezon's opinion that civilian stockpiles of food, fuel, and medicine be left for the Philippine population. The Japanese had no such scruples and later seized warehouses in Manila and across the Central Luzon Plain containing tons of material that would have been of invaluable assistance to the defenders of Bataan. Even storerooms of supplies owned by Japanese businesses were declared off-limits by MacArthur and could not be seized by retreating U.S. and Philippine soldiers. The invaders would depend on these stores while the defenders of Bataan went hungry. As a history published later by the U.S. Army states, "The shortage of supplies of all types, and especially of food, had a greater effect on the outcome of the siege of Bataan than any other single factor."[50]

CHAPTER 4

Bataan

Douglas MacArthur ensconced himself on the fortress island of Corregidor adjacent to the southern end of Bataan, where most of his men were digging in and preparing to endure a long siege. A lack of food and the 26,000 civilian refugees who had been allowed into Bataan forced an immediate reduction to half rations of around 2,000 calories a day. At first, this was not a significant problem as local farms on Bataan were scoured for food, and hunting in the jungle yielded game. There was a lull in the fighting as the Japanese focused on the capture of Manila, morale of the garrison was generally good, and there was optimism that reinforcements would soon arrive.

MacArthur later claimed that retreating to Bataan and Corregidor was a stroke of genius on his part that significantly impacted the entire future of the Pacific conflict to Japan's great detriment:

> The entrance to Manila Bay was completely covered by Corregidor and Bataan, and as long as we held them, its use would be denied the enemy. He might have the bottle, but I had the cork. The Japanese had not expected that our forces would be withdrawn from Manila, intending to fight the decisive battle of the campaign for control of the city. The devastating attack on Pearl Harbor and the subsequent thrusts in Asia left only this one important obstacle in the path of the Japanese onslaught in the Southwest Pacific. Our tenacious defense against tremendous odds completely upset the Japanese military timetable, and enabled the Allies to gain precious months for the organization of the defense of Australia and the vital eastern areas of the Southwest Pacific. . . . As for myself, I have always regarded my decision as not only my most vital one of the Philippine defense campaign, but in its corollary consequences one of the most decisive of the war.[1]

This shocking claim by MacArthur has been trumpeted by his admirers in the many decades since the end of World War II. After all, the General's decision to retreat was not a novel one: for more than twenty years, War Plan

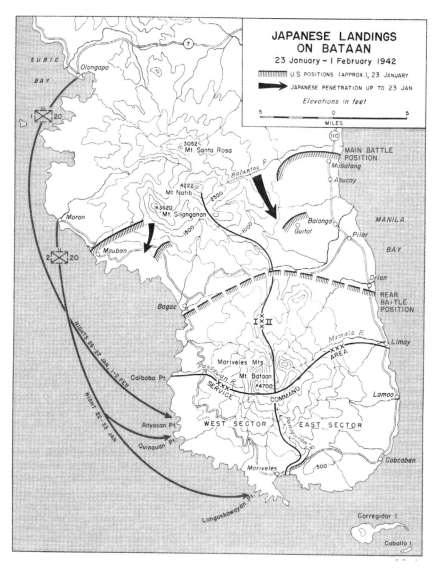

Orange (WPO) had envisioned the Philippine garrison focusing on a defense of Bataan and Corregidor to deny the use of Manila Bay to the Japanese. It is particularly ironic that MacArthur would claim credit for the brilliant idea of retreating to Bataan as he had fought against this very focus of WPO for a decade—first as army chief of staff and then in his subsequent posting to the colony. Also, arguing that the Philippine garrison's success in slowing the

Japanese advance across the Pacific in 1941 and 1942 was one of the most decisive events of World War II is laughable. Does it really stand in similar company to the Wehrmacht's gamble to push its panzers through the Ardennes in 1940, Winston Churchill's refusal to enter into peace negotiations with Germany after France's capitulation, Isoroku Yamamoto's attack on Pearl Harbor, Adolf Hitler's invasion of the Soviet Union, Georgy Zhukov's double envelopment of the German 6th Army at Stalingrad, or Harry Truman's decision to use the atomic bomb?

Next, and this is a question of greater importance in an analysis of MacArthur's military leadership, did the lengthy siege of Bataan and Corregidor "completely upset the Japanese military timetable" and give the Allies time to prepare to defend Australia and its lines of communications? The answer is no. WPO had for years imagined that the Philippine garrison could hold out on Bataan and Corregidor for six months. With the expansion of the Philippine Army (PA) and the increase in reinforcements to the Philippines, which arrived in the second half of 1941, war planners in Washington could have reasonably hoped for MacArthur's forces to hold out for a period that exceeded earlier projections. Bataan finally surrendered on April 9, 1942, and Corregidor followed on May 6, almost exactly six months to the day from the attack on Pearl Harbor. Thus, the siege did not last any longer than the U.S. military had predicted despite all the B-17s, tanks, and reinforcements rushed to Manila in the final months of peace.

In addition, it is well documented that the Japanese were surprised by the speed with which they defeated MacArthur's army. The Japanese expected a protracted fight from the enlarged PA and U.S. garrison but still planned for the 14th Army's best unit, the 48th Division, along with the invasion force's main air formation, the 5th Air Group, to be withdrawn from Luzon fifty days after the start of the war. With the fall of Manila and the rapid retreat of the American forces into a small peninsula, the attackers were able to accelerate their plans. The history compiled by MacArthur's own staff relates, "While the Japanese units were engaged in these preliminary operations against Bataan, Southern Army Headquarters at Saigon had reached a decision which was to profoundly affect General Homma's campaign. General [Hisaichi] Terauchi, Commander-in-Chief of the Southern Army, had become convinced that operations in the Philippines were all but completed and that the Japanese drive in the Netherlands East Indies could safely be put forward a month."[2] In other words, American resistance had been overcome significantly faster than expected, allowing the Japanese to move up their timetable of additional conquests further to the south.

While the Japanese certainly wanted to make use of Manila Bay and to remove MacArthur's "cork," that was not their primary goal. Their invasion of the Philippines, as already discussed, was driven by a need to eliminate U.S. naval and air forces in the region, which could interdict shipping of raw materials streaming north to Japan from conquests in the resource-rich areas of Malaya, the Dutch East Indies, and French Indochina. They had expected a longer and harder fight to seize the airbases of Clark, Nichols, and Iba airfields, the naval base at Cavite, and Manila itself. With the destruction of the American B-17 force, the retreat of the U.S. Asiatic naval squadron to the south, and the capture of all major airfields and port facilities on Luzon, MacArthur's forces no longer constituted a threat to Japanese military goals.

Thus, not only did the actions of MacArthur's forces in December 1941 fail to disrupt the Japanese offensive in the Southwestern Pacific, but it can be argued that they actually allowed the enemy to advance his schedule of conquest. One can easily imagine a scenario where MacArthur lost his aircraft more slowly by dispersing his P-40s and B-17s prior to their destruction on December 8. With local air cover, Adm. Thomas Hart's surface ships could have remained in the area for longer and potentially sortied to oppose the Japanese invasion fleet. A concentration of ground forces around the capital might have allowed the garrison to hold Clark Field, Cavite Naval Base, and Manila for a longer period, while Bataan was prepared for a siege. Certainly, Gen. Brereton's planes would still have been destroyed and Hart's surface ships sunk in the initial months of the conflict, but they might have been able to do Japanese shipping greater damage and slowed the enemy advance. Such a counterfactual scenario is only conjecture. What we can definitely conclude is that the siege of Bataan and Corregidor in no way disrupted Japanese offensive plans in the first half of 1942. The American and Filipino defense of Bataan was heroic, but it should not be given credit for something it did not accomplish.

With the reassignment of the 48th Division and most of his aircraft, General Homma ordered the 65th Brigade to the frontlines of Bataan to join elements of the 16th Division. The 65th, composed of 6,500 generally inexperienced soldiers, was intended to be used for garrison duty rather than frontline combat operations. In addition, during the siege, the defenders outnumbered the attackers by approximately three to one.[3] The Japanese leadership realized that this weakening of the 14th Army might slow the reduction of MacArthur's remaining U.S. forces on Luzon but was willing to bypass this concentration of U.S. force and leapfrog ahead to secure the conquest of the Dutch East Indies. As the siege dragged on and both sides suffered casualties in a battle of attrition, General Homma asked for reinforcements and received the Japanese 4th Division, which, as previously discussed, arrived from China in April 1942. After Bataan's capitulation, this unit was transferred back to Japan and was not engaged in any significant fighting for the remainder of the war. The 16th Division remained in the Philippines until it was wiped out in the Battle of Leyte in 1945. The 65th Brigade moved to the Japanese base at Rabaul in late 1942, where it acted in its planned role as a garrison force.

MacArthur spent his days on the island of Corregidor as the siege dragged on into the spring of 1942. In World War I, MacArthur had often accompanied his men on operations where he placed himself in great danger. During World War II, the General occasionally walked confidently along the frontlines or stood imperiously while Japanese aircraft bore down on his position. He said many times, and probably believed, that he was a man of destiny and that no bullet could hit him. However, such acts of bravery often needlessly placed all those accompanying him at extreme risk for no other apparent purpose than to create positive press copy about his unflinching courageousness. An example of this occurred in the early days of the war.

> No one could forget that day back in December when his house on Corregidor had been bombed. Jean had grabbed their four-year-old son and run outside to the air-raid shelter, totally ignored by MacArthur. Any other husband would surely have attempted to protect his wife and child, but not Douglas MacArthur. He seemed oblivious of their presence as he stood there glaring at the enemy bombers that had dared defy him and were once again plastering the Rock, nearly killing his own family in the process.[4]

In contrast to such bravado, MacArthur only traveled once to visit Bataan on January 10, 1942. He promised the men that help was most certainly on the way and then left the peninsula, not to return for more than three years. Thus he had to rely on the reports of others regarding disposition of his troops and their morale—despite the fact that the trip between Corregidor and Bataan could easily be accomplished at night via PT boat in less than ten minutes. Even historians who idolize the General have difficulty explaining away what many would call a dereliction of duty. Some attribute MacArthur's absence to his guilt that he had led his men into a siege woefully short of food, ammunition, and other supplies. They suppose that he couldn't bring himself to look his doomed men in the eye. However, he still demanded that they fight to the death and vehemently opposed capitulation even after he had been evacuated to safety and continued resistance by the garrison had become futile. The men doing the fighting on Bataan heard radio reports issued from MacArthur's headquarters on Corregidor that attested to their General's bravery and proclaimed that he was actively leading them in victorious operations. As the American lines were pushed back and food distribution was reduced, eventually to one-quarter rations (about 1,000 calories a day), morale declined, as did the men's view of their commander. The soldiers on Bataan who waited in vain to catch even a glimpse of MacArthur began calling him "Dougout Doug" and singing a song to the tune of "The Battle Hymn of the Republic":

> *Dugout Doug MacArthur lies ashakin' on the Rock*
> *Safe from all the bombers and from any sudden shock*
> *Dougout Doug is eating of the best food on Bataan*
> *And his troops go starving on . . .*
>
> *Dougout Doug, come out from hiding*
> *Dougout Doug, come out from hiding*
> *Send to Franklin the glad tidings*
> *That his troops go starving on![5]*

In the face of the declining morale, MacArthur either wanted to cover up that he didn't visit his men on Bataan or wished to remember things differently. In his memoirs he fondly recalls his "visits" to his men on the peninsula late in the siege, saying that they

> cursed the enemy and in the same breath cursed and reviled the United States; they spat when they jeered at the Navy. But their eyes would light up and they would cheer when they saw my battered, and much reviled in America, "scrambled egg" cap. They would gather round and pat me on the back and 'Mabuhay Macasar' me. They would grin—that ghastly skeleton-like grin of the dying—as they would roar in unison, "We are the battling bastards of Bataan—no papa, no mama, no Uncle Sam."[6]

This recollection is clearly a fabrication. MacArthur's one visit to Bataan in January took place long before reduced rations would have led to much weight loss by the men of the garrison. Also, documented reports of anger toward the battered U.S. Navy in the besieged Philippine garrison primarily come from MacArthur himself and his immediate staff.

The General certainly took out much of his anger and frustration on the navy. First, he complained about the retreat of the Asiatic Squadron's surface units. His view of the navy only got worse when the main Japanese invasion force arrived along the Lingayen Gulf. While MacArthur's few remaining B-17s made one bombing attack on the invasion convoy and scored no hits before flying off to Australia, the General focused his ire on the U.S. submarines of the Asiatic Squadron. The submarines did little damage, with two U.S. boats each sinking a single Japanese transport vessel. True, U.S. sub skippers were not aggressive enough early in the war. However, the primary problem was the Mark XIV torpedo, which had significant defects: it often ran too deep, the magnetic exploder triggered too early, and the contact exploder often failed when it hit its target. Even worse, the Mark XIV was also prone to circular runs due to a failed rudder and would strike the launch platform.

While besieged, MacArthur repeatedly cabled Washington demanding aid be sent via ship to Bataan. He accused the navy of defeatism and for failing to run its vessels through the "paper blockade" to save his force. Even after the war, he continued to argue that Adm. Ernest King, Chief of Naval Operations, was derelict in not ordering his fleet to fight its way across the Pacific to the Philippines before the garrison was forced to surrender.[7] Had the navy taken MacArthur's advice and attempted to sail a task force to Manila in early 1942, the outgunned U.S. squadron, running a gauntlet of land-based aircraft and a picket of submarines before encountering the Japanese fleet, would have likely suffered a major defeat. Finally, even though MacArthur was personally protected for months on Corregidor by the 4th Marine Regiment, he refused to recommend it for a presidential unit citation while nominating his army forces for that honor because "the Marines had enough glory in World War I."[8]

A result of this stream of recriminations was mutual antipathy between MacArthur and the officers of the U.S. Navy and Marines, which continued even after the conclusion of the war. Individual naval commanders (for example, Thomas Kinkaid, William Halsey, and Daniel Barbey) worked well with the General in the furtherance of their mission and their orders. However, resentment was unsurprisingly heavy against MacArthur for calling the U.S. Navy defeatist and incompetent. The General was frequently vocal that the navy was out to get him in what often became a self-fulfilling prophesy. MacArthur's chief of staff, Sutherland, amplified these negative feelings. When Sutherland was sent as MacArthur's representative to strategic Joint Chiefs of Staff (JCS) military conferences, he publicly repeated many of his boss's complaints. General Marshall called Sutherland "the chief insulter of the Navy"[9]

While relations between the army and the navy were strained in many places in World War II, nowhere did they sink to such levels of mutual reproach as prevailed around MacArthur. For example, army forces generally performed competently under naval authority in the Central Pacific. Conversely, the navy served under Dwight Eisenhower's command with few difficulties in the Mediterranean and at Normandy. However, navy resistance to a similar command structure in the Pacific was resolute after MacArthur escaped to Australia and lobbied to be put in charge of all American forces fighting the Japanese. After allowing his air force to be destroyed on the ground and his outnumbered land forces to be routed, then accusing the Navy of cowardice, it should come as little surprise that the admirals resisted the General's efforts to become their overall commander. Many navy and marine officers held feelings ranging from distrust to loathing toward MacArthur that prevailed long after the end of the war. Of course, many in the army also came to hold similar views of the General.

Once the retreat to Bataan was complete, MacArthur chose to make his stand where the great bulk of Mount Natib divided the peninsula, and as he based himself on Corregidor, Gen. Jonathan Wainwright was placed in command of the defenders of Bataan. There MacArthur had ordered a division of his force into two corps—one to hold the front in the east and the other in the west. The steep slopes of the mountain in the center divided the defensive lines. During a visit to Bataan from Corregidor, Sutherland expressed concern to Wainwright that the Japanese would exploit the gap in the center of the lines between the two corps. Wainwright disagreed, believing that the intervening terrain was inaccessible by either the defenders or any attacker, and this tactical positioning was not addressed.[10] It is unclear why Sutherland did not bring up this issue with MacArthur or personally see to it that the gap was closed.

Thus, the two corps were not connected and were unable to easily communicate with or reinforce each other. In contrast, the Japanese did not think the terrain too difficult when they attacked on January 17. Enemy units were able to move through this central gap, and the defenders "were unable to prevent the Japanese from infiltrating across the steep jungle-covered slopes of Mount Natib in the center of the general defense line."[11] The Japanese turned the flanks of the USAFFE and forced a retreat further south down the peninsula. Subsequent attritional attacks resulted in MacArthur's army being gradually forced back into a compressed defensive perimeter.

Few have noted that at the start and at the conclusion of MacArthur's wartime command, he chose to separate his force on a peninsula divided by mountainous terrain and was subsequently defeated on both occasions by a smaller attacking enemy force. In Bataan, this oversight was overshadowed by the positive communiqués issued from MacArthur's headquarters, which trumpeted significant tactical victories and large numbers of casualties inflicted on the enemy. Few in Washington apportioned blame for this retreat to American leadership. After all, they did not realize that the Japanese invasion force was outnumbered and had been shorn of much of its infantry, artillery, and air power. Also, MacArthur's superiors did not know that, due to a lack of supplies, the U.S. and Filipino forces "were already beginning to suffer from malaria and their daily rations, which had been sharply reduced, were to become even more meager as time went by."[12]

The outnumbered Japanese were unable to break through the new continuous defensive perimeter further south. They pulled back their lines a few miles to dig in along better terrain and settled in to starve out the defenders while General Homma called for reinforcements.[13] Along with the 4th Division,

Imperial Japanese Headquarters sent him the Kitajima Artillery Group of around 150 guns from Hong Kong.[14] These forces arrived in Luzon in March and trained north of Bataan for an attack scheduled for early the next month. While the Japanese prepared, the USAFFE force waited within its siege lines as malnutrition and disease took their toll: "The absence of mosquito netting, shelter halves, blankets and sun helmets was as serious as the shortage of clothing. The physical deterioration of the troops and the high incidence of malaria, hookworm, and other diseases were caused as much perhaps by the lack of proper protection against the weather and the jungle as the unbalanced and deficient diet."[15]

During February and March, the 20,000 U.S. Army forces and 60,000 PA soldiers still under MacArthur's command in Bataan could have staged a counterattack, which would have likely led to a significant victory.[16] While the American forces were ravaged by malnutrition, malaria, and other disease, the Japanese besiegers were suffering as well. In fact, by late February, the 16th Division and the 65th Brigade were down to a shockingly small combined total of only about 3,000 effective troops able to man the siege lines. This number rose with the arrival of around 7,000 replacements from overseas over the course of March.[17]

MacArthur thought it quite possible that he could retake Manila had he chosen to go over to the attack during this period, though he did not know how outnumbered the Japanese besieging force was. To take the offensive held risks, but the USAFFE desperately needed food, ammunition, weapons, fuel, and medicine. While MacArthur repeatedly called for delivery of supplies by sea, weapons, ammunition, and fuel on the other side of the frontlines were ripe for the taking from the Japanese. Had the USAFFE been able to break out toward Manila, the local Philippine population was likely to have shared what food, clothing, and other supplies it could spare. In the end, MacArthur chose not to counterattack, as he believed that eventually he would have to retreat back into Bataan.[18] Thus, rather than take the initiative, MacArthur's men settled down in their trenches for the next several weeks and starved.

The U.S. military establishment in Washington had decided early on against an all-out attempt to relieve the men in Bataan. The battered Pacific Fleet was not strong enough to confront the IJN, the U.S. Army was not ready to take the offensive, and the "Germany First" policy dictated the decision. General Marshall assigned Eisenhower (now a colonel) to his planning staff due partially to his experience serving in the Philippines with MacArthur. Marshall asked for an opinion on the best course of action regarding the isolated garrison. It only took a few hours for Eisenhower to crystalize a formal written reply:

It will be a long time before major reinforcements can go to the Philippines, longer than the garrison can hold out with any driblet assistance, if the enemy commits major forces to their reduction. But we must do everything for them that is humanly possible. The people of China, of the Philippines, of the Dutch East Indies will be watching us. They may excuse failure but they will not excuse abandonment. Their trust and friendship are important to us. Our base must be in Australia, and we must start at once to expand it and to secure our communications to it.[19]

Eisenhower later wrote, "If we were to use Australia as a base it was mandatory that we procure a line of communications leading to it. This meant that we must instantly move to save Hawaii, Fiji, New Zealand, and New Caledonia, and we had to make certain of the safety of Australia itself."[20] Marshall and the rest of the JCS agreed with this assessment, as did Secretary of War Henry Stimson and Franklin Roosevelt.

While the leadership in Washington wanted to aid the Philippine garrison, the focus remained on an initial defeat of Germany. As Eisenhower wrote in February 1942, "The United States interest in maintaining contact with Australia and . . . preventing further Japanese expansion to the southwestward is apparent . . . but . . . not immediately vital to the successful outcome of the war. The problem is one of determining what we can spare for the effort in that region without seriously impairing performance of our mandatory tasks."[21] Stimson summed up the American strategy regarding the Philippine garrison with the brutal statement, "There are times when men have to die."[22] Eisenhower's view of MacArthur's defense of the Philippines was quite poor. In a private diary kept during the war, the future president wrote, "I still think he might have made a better showing at the beaches and passes, and certainly he should have saved his planes on Dec. 8—but he's still the hero!!! . . . MacArthur is as big a baby as ever. But we've got to keep him fighting. . . . Today, in a most flamboyant radio, MacArthur recommends successor in case of 'my death.' He picked Sutherland, showing he still likes his boot lickers"[23]

MacArthur was promised assistance, but few surface vessels loaded with supplies braved the Japanese blockade. A few did make it to Cebu in the central Philippines but only days before the island fell to the Japanese. However, several U.S. submarines completed the trip to Corregidor, bringing more than fifty tons of desperately needed ammunition, fuel, food, and other supplies to the garrison. These boats also evacuated military intelligence codebreaking personnel along with President Manuel Quezon and his party.

Before departing, Quezon offered MacArthur $500,000 from the Philippine Commonwealth's treasury for his "exemplary past service." As the General was an active member of the U.S. military, this emolument was of extremely dubious legality, but he accepted it, and the funds were sent to his bank account back on the American mainland. If this payment was a factor in space being found in a heavily loaded submarine to evacuate Quezon and his family, or if it fired MacArthur's relentless drive to lead an army back to the Philippines at the earliest possible date, we will never know. What is certain is that he never mentioned the transaction in public, and it only came to light after his death. To put the size of this payment in context, the average home price in America in 1940 was $2,900.[24]

As the garrison's defenders weakened, FDR became concerned that the capture of MacArthur along with his wife and young son would be a powerful propaganda victory for the Japanese. He ordered the General to leave Corregidor and travel to Australia. After a great deal of loud complaining that he should remain to die fighting the final Japanese assault, MacArthur boarded a PT boat with his family, domestic servant, and a few aides after sunset on March 12. His immediate staff accompanied their leader in two more of these small vessels, which together motored off into the night.

Wainwright took charge as commander of USAFFE and for the first time provided Washington with an accurate headcount of the size of the garrison. General Marshall was shocked to find out that there were still 90,000 fighting men on Bataan, of which 20,500 were U.S. Army personnel. The army chief of staff wired back, demanding details and stating that the garrison's size was "greatly in excess of what we understood was there."[25] Even these large numbers did not include an additional 11,000 men defending Corregidor. Somehow, after months of fighting, retreat, disease, and starvation, Wainwright had inherited a force more than twice the size of the one MacArthur claimed he commanded on Luzon when the Japanese first landed along Lingayen Gulf. However, large as it was, starvation, disease, and lack of supplies had dramatically reduced the combat efficiency of the garrison. When General Homma launched a new offensive, the smaller Japanese force surged forward and broke through the USAFFE lines despite desperate resistance. The last significant attempt at an American counterattack failed on April 6, and the garrison of Bataan surrendered on April 9.

The Japanese then turned their full attention to Corregidor. Intensified bombardments were followed by an amphibious assault that overran the island. On May 6, General Wainwright surrendered along with Corregidor's defenders. These men, along with those who had capitulated earlier, were then forced to endure the infamous "Bataan Death March." The defeat represented the largest surrender of an American fighting force in U.S. history. MacArthur raged against these capitulations and successfully lobbied to block Wainwright, now a prisoner of war, from receiving the Medal of Honor.

FIRST ADVANCE

The Hard Way Back

"Thinking it over, MacArthur's two hour talk gives me the impression of a brilliant mind, obsessed by a plan he can't carry out; frustrated, dramatic to the extreme, much more nervous than when I formerly knew him, hands twitch and tremble, shell-shocked."[1]

—General of the Army Henry "Hap" Arnold, 1886–1950

CHAPTER 5

I Shall Return

The small flotilla of PT boats successfully delivered Douglas MacArthur, his family, and his staff to an area of Mindanao that was still under American control. He then flew the rest of the way to northern Australia, where he was appointed supreme commander of Allied forces in the Southwest Pacific Area (SWPA), which consisted of Australia, the Dutch East Indies except Sumatra, the portion of Malaya on the island of Borneo, and the Philippines. To his west in the Indian Ocean were the British, and the Pacific Ocean Areas (POA) to the east and north were under command of Adm. Chester Nimitz based in Hawaii.

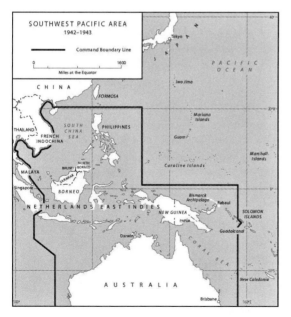

Courtesy of the U.S. Army Center of Military History.

Immediately upon his arrival in Australia on March 17, MacArthur made the most famous pronouncement of his career: "The President of the United States ordered me to break through the Japanese lines and proceed from Corregidor to Australia for the purpose, as I understand it, of organizing the American offensive against Japan, a primary object of which is the relief of the Philippines. I came through and I shall return."[1] A few days later, on March 21, his remarks in an interview with the Australian Broadcasting Company included,

> I have every confidence in the ultimate success of our joint cause; but success in modern war requires something more than courage and a willingness to die: it requires careful preparation. This means the furnishing of sufficient troops and sufficient material to meet the known strength of the potential enemy. No general can make something out of nothing. My success or failure will depend primarily upon the resources which the respective Governments place at my disposal. My faith in them is complete.[2]

Finally, on March 26, he went even further in his interpretation of U.S. foreign policy and how the United States would fight World War II: "There can be no compromise. We shall win or we shall die, and to this end I pledge you the full resources of all the mighty power of my country and all the blood of my countrymen."[3]

In other words, MacArthur felt it acceptable to state in public what the course of U.S. war strategy would be and to dare his superiors and the president in Washington to disagree with him. These comments clearly indicate his disagreement with the quantity of men and material being sent to the Pacific in a manner likely to invite the Australians to complain that they were not receiving as much as necessary. In contradicting "Germany First," MacArthur's remarks implied that the "full resources" of the United States were being directed to mightily reinforce Australia in the middle of 1942. This was simply not true. Such an undermining of President Franklin Roosevelt's policy would have been bad enough if the General had only made his case to the Australian and American press. However, he went further and radioed Marshall to express his opinion regarding the error of America's global strategy and the need for the U.S. Navy to sortie to relieve the Philippines immediately:

> You must be prepared to take heavy losses, just so heavy losses are inflicted in return. I wish to reiterate that his [Japanese] bomber strength is practically entirely engaged on his southern front and represents little menace to such a naval thrust. With only minor threat from the fleets of Germany and Italy the American and British navies can assemble without serious jeopardy the force to make this thrust. I unhesitatingly predict that if this is not done the plan

upon which we are now working, based upon the building up of air supremacy in the southwest Pacific, will fail, the war will be indefinitely prolonged and its final outcome will be jeopardized.[4]

MacArthur's comments were so strident and public that Marshall felt compelled to apologize to British field marshal Sir John Dill: "The measures General MacArthur advocates would be highly desirable if we were at war with Japan only. In our opinion, the Pacific should not be made the principal theatre."[5] Marshall then sent a similar message to Australian prime minister John Curtin to make it clear to the ally "down under" that U.S. global military strategy remained committed to "Germany First."[6] Again, as with his efforts to negotiate a Soviet attack on Japan, MacArthur was allowed to interfere with global U.S. policy and received no censure from his superiors in Washington. The only pushback was minor: the Office of War Information asked if it could modify his statement from "I shall return" to "we shall return." True to character, the General refused. Historians Richard Rovere and Arthur Schlesinger Jr. point out that the request was a reasonable one in U.S. military tradition and that MacArthur's use of "the first person singular had left a rather ashen taste in the mouths of the men who knew they would be called on to return somewhat in advance of him."[7]

U.S. policy at the time clearly intended a "return" to the Philippines, and MacArthur was not out of line to state that fact. However, the Philippines could be the final territory retaken by U.S. forces in World War II, but MacArthur's statements implied that the U.S. primary goal was to reconquer the colony at the earliest possible date. He argued that a return to the Philippines was urgent for American honor, vital to the standing of the United States among the people of Asia, and more important than victory over Germany and Italy. Of course, FDR had publicly promised to free not only the Filipinos but also the peoples of France, Norway, Denmark, Luxembourg, Belgium, Poland, the Netherlands, the Dutch East Indies, Malaya, Burma, Guam, New Britain, Indochina, Czechoslovakia, Yugoslavia, and Greece, while also assisting China and the Soviet Union in the recovery of their occupied territories.

MacArthur highlighted that American civilians were trapped in Manila and must be freed, but even larger numbers were imprisoned behind Axis lines in mainland Asia and continental Europe. Under the U.S. constitutional system, it was FDR's prerogative to allocate U.S. resources, determine which of these enslaved peoples were to be liberated first, and decide what policy constituted the optimal path to uphold American honor. Perhaps the U.S. Senate is empowered to have a consultative role in such decisions, but nowhere is it written that an American regional military commander is imbued with the authority to determine global U.S. foreign policy.

Many supporters of MacArthur claim that he was simply lobbying for the maximum resources possible to achieve his mission, just as were other Allied generals around the world. It is an axiom that all commanders believe their theater of operations to be the "most important" in wartime. However, America had a dire need to ensure that the Soviet Union, Britain, and China were all sufficiently supplied and supported. Otherwise, they might capitulate and enter into separate peace negotiations with the Axis. In addition, to win the war in the shortest period, it was imperative that the Allies focus on depriving Germany and Japan of use of the highly industrialized regions they had conquered such as French Lorraine, Flanders, eastern Ukraine, and the central Chinese coast. Retaking relatively impoverished agricultural colonies was decidedly of lower strategic importance.

MacArthur did not acknowledge these imperatives and believed that retaking the Philippines should be the primary goal of U.S. military strategy. Only then could the nation turn to assisting its allies and complete the final defeat of the Axis nations. To frame how unusual MacArthur's statements were, imagine if Britain's Gen. William Slim had loudly argued in public that liberating the people of Burma was of utmost importance and took precedence for British prestige in the world and that Churchill and FDR should divert a preponderance of force to India even though that would delay the defeat of Nazi Germany. Or consider the absurdity of a scenario where Admiral Nimitz stridently and repeatedly proclaimed that U.S. standing in a postwar Asia was dependent on the earliest possible release of the Chamorro people of Guam from Japanese bondage.

While MacArthur's actions were outrageous and detrimental to the U.S. war effort, we can at least give him credit in that there was no subterfuge, and his goal was clear to all. He insisted that the switchboard operator at the Australian hotel hosting his headquarters answer the phone, "Hello, this is Bataan." The mansion he used later as his command post in New Guinea was named "Bataan," and of course his personal B-17 plane was emblazoned with the name . . . *Bataan*.

THE LUCKY GENERAL: KING, DIGGERS, AND ULTRA

When MacArthur took over SWPA, his orders and those of Nimitz in the POA were primarily defensive in nature: to protect Hawaii and Australia and the communication links between these two points. This required that New Zealand, New Caledonia, Vanuatu, Fiji, and Samoa remain in Allied hands. Despite initial orders to hold a defensive line in the Pacific, MacArthur insisted that a counteroffensive out of Australia to reconquer the Philippines was paramount and complained bitterly that he received such a small portion of

America's flow of men and material. However, a consideration of the global strategic challenges from Washington's viewpoint in 1942 explains why SWPA was relegated to the bottom of the list:

- A Nazi victory over the USSR and/or an invasion of England would have had devastating strategic implications for the United States— hence the strategy of "Germany First."
- A Japanese invasion of Hawaii and follow-on raids on California would have cut off Australia and put West Coast centers of U.S. industrial production at risk.
- A Chinese Nationalist government collapse or acceptance of a separate peace could free up more than a million Japanese troops along with massive numbers of supporting planes, tanks, and artillery to strengthen Tokyo's island defense line in the Pacific.
- A successful Japanese advance out of Burma into India would have cut off large manpower, industrial inputs, armaments, and food to the British war effort. An occupation of India would have then threatened the outbound shipment of Middle Eastern oil and Lend-Lease aid to the USSR via Persia and potentially led to a Japanese linkup with the Germans and Italians at Suez, allowing the Axis nations to transfer military technology and supplies.
- A Japanese severing of communication lines between Australia–New Zealand and the United States would not have had a significant impact in the great strategic balance of World War II or accrued large strategic benefits to Tokyo. A strong case can be made that MacArthur was placed in charge of the least strategically important Anglo-American Allied theater in that conflict.

Despite fears in Canberra of an enemy invasion of Australia and MacArthur's repeated warnings that one was imminent, Japanese intentions to land troops on the continent never got past the planning stages at the IJN, and the IJA was always opposed to the idea. Even so, by the spring of 1942, Japan's efforts had been so successful in such a short period that its military leaders succumbed to what they later referred to as "victory disease." This led them to embark on additional offensives that took them far outside their planned imperial perimeter.

To the west, in the Indian Ocean, they seized the Nicobar and Andaman Islands from the British and contemplated a landing in Ceylon. In the east they planned an invasion of Midway Island, as well as the Aleutian Islands of Attu and Kiska, to push back American naval and air power. In the southeast they decided against invading Australia.[8] Instead, the Japanese planned to focus on their naval and aviation advantages to isolate the continent by cutting off its communication lines to the United States. Operation FS called for a thrust from the military base of Rabaul on the island of New Britain to conquer eastern New Guinea, the Solomons, New Caledonia, Fiji, and Samoa.[9] The downside of this plan was that it envisioned a projection of the Japanese defense perimeter more than 2,000 miles to the east. Such an exposed salient could subsequently be attacked, pinched off, or simply bypassed by Australian forces from the south and American ones from the north.

In his quest to return to the Philippines, MacArthur was in many ways lucky that Adm. King was the commander of the U.S. Navy throughout World War II. While his name is by no means as famous as those of Marshall, Nimitz, MacArthur, or Eisenhower, King was one of the true architects of America's victory and responsible for shifting significant resources away from Europe to the Pacific, which accelerated the defeat of Japan. The admiral was a lifer in the navy as much as MacArthur was dedicated to the army. King could be abrasive, abusive, and obstinate. His daughter once said that her father was "the most even-tempered person in the U.S. Navy, he is always in a rage."[10] King's style of leadership can be compressed down to one of his quotes: "I don't care how good they are, unless they get a kick in the ass every six weeks they'll slack off."[11]

FDR knew exactly what he was getting when he promoted King to run the navy in 1942 and joked that the admiral "shaves with a blowtorch every morning."[12] Friction between such a head of America's fleets and the upper echelons of the U.S. Army was almost a given. Eisenhower wrote in his diary in early 1942, "One thing that might help win this war is to get someone to shoot King."[13] While the admiral argued with the army, with the British, and perhaps even with FDR, the president wanted him just the way he was. When King informed FDR in writing that he was approaching the navy's mandatory retirement age in late 1942, the president replied, in a handwritten note, "So what old top? I may even send you a present."[14] Indeed, the admiral was given an autographed photo of the president, and the man FDR referred to as a "formidable old crustacean" remained at his post through the end of the war.[15]

King relentlessly pressed the British to join in an early invasion in France and, if they resisted, advocated increasing the 15 percent of U.S. military output that the Allies had agreed would be allocated to the Pacific. Marshall backed his navy counterpart in these efforts. As Winston Churchill and his colleagues temporized and made clear that they would not support a decisive landing in France in 1943, King was able to send more U.S. resources west and pivot in the war against the Japanese. While he accepted the strategy of "Germany First," King believed "Japan was not likely to wait to be defeated at a time and place convenient to the Allies. . . . Thus, he continually pressed for a faster tempo of offensive activity than that proposed by his British and American colleagues."[16]

The navy's commander clearly saw the threat to the Allied position posed by Japan's Operation FS. King decided to rush what forces he could spare to the Solomons to blunt the enemy offensive in what became turning point battles of the war on, above, and in the seas around the island of Guadalcanal. The admiral's efforts surely led to more men, planes, ships, ammunition, tanks, and supplies being sent to fight in the Pacific in 1942 and 1943 than would have been otherwise. In this, King's presence atop the U.S. Navy was greatly beneficial to MacArthur's cause.

However, King believed that the nature of operations in the Pacific theater required that the navy should be predominant, just as the complexion of the war in Europe meant that the army naturally took the lead there.[17] He also believed America's route to victory was west from Hawaii to the Mariana Islands and, after that, either onward to China's coast first or directly toward Tokyo. This was a shorter and more direct path than MacArthur's, which swung thousands of miles south to Australia before moving through the malarial jungles of New Guinea to the Philippines and then on to Japan. On King's route, dominated by ocean rather than large landmasses, the army would have only a supporting role. As the most senior four-star U.S. military officer in the Pacific and protective of army prestige, MacArthur was never going to serve under an admiral like Nimitz, who was his junior. He also consistently argued that the only plausible way to defeat Japan was via his longer southern route, which many in SWPA accurately referred to as "the hard way back."[18]

While King pushed for the navy to be ascendent in the Pacific, he and Marshall got along well enough, traveled and dined together often, and, when necessary, agreed to disagree without rancor. In return for army leadership in Europe, King did not specifically demand a quid pro quo in the Pacific but resisted U.S. Army control of marine divisions and major naval squadrons in the theater. His argument for a member of the U.S. Navy exercising primacy of command in the war against Japan was as follows:

> The campaign in the Pacific differed markedly from the campaign in Europe. While the European war, in its offensive stages, was a land campaign in which the role of the Navy was to keep open the transatlantic sea routes against an enemy whose principal naval strength was in his submarine activities, in the Pacific the war remained throughout 1944 in the military-naval "crossing the oceans" phase. Although there were times when troops got beyond the range of naval gunfire support in the Pacific, much of the fighting was on beaches where Army and Navy combined in amphibious operations. Therefore the essential element of our dominance over the Japanese was the strength of our fleet.[19]

King's viewpoint led to friction with MacArthur, who believed that due to his seniority, genius, and experience, the obvious decision was to put him in charge of the war in the Pacific. On balance, King's efforts were still of great help to the General, who wanted desperately to begin winning victories over the Japanese.

MacArthur's good fortune was not confined to the additional U.S. forces King was able to divert to the Pacific. That the General also took command in the "lucky country" dramatically increased his command's striking power. Australia's military in 1942 was generally better trained, with higher morale, than most ground forces being shipped out of America at the time. Rather than green U.S. Army units then available, many of the Australians MacArthur commanded were veterans and ready to fight in exceedingly difficult conditions. Prime Minister John Curtin and his cabinet gave up a surprising amount of the nation's sovereignty in return for American support in holding back the Japanese. Despite the historic ties between Canberra and London, the British military in the Far East had performed so poorly against the Japanese that Australia announced its willingness to transfer its primary allegiance to the United States. As Curtin wrote in Melbourne's *The Herald* on December 27, 1941,

> We refuse to accept the dictum that the Pacific struggle must be treated as a subordinate segment of the general conflict. By that it is not meant that any one of the other theatres of war is of less importance than the Pacific, but that Australia asks for a concerted plan evoking the greatest strength at the Democracies' disposal, determined upon hurling Japan back. . . . Without any inhibitions of any kind, I make it quite clear that Australia looks to America, free of any pangs as to our traditional links or kinship with the United Kingdom. We know the problems that the United Kingdom faces. We know the constant threat of invasion. We know the dangers of dispersal of strength, but we know too, that Australia can go and Britain can still hold on. We are therefore determined that Australia shall not go, and we shall exert all our energies towards the shaping of a plan, with the United States as its keystone, which will give to our country some confidence of being able to hold out until the tide of battle swings.[20]

By the middle of 1942, despite its small population of only seven million, Australia's early start in going to war allowed it to field significant ground forces that were better prepared to take on the Japanese than those the U.S. Army could supply at the time. By the time of MacArthur's arrival from the Philippines, the Australians, or "Diggers," as they were nicknamed, had raised ten divisions, of which two were armored. When SWPA was established, there were 46,000 Australian Imperial Force (AIF) veterans back from fighting the Germans and Italians in the Mediterranean, along with an additional 63,000 men who had completed their military training.[21] This was more than the Japanese, at the end of a very long supply line, could deploy to eastern New Guinea, where the battle was joined.

Australian troops, man for man, arguably performed better than those of any other Allied nation over the course of World War II. The Diggers fought well and were generally competently commanded by their own officers at the brigade level and below.[22] Failures that they suffered in 1940 and 1941 were rarely attributable to tactical execution in the field but rather were due to poor British strategic command decisions, as when Australian units were deployed to Greece, Malaya, and Singapore. When MacArthur was put in charge of SWPA, his command included three battle-hardened divisions—three more than any other U.S. general had at the time. The early battles that took place after the formation of SWPA, along the Kokoda Track, at Milne Bay, Buna, Lae, and on the Huon Peninsula, were primarily won by the weight of Australian boots on the ground.

While MacArthur was glad to send Diggers into bloody attritional slug fests in the jungles of New Guinea, he resented having to win his victories using men who were not part of his beloved U.S. Army. He held his allies in low regard despite their accomplishments under his command and denigrated them in messages to both Washington and Canberra.[23] When hard fighting and success were achieved by Americans, he announced as much through his communiqués, but when the credit was due to Australian valor, he often cited "Allied forces." This irritated the average Australian soldier at the front, who knew who was doing the fighting, but made the American public think that it was their men winning victories over the Japanese. That green U.S. troops in SWPA often failed to perform in combat while the Australians pushed on resolutely was an embarrassment to MacArthur. He refused to incorporate AIF commanders into his senior staff and discarded his allies as soon as he could replace them in the vanguard of his offensive.

The General's final great piece of luck as the new SWPA commander was the massive advantage the United States gained in deciphering Japanese coded radio communications. This intelligence operation, called Ultra, was to have a dramatic impact on the course of the conflict. While American codebreakers had broken the ciphers of Japanese diplomatic messages, referred to as Magic, prior to the war, success was increasingly achieved against both IJN and then IJA message traffic. At first, the impact was mostly focused on naval operations with the cracking of the JN25 code. This was instrumental in ending Adm. Yamamoto's six months of "running wild." The American naval victories at Coral Sea and Midway were directly the result of Ultra intelligence. Similarly, signals intelligence mightily aided the U.S. Submarine Force in achieving spectacular successes that crippled Japan's ability to relocate and resupply forces across its maritime empire. The blunting of the Japanese advance and shift of the Allies onto the offensive was hugely aided by signals intelligence.

The Ultra codebreaking effort improved in accuracy and specificity over time. In the middle of 1942, it told Nimitz the approximate date and direction from which the Japanese carriers were likely to attack Midway. By the Battle of the Bismarck Sea in March of the following year, MacArthur was able to send his air force to attack a Japanese supply convoy heading to New Guinea knowing the specific vessels involved and the day they were to arrive. The next month Ultra was able to pinpoint the exact time and place to send American fighters to intercept Admiral Yamamoto's plane, resulting in the aerial ambush that killed him. By the spring of 1944, U.S. signals intelligence could provide an almost complete picture of the location of every significant Japanese unit based on New Guinea, allowing MacArthur to bypass large enemy concentrations and land troops where there was little resistance.

One cannot understand the success of MacArthur's offensive from New Guinea to Manila without a clear understanding of Ultra. It allowed the General to portray himself to the American public as smarter and more daring than he actually was. Because Ultra was kept secret, few outside certain military intelligence units and high command staffs knew that the Allies were often able to read Japanese messages as quickly as their intended recipients. Without the impact of Ultra leading to the Coral Sea, Midway, Milne Bay, Bismarck Sea, and Hollandia victories, the U.S. offensive to retake the Philippines would have been pushed back significantly.

As MacArthur's command moved onto the offensive across the Pacific, he regularly received specific information as to where and when his forces would encounter the Japanese, and those enemy formations were less numerous, more poorly supplied, and hindered in receiving reinforcements due to the remarkable assistance of U.S. signals intelligence. The leading historian of American cryptography in the Pacific, Edward Drea, concluded, "MacArthur's carefully constructed persona as a daring gambler was diminished because ULTRA showed that as often as not he was betting on a sure thing. ULTRA's portrayal of the opponent's condition was the ace up MacArthur's sleeve. In most showdowns with the Japanese, he held the winning cards."[24]

That the General held an informational advantage over the enemy does not mean he always chose to use it. He launched several attacks, on Buna, Los Negros, Biak, and Luzon, after discrediting Ultra reports of large Japanese force concentrations ready to oppose his operations. This led to higher Allied casualties and a slower advance toward Tokyo, but the growing ability of the United States to provide reinforcements to imperiled landing forces, while at the same time its air and naval superiority interdicted Japanese reinforcements and supplies, allowed MacArthur to eventually achieve repeated victories.

To conclude this section, MacArthur benefited from significant good fortune when he set up his new headquarters in Brisbane in contrast to what might have initially appeared to be a bleak Allied situation in the Pacific. To review: First, Tokyo's plan was not to invade the General's new base in Australia but instead to push the borders of Japan's already extended empire eastward across more than 2,000 miles of scattered Pacific islands. Rather than conform to the prewar plan of fortifying a perimeter and moving along interior lines to repel Allied counterattacks, Tokyo's offensive exposed its forces to attack from the building power of Allied forces in both Hawaii to the north and Australia to the south.

Second, British trepidation regarding an early invasion of northern Europe allowed Admiral King to divert a larger percentage of the surging flow of U.S. forces to fight the Japanese rather than the Germans. In contrast to MacArthur's accusations of the navy's defeatism, King and Nimitz supported repeated aggressive attritional fleet actions at Coral Sea and Midway and off Guadalcanal. Next, MacArthur took over command of an Australian military that supplied him with well-trained veteran divisions that could stand against the advancing Japanese, while U.S. Army divisions were still green and of variable effectiveness.

Finally, Ultra intelligence was decisively important in MacArthur's victories in New Guinea. He increasingly had advance knowledge of where the Japanese were and where they were not, while the U.S Navy and Army Air Force received precise intelligence facilitating successful attacks on Japanese aviation concentrations and supply convoys. These advantages were so great that MacArthur could afford to treat his Australian forces with disrespect, feud with the navy, and ignore Ultra intelligence when it did not suit the narrative he chose to believe and still emerge victorious.

BUILDING THE TEAM

Upon being given command of SWPA, MacArthur immediately began building out his complement of command staff and battlefield leaders to prepare for a counteroffensive to retake the Philippines. In his choice of field commanders, he did extremely well. MacArthur's luck with the Australian military extended to its commander in chief, Gen. Thomas Blamey, a seasoned officer who had led troops in Libya and Greece against German and Italian forces. Blamey's leadership of his Diggers was critical in several of the early SWPA victories across eastern (Papua) New Guinea. This was especially important as only two of MacArthur's twelve divisions in April 1942 were from the United States. Thus, Australians were the ones doing most of the fighting on the frontlines to blunt the Japanese offensive.

However, by early 1943, reinforcements from America had increased SWPA's strength to slightly over fifteen divisions with two more on the way.[25] The U.S. commanders MacArthur chose to lead these growing forces won for him the campaign across western New Guinea and the Philippines. An early MacArthur selection was Maj. Gen. George Kenney, who flew across the Pacific in July 1942 to assume command of all Allied air assets in the theater. This included what remained of the FEAF, which had been reorganized as the U.S. 5th Air Force.

Kenney was the most effective and innovative American tactical aviation leader of the war. He made the most of what he had and gladly accepted models of aircraft that were not in demand in Europe. This helped expand his striking power as SWPA experienced dramatic growth from only 85 operable combat aircraft in the spring of 1942 to 1,000 mostly new planes by the start of 1943.[26] Kenney was an aggressive commander, a proponent of close air support who put a focus on destruction of enemy aircraft and airbase infrastructure to achieve dominance over the battlefield. This fit well with the geography of the Southwest Pacific, where there were few major population/production centers to hit with strategic bombing. Infantry forces in the theater generally had to advance with limited artillery in terrain unsuitable for tanks, so air support often represented the difference between victory and defeat.

Upon taking command, Kenney immediately ordered that fighter cockpits be retrofitted with protective armor and that his pilots be more aggressive. An inventor of parachute fragmentation bombs in the 1920s, he had them utilized to great effect in SWPA: they allowed pilots to drop their loads from lower altitudes at slower speeds, which increased both accuracy and effect most notably in raids on Japanese airfields.[27] Kenney's attack-minded philosophy led him to order the installation of heavy .50-caliber machine guns on as many aircraft as possible, ranging from the smallest fighters to his heaviest bombers. His pilots were ordered to make multiple strafing runs on enemy targets after their bombs had been released.[28]

Next, while the Americans may not have invented skip bombing, which utilized low-level attacks on naval targets (that honor likely belongs to the British), Kenney had been a proponent of the tactic prior to the war, and it was perfected in SWPA to target Japanese ships after his arrival. Finally, he was also an enthusiastic consumer of Ultra intercepts and consistently used this intelligence to time the launch of raids on Japanese aircraft concentrations and maritime convoys. In a mostly roadless theater full of narrow waterways where few carriers and battleships dared sail, his 5th Air Force relentlessly hunted Japanese coastal vessels and wore down enemy aviation assets.

MacArthur also asked for Lt. Gen. Robert Eichelberger, who was transferred to Australia in August 1942. Once in SWPA, Eichelberger proved his worth as one of the best U.S. field generals of World War II. MacArthur came to rely on him as a fireman who turned bloody stalemate into victory on multiple occasions. Eichelberger regularly operated at the front in difficult and dangerous conditions for long stretches of time and moved seamlessly from heading a division to commanding a corps and then the entire 8th Army when it was formed in 1944. MacArthur also brought Lt. Gen. Walter Krueger over from the United States in early 1943 to lead the newly created 6th Army. Krueger had spent years planning combined operations and building relationships with the U.S. Navy and was the perfect man to execute complicated amphibious landings that became ever larger in size and scope as American power grew in SWPA. MacArthur chose the islands he wanted to seize; Krueger and his staff did the work of making sure the operations took place successfully. Krueger was a competent field commander and prudently refused to be rushed by MacArthur, who often wanted victories to take place based on arbitrary calendar dates rather than military realities on the ground.

The SWPA commander was also well served by his subordinates in the U.S. Navy. The flotilla under his command, the Southwest Pacific Force, was officially renamed the 7th Fleet in early 1943 and often called "MacArthur's Navy." While initially quite small, it grew steadily in both size and effectiveness. The fleet's first commander, Adm. Arthur Carpender, was too timid for MacArthur's taste, and Adm. Thomas Kinkaid took over the job in late 1943. Kinkaid had a reputation for getting along well with the U.S. Army and soon gained MacArthur's trust. The SWPA commander was also well served by Adm. Daniel Barbey, who was placed in charge of the fleet's amphibious force. His ships successfully landed American troops in more than forty combat operations over the course of the war.

In contrast to his choices of field commanders, the SWPA staff officers MacArthur selected were of decidedly more mixed quality. Most of his men in the latter category had come out of the Philippines with MacArthur by PT Boat and bore him a strong personal loyalty; they were known as the "Bataan Gang." The most prominent of these was Richard Sutherland. Despite his culpability in the defeat of the FEAF on December 8, his failure to properly supply Bataan, and his negligence in overseeing the closing of the gap that the Japanese exploited along the slopes of Mount Natib, he remained chief of staff and eventually rose to the rank of lieutenant general in 1944.

Every commander may need a hatchet man, and MacArthur certainly had found one. However, Sutherland was a man of such acrimonious temperament and poor judgment that he clearly acted as a detriment to the war effort. Marshall expounded his distaste for the U.S. Navy's "chief insulter" when he wrote, "He antagonized almost every official in the War Department with whom he came in contact and made our dealings with the Navy exceptionally difficult.

Unfortunately he appears utterly unaware of the effects of his methods, but to put it bluntly, his attitude in almost every case seems to have been that he knew it all and nobody else knew much of anything."[29]

MacArthur's chief of staff was no better liked at SWPA headquarters. Kenney wrote that Sutherland's "arrogance combined with his egotism had made him almost universally disliked."[30] Attempts by Sutherland to block access to MacArthur and micromanage the 5th Air Force led an angry General Kenney to draw a dot on a piece of otherwise blank paper and declare, "This dot represents what you know about air operations. The entire rest of the paper what I know."[31] Eichelberger wrote to his wife that Sutherland treated him "more like a Lieutenant than a Lieutenant General" and that he never trusted the chief of staff.[32] The most scathing rebuke from a MacArthur lieutenant came later. After the war, when informed that Sutherland had died, General Krueger replied that "it was a good thing for mankind."[33]

Sutherland had other unattractive qualities common to staff officers in SWPA headquarters: a sycophantic relationship with MacArthur, an active paranoia that many were out to sabotage his boss, and little respect for America's democratic form of government.[34] MacArthur valued loyalty in staff subordinates without respect to competence. However, even he had limits: Sutherland disobeyed his superior's direct order and had his Australian mistress (who was married to an Allied officer) secretly transported to be with him at advanced headquarters locations in New Guinea and, later, the Philippines. When MacArthur found this out in 1945, the mistress was abruptly flown back to Brisbane. Sutherland then announced he had a toothache and claimed he would have to return to Australia for treatment. Of course, this brought him to Brisbane as well, where he was reunited with his mistress for a time. After he finally returned to SWPA Headquarters, Sutherland never regained the supreme commander's full trust.

As Sutherland's star faded, a new one rose in MacArthur's court in the person of Col. Cortney Whitney. He joined the army in 1917 as a second lieutenant, became a fighter pilot, and went to night school to obtain his law degree after World War I. He left the service in 1927 and moved to Manila, where he developed a very successful legal practice. This allowed him to accumulate significant wealth, become a member of the monied elite of the colony, and develop a friendly relationship with MacArthur. He rejoined the army as a major in 1940, and MacArthur had him transferred to his headquarters in Australia, where he was rapidly promoted. The new colonel made himself indispensable to MacArthur and played off the SWPA commander's enormous ego: "Whitney was a consummate flatterer. . . . He poured it on and the General ate it up ."[35]

The sycophant often positioned himself outside his boss's door so he could listen in on every meeting and became MacArthur's alter ego. Whitney was known for being as reactionary, undiplomatic, and belligerent as Sutherland, and the *New York Times* wrote in his obituary, "He possessed a temperament that virtually matched that of the Supreme Commander, and an ability to read and react to situations as would MacArthur himself."[36] Loyalty had its rewards, and Whitney rose to the august rank of major general. This did not keep other aides from complaining. When confronted about Whitney's "deplorable influence," MacArthur replied, "I know. Don't tell me. He's a son-of-a-bitch. But, by God he is *my* son-of-a-bitch."[37] Regarding Whitney, MacArthur biographer William Manchester concluded, "The General's talents were rare and varied, but his judgement of men was often appalling. . . . Surely he could have found a better officer, equally loyal."[38]

In addition to Sutherland and Whitney, MacArthur chose to keep Col. Charles Willoughby on as his G-2, or head of military intelligence—this despite glaring errors in predicting enemy intentions, strength, and capabilities in the campaign to defend the Philippines. Somewhat shockingly in a U.S. military fighting an existential war against right-wing totalitarianism, Willoughby was an open admirer of authoritarian dictators and looked up to Spanish dictator Francisco Franco as a great hero. MacArthur even referred to his G-2 as "his pet fascist," and after Willoughby retired from the army in the 1950s, he traveled to Spain and worked for the Generalissimo as an advisor and a lobbyist. Perhaps Willoughby could have made up for such personality traits with excellent staff work, but the colonel was a terrible appointment. MacArthur knew it and once stated, "There have been three great intelligence officers in history. Mine is not one of them."[39] Nevertheless MacArthur saw to it that Willoughby, like Whitney, was eventually promoted to the rank of major general.

Edward Drea is quite harsh in his assessment of the intelligence chief, writing disparagingly of

> Willoughby's idiosyncrasies, particularly his disconcerting gambit of reversing major interpretations overnight for no apparent reason. . . . In addition, Willoughby often projected his military appreciation of events onto opponents, a cardinal sin for an intelligence chieftain who aims to understand, not transform, the enemy. These traits resurfaced throughout the war in the highly personalized brand of intelligence assessments that were characteristic of MacArthur's campaigns.[40]

Finally, while MacArthur had been advised by the War Department to promote Australian officers to high staff positions, none were. The upper ranks of SWPA headquarters were an all-American affair, even when the preponderance of the fighting and dying was being done by the Diggers. This caused stress between the two armies, which could not have improved morale at the front. However, all was well at the top as MacArthur maintained good relations with Prime Minister Curtin. MacArthur's vocal efforts and political clout arguably led to more American support being shipped to SWPA than would have been obtained by any other commander. Thus, Australian fears of a Japanese invasion were eased, and acceptance of U.S. Army control over all major SWPA military decisions was accepted.

CHAPTER 6

The Offensive-Defensive

Almost immediately after MacArthur's arrival at his new command, Allied forces began to check the Japanese advance and, by the end of 1942, had moved on to the offensive. Certainly, the General deserves some of the credit for this change in fortune, but, as we will see, his claim of predominance in this was a blatant exaggeration. If there was a principal driver behind the 1942 Allied resurgence in the Pacific, it was the U.S. Navy. As the British resisted an invasion of France, Adm. King pushed to send more force to fight the Japanese. This led to a new posture in the Pacific, which King described as "the Offensive-Defensive." The first major battles of this effort were fought and waged by the U.S. Navy and its 1st Marine Division under Adm. Chester Nimitz's command. Despite being repeatedly outnumbered in these engagements, the commander of the Pacific Ocean Areas (POA) achieved remarkable victories.

Papua New Guinea and New Britain Island.

Wikimedia: https://commons.wikimedia.org/wiki/File:New_guinea.png.

Further south, MacArthur had arrived in an Australia fearful of an imminent Japanese invasion and preparing battle plans to defend its major cities.
The General and his supporters have used this situation to try to convince
posterity that his particular genius led to the decision to "defend Australia from
New Guinea." In 1950 his staff in Tokyo wrote,

> General MacArthur felt strongly that passive defense was strategically un-
> sound. He decided to move forward more than a thousand miles into eastern
> Papua and beat the Japanese to the punch. By making the first move, he could
> force them to fight on his terms—across the barrier of the Owen Stanley
> Range. . . . The results achieved completely vindicated his judgement. This
> bold and imaginative decision was one of the most crucial and decisive of the
> war and the final successful culmination of the Papuan operations undoubt-
> edly saved Australia.[1]

MacArthur published a similar narrative in his memoirs.[2]

Such statements engage in significant hyperbole, as "saving" Australia
could hardly be viewed as one of the most decisive turning points of the global
war. The new SWPA commander's orders from Washington were to defend
the communication lines between Australia and Hawaii—not just Australia
itself—and Papua anchored the western end of that line. In addition, there
is the inconvenient fact that the Australian army had already decided to "defend Australia from New Guinea" and had deployed forces to Papua prior to
MacArthur's flight from Corregidor. In fact, in late 1941, the 39th Infantry
Battalion departed Sydney for the north coast of New Guinea to join the Papuan Infantry Battalion already there.

Of course, by far the most powerful force defending Australia from New
Guinea was not even in SWPA; it was the U.S. Navy operating out of Nimitz's POA. In early May 1942 Ultra intercepts indicated that a Japanese landing force planned to seize the island of Tulagi in the Solomons while another
would sail around the eastern end of New Guinea to land at the SWPA forward
base at Port Moresby. Nimitz sent a task force south from Hawaii to stop the
invasion convoy in what became known as the Battle of the Coral Sea. The
Americans lost the carrier USS *Lexington*, and the USS *Yorktown* was heavily
damaged. However, the enemy suffered similar losses, and Nimitz achieved a
strategic victory as the Japanese landing force bound for Port Moresby turned
back due to fears of a U.S. air attack.

A much more significant triumph was achieved two months later at the
Battle of Midway. This time Ultra analysis of JN25 communications predicted

a Japanese attempt to seize that atoll 1,000 miles northwest of Honolulu along with a diversionary attack on Alaska. Nimitz sent his three remaining carriers to ambush the enemy force as it approached Hawaii from the northwest. As MacArthur relates in his memoirs, "Our carrier aircraft, supported by land-based planes from Midway, sank one heavy cruiser, severely damaged a destroyer, and destroyed 250 aircraft. Our losses totaled one carrier, one destroyer and 150 aircraft."[3] It is difficult to understand how MacArthur (and his publisher) could have innocently forgotten to mention that the U.S. Navy fliers also sank four Japanese fleet carriers in this famous battle that forever ended the dominance of the air arm of the IJN in the Pacific.

In the aftermath of the Battle of Midway, the Japanese surprisingly did not consider that they might need to completely revamp their military cipher codes. The depth of incompetence of Japanese military communications security became even more shocking after the *Chicago Tribune* published an account describing how the U.S. military was reading Japanese radio traffic under the front-page headline "Navy Had Word of Jap Plan to Strike at Sea, Knew Dutch Harbor Was a Feint" on June 7, 1942.[4] For reasons that remain unclear, the IJN continued to use the same compromised base code through the end of the war.

After the victory off Midway, King argued that the United States should step up efforts to stop the enemy drive in the South Pacific, and "on 2 July 1942 the U.S. Joint Chiefs of Staff ordered Allied forces in the Pacific to mount a limited offensive to halt the Japanese advance toward the line of communications from the United States to Australia and New Zealand."[5] MacArthur proposed the "Elkton Plan," according to which he would command a campaign to retake Rabaul and the island of New Britain with attacks pushing northward through New Guinea and the Solomons. King approved in concept but demanded that the navy be in charge of the initial phase of the offensive as its sailors and marines would be doing the fighting.

General Marshall worked out a compromise in which Elkton was renamed Operation Cartwheel, and Adm. Robert Ghormley (later succeeded by Adm. William Halsey) under Nimitz's command would oversee the capture of Guadalcanal and Tulagi in the central Solomons from the Japanese. At the same time, MacArthur was to direct the Australians and his two U.S. Army divisions in the conquest of eastern Papua. Then the General would take command of both advances to close on Rabaul. Concurrently, the Japanese decided to redouble their efforts to execute the initial stages of Operation FS and take the Solomons and Papua. This triggered a bloody attritional conflict in which both sides fought at the extreme ends of extended supply lines in pestilential jungle conditions near the equator.

The 1st Marine Division landed on Guadalcanal in early August and seized the airstrip the Japanese were building there. The fighting to hold it became a slug fest on land and sea and in the air. The Japanese also landed units at Buna on the north coast of Papua. Willoughby, recently promoted to brigadier general, insisted that the correct move for the Japanese was to dig in, hold a perimeter, and use the area as an airbase. He disregarded intelligence that indicated the enemy would make a significant effort to take Port Moresby by advancing across the Kokoda Track, which traced a path over the mountains of the Owen Stanley Range. When the defending Australian forces were pushed back along the Kokoda, MacArthur failed to relieve his intelligence chief and instead turned on the Diggers for retreating.[6] Among several denigrating statements, he cabled Marshall, "The Australians have proved themselves unable to match the enemy in jungle fighting. Aggressive leadership is lacking."[7] The Japanese pushed to within twenty miles of Port Moresby and seemed on the verge of taking all of New Guinea. However, the Australians most certainly did "match the enemy in jungle fighting," inflicted large casualties, and eventually ground the Japanese offensive to a halt. Many Australian officers resented that MacArthur complained to Gen. Blamey and his staff in 1942 that the Diggers were not fighting hard enough and were poorly led.[8]

Another threat to Port Moresby emerged as Ultra indicated a likely amphibious landing by the enemy to seize Milne Bay on New Guinea's eastern tip. Australian reinforcements were rushed to the small garrison already there while Kenney prepared his air force to strike the invasion flotilla. This led to MacArthur's first victory of World War II. Unaware of the increased size of the defensive garrison, the Japanese only put ashore about a battalion of its Special Naval Landing Forces in late August near Milne Bay. Despite receiving reinforcements, the invaders remained outnumbered, and while many of the defending Australian units were green militia, they performed well in the subsequent bitter fighting.

The Japanese withdrew by ship two weeks later, leaving almost a third of their force dead along the shore. Setting the tone for much of the subsequent fighting in New Guinea, the advancing Australians found the remains of their comrades who had been taken prisoner: all had been executed, and many of the bodies had been mutilated. A similar fate befell Papuan civilians captured by the Japanese around Milne Bay. The Allies had won a small but important victory, as it was the first time a Japanese amphibious assault had been defeated. MacArthur released a public statement that the Japanese move had been "anticipated . . . and prepared for with great care. With complete secrecy the position was occupied by our forces and converted into a strong point. The enemy fell into the trap with disastrous results to him."[9] As with the defeat at

Midway, the Japanese failed to consider that their maneuvers were expected due to compromised military communications.

Fighting also continued on Guadalcanal as both sides reinforced their positions on the island. However, the Americans increasingly gained the upper hand and expanded their perimeter around the airfield. At about the same time that the first elements of the U.S. Army's "Americal" Division landed on Guadalcanal, the Japanese concluded they did not have the resources to maintain two offensives in the region. The overland attack in New Guinea was called off and the Japanese 17th Army concentrated on achieving a victory in the Solomons while the newly established 18th Army focused on holding the north coast of New Guinea.

In late September, Gen. Arnold, commander of the U.S. Army Air Force, paid a visit to SWPA headquarters. He found many of the senior Allied generals in the theater to be upbeat, including Eichelberger, Kenney, and Blamey. In contrast, despite the Allies' recent successes in the Pacific, MacArthur gave a particularly dour report to this representative from the Joint Chiefs of Staff. Arnold committed the SWPA commander's opinions of the Pacific conflict to his diary:

- The Japanese were better fighting men than the Germans and had better command and control of their forces.
- Japan had sent only its very best soldiers to the southern Pacific.
- SWPA's untrained U.S. troops were too few to hold the enemy back. In addition, he would need an additional 500 aircraft to stabilize the front and was receiving no assistance from the navy. The Australians were of little assistance and poor soldiers.
- The Japanese could take New Guinea at will, then move to conquer Fiji, and would control the Pacific for 100 years.
- Allied strategic positioning in the Pacific was flawed and out of date.
- The Japanese would soon move into Siberia.

Furthermore, MacArthur launched into his opinions regarding the broader war:

- England was no more than a besieged citadel, could never support enough airbases to provide air cover for a cross-channel invasion of France, and no second front in Europe could be launched from Britain.
- Any move into North Africa would be a wasted effort.
- The United States should send army divisions to the Soviet Union to fight against both Germany and Japan.
- The United States should stop building tanks, trucks, and other ground vehicles because they could not be successfully transported overseas.[10]

Arnold then wrote, "Thinking it over, MacArthur's two hour talk gives me the impression of a brilliant mind, obsessed by a plan he can't carry out; frustrated, dramatic to the extreme, much more nervous than when I formerly knew him, hands twitch and tremble, shell-shocked."[11] Thus, the Army Air Force general drew a dire conclusion regarding MacArthur's fitness to remain in command. While Arnold did not press for a change in SWPA, if MacArthur believed Australian ground forces were not of a sufficient quality to stand against the Japanese and that he needed huge reinforcements of planes and pilots to have a chance at victory, then perhaps someone else should have been in charge of SWPA.

Even though the tide was turning in the Allies' favor in the Pacific, MacArthur's messages to Washington became ever more frantic. On October 17, he sent a cable demanding an immediate reallocation of all available Allied military power to his theater:

> If we are defeated in the Solomons, as we must be unless the Navy accepts successfully the challenge of the enemy surface fleet, the entire Southwest Pacific Area will be in the gravest danger; information derived from enemy sources indicates that an attack on Milne Bay and possibly elsewhere in New Guinea is contemplated for mid-November; urge that the entire resources of the United States be used temporarily to meet the critical situation; that shipping be made available from any source, that one corps be dispatched immediately; that all available heavy bombers be ferried here at once and that urgent action be taken to increase the air strength at least to the full complement allotted for this area; that immediate action be taken to prepare bases for naval operations on the east coast of Australia; that the British Eastern Fleet be moved to the west coast of Australia.[12]

MacArthur was once again asking for an immediate and major change in President Franklin Roosevelt's war policy. Of course, the SWPA commander was unaware that following through on his demands would have delayed Operation Torch, the imminent Allied invasion of North Africa. In addition, MacArthur's suggestion to move the Royal Navy's Indian Ocean forces to Australia would have left shipping transiting the Persian Gulf exposed to raids by the IJN, putting at risk critical oil deliveries to England as well as U.S. Lend-Lease aid flowing to the USSR via Persia. Once again, FDR declined to take MacArthur's advice, but also little was done to silence the SWPA commander's vocal attempts to dictate the Allies' global policy and concentrate its military power in the Pacific.

The General also made a separate complaint that Adm. Louis Mountbatten, the newly appointed commander of British forces in India, might possibly infringe on MacArthur's authority. When Churchill heard this, he calculated the distance between Brisbane and the admiral's base in northern Burma as 6,660 miles and wryly asked a visiting British diplomat, "Do you think that's far enough apart?"[13] MacArthur clearly comported himself differently than other theater commanders in the global war against the Axis powers.

MacArthur's implication in his October 17 cable that the U.S. Navy was failing to "challenge the enemy surface fleet" in the Solomons was an unfair one. There had already been three large surface engagements off Guadalcanal by that date, resulting in the deaths of thousands of American sailors and the sinking of several major combat vessels. By the end of the campaign, seven major surface battles and many smaller actions had taken place in which the Japanese sank twenty-nine Allied ships, including two fleet carriers, six cruisers, and fourteen destroyers.[14] However, the IJN suffered even greater losses in these bloody attritional battles. The United States also slowly wore down the enemy land forces on Guadalcanal with the arrival of the 2nd Marine Division and the army's 25th Division. As the campaign dragged on, the Japanese were only able to land 35,000 men on the island over the course of the fighting, compared to almost twice that number on the American side. Eventually the shattered remnants of the Japanese 17th Army were evacuated from Guadalcanal.

As the Japanese directed the bulk of their efforts at the Solomons and went on the defensive in Papua, MacArthur's forces were able to advance. Australian and American forces pushed their way north over the Owen Stanleys. Other Allied forces converged on the area by sea and air. However, it soon became clear that transporting light infantry to the northeast coast of New Guinea was one thing; supporting the troops with proper supplies, vehicles, and artillery through a lengthy jungle campaign was another.

The SWPA contingents soon pushed up against Japanese fortified lines that had been constructed around the coastal villages of Buna and Gona. As during his command of the siege of Bataan, MacArthur remained in Port Moresby and chose not to visit the front on Papua's north coast. Thus, he failed to understand the nature of the fighting in the disease-ridden swamps from which his men assaulted the enemy's well-prepared defenses. Attempts to advance were stymied by fanatical resistance in which the Japanese defenders often cannibalized the dead for food and wore gas masks to tolerate the stench of decomposing fallen comrades.

Logistics and terrain meant that Buna/Gona was a campaign of small-unit tactical combat totally divorced from the orders for the sort of mass advances that emanated from SWPA Headquarters. Also, MacArthur's U.S. 41st and 32nd divisions—green and unprepared for jungle warfare—performed poorly when they arrived at the front. General Eichelberger had warned that the 32nd, commanded by Brig. Gen. Edwin Harding, was unready to meet Japanese troops on equal terms and accurately assigned the unit a "barely satisfactory" combat rating. Reports came back to headquarters of Americans throwing down their weapons and fleeing to the rear.[15] Such results were not surprising as Harding's men were poorly supplied and insufficiently equipped for the job to which they had been assigned. Not only did they want for artillery and flame throwers, but they did not have even basic supplies necessary for jungle fighting: machetes, insect repellent, and oil to keep rifles free of rust. Blamey told the SWPA commander that he could win at Buna and Gona with reinforcements but asked only for more Australians in light of the poor showing of the American GIs—ironic in light of MacArthur's earlier denigration of the fighting prowess of the Diggers.[16]

Embarrassed and feeling pressure as Nimitz's command was gaining the upper hand in the Solomons, MacArthur summoned Eichelberger to his headquarters in Port Moresby. MacArthur announced, "Bob, I'm putting you in command at Buna. Relieve Harding. I am sending you in, Bob, and I want you to remove all officers who won't fight. Relieve regimental and battalion commanders; if necessary, put sergeants in charge of battalions and corporals in charge of companies—anyone who will fight. Time is of the essence. . . . Bob, I want you to take Buna, or not come back alive. And that goes for your chief of staff too. Do you understand?"[17]

At least MacArthur offered potential rewards to Eichelberger for his "win or die" mission. He promised, "If you capture Buna, I'll give you a Distinguished Service Cross and recommend you for a high British decoration. Also, I'll release your name for newspaper publication." Some MacArthur supporters deny this exchange took place, but Eichelberger's chief of staff, Gen. Clovis Beyers, corroborated it. In addition, MacArthur later said of Eichelberger to an Australian officer, "I want him to die if he doesn't get Buna."[18] This unwillingness to understand the field of battle, honestly assess the strength of the enemy, and properly supply his forces, combined with his ordering others forward to win or die in the attempt, has been described by Richard Frank as the low point of MacArthur's military leadership.[19]

Luckily for the Allies, Eichelberger proved to be an extremely effective and brave field commander. He shared his men's hardships in the jungle, lost thirty pounds in a month at the front, and continued to wear his three stars on his uniform near the fighting despite the presence of Japanese snipers in the area. During the course of the campaign, three subordinate brigadier generals were shot, as was another officer who happened to be standing next to Eichelberger when he was hit. While Harding was relieved as ordered, Eichelberger listened to the brigadier general's advice: victory required supplies, reinforcements, artillery, and tanks. The new commander found that his U.S. troops were "riddled with malaria, dengue fever, tropical dysentery and were covered with jungle ulcers"; entire companies were running fevers even as they were ordered forward into battle.[20]

Eichelberger temporarily halted the offensive, the men received their first hot food at the front, and supplies were airlifted to the area. The U.S. 127th Regiment soon arrived, as did the Australian 18th Brigade, which had recently fought at Milne Bay. With these Allied reinforcements, the Japanese were now outnumbered. Eichelberger also supervised transport to the front of additional artillery along with a force of U.S. M-3 light tanks operated by Australians. While the Allied situation on the ground began to improve, victory or defeat remained finely balanced.

MacArthur constantly urged Eichelberger to intensify the offensive regardless of casualties. On December 13, he sent a message to Eichelberger that began, "Time is fleeting and our dangers increase with its passage. However admirable individual acts of courage may be; however important administrative functions may seem; however splendid and electrical your presence has proven; remember that your mission is to take Buna. All other things are merely subsidiary to this."[21] The M-3 tanks, which had been secretly brought up to the front, were successful in leading an assault that broke through the enemy lines. Slowly the Japanese were compressed into increasingly smaller pockets. First Gona, then Buna, and finally the additional fortified positions around the village of Sanananda were taken in early 1943.

With the conquest of Guadalcanal and the eastern end of the Papuan peninsula, the Japanese had been decisively defeated in their offensive to sever the lines of communication between Hawaii and Australia. Rather than relying on interior lines and a prepared defensive chain of fortified islands, as had been their prewar plan, the Japanese empire had squandered massive numbers of fighting men, warships, and aircraft at the end of tenuous supply lines for objectives of questionable strategic value.

"MOVE OVER, GOD, IT'S MAC"

At last MacArthur had won a major victory over the Japanese, though it came at great cost. The end of the Papua campaign highlighted how the daily communiqués emanating from SWPA Headquarters had become increasingly inaccurate. They represented a major effort of the General's personal public relations campaign to flatter his image rather than provide factual information to the War Department and the American public. For example, while the battle raged around Buna on December 26 (December 25 back in the United States), SWPA HQ announced, "On Christmas Day our activities were limited to routine safety precautions. Divine services were held throughout the command where possible."[22] In actuality, Eichelberger reports, fighting was particularly fierce over the holiday, and his forces suffered through a major Japanese air attack.[23]

After the fall of Buna and Gona, MacArthur's communiqué of January 28, 1943, trumpeted,

> Our losses in the Papuan Campaign have now been compiled and are low. As compared to the enemy they are less than half that of his ground force losses, including not only our battle casualties but our sick from natural causes; in the air they amount to a very much lower proportion, and on the sea our losses were negligible. These figures reverse the usual results of a ground offensive campaign, especially against prepared positions defended to the last when losses of the attacker are usually several times that of a defender. Two factors contributed to this result: First, there was no necessity to hurry the attack because the time element, in this case, was of little importance; and second, for this reason, no attempt was made to rush the positions by mass and unprepared assault. The utmost care was taken for the conservation of our forces with the result that probably no campaign in history against a thoroughly prepared and trained army produced such complete and decisive results with a lower expenditure of life and resources.[24]

This communiqué contained multiple blatant untruths. First, there is significant documentation that MacArthur insisted to his subordinates that time was of paramount importance and victory be achieved before the navy conquered Guadalcanal. In addition, losses were not low; they were high. Eichelberger noted that casualty ratios for units fighting in Papua were similar to the bloodletting of many major battles in the U.S. Civil War. Even more outrageously, MacArthur soon made additional statements that the navy had incurred great and unnecessary losses in the ground fighting on Guadalcanal that compared poorly to those his forces recorded at Buna and Gona. This was true if one counted only casualties suffered by Americans in the fighting in Papua. Of course, the Australians supplied most of the Allied manpower on New Guinea in 1942 and early 1943 and also did most of the dying. MacArthur's command suffered 250 percent the number of fatalities suffered by U.S. ground forces in the central Solomons while utilizing only half the number of men.

In addition, illness rates in Papua were an order of magnitude higher than at most other battlefields in the Pacific War. Diseases like malaria and dengue fever may have killed few soldiers, but they forced thousands into field hospitals and left many with long-term negative health impacts. William Manchester, who claimed in *American Caesar* that MacArthur was "America's greatest ever man-at-arms," concluded that the communiqué of January 28 was a stain on the General's record and that "except for Bataan and Corregidor, this was his darkest hour."[25] Historian William O'Neil noted that the fighting at Buna and Gona was particularly bloody for the Allies and that "only MacArthur had the audacity to stand these facts on their head."[26] Many of MacArthur's GIs and Diggers agreed wholeheartedly with such disparaging sentiments.

MacArthur's communiqués also began to use the term "mopping up" at this time to imply that only small, residual actions in an area were still required to complete the annihilation of enemy forces.[27] This allowed the General to announce to the American public that a battle was effectively over on his schedule, even if it was still long before the heavy fighting had ceased. Eichelberger complained that the mopping up in Papua was a "completely savage and expensive battle."[28] SWPA infantrymen came to despise the term, and Eichelberger spoke for many when he wrote after the war,

> I never understood the public relations policy that either he or his immediate assistants established. It seemed to me, as it did to many of the commanders and correspondents, ill advised to announce victories when a first phase had been accomplished without too many casualties. Too often, as at Buna and Sanananda, as on Leyte, Mindanao and Luzon, the struggle was to go on for a long time. Often these announcements produced bitterness among combat troops, and with considerable cause. . . . If there is another war, I recommend that the military, and the correspondents, and everyone else concerned, drop the phrase "mopping up" from their vocabularies. It is not a good enough phrase to die for.[29]

The communiqués from Corregidor had always depicted MacArthur in the most heroic and successful light possible and were often overly upbeat regarding the course of the campaign in what was a doomed cause. However, once in command of SWPA, his press releases took on greater importance as ever larger numbers of men fell under his command in a war in which there were many possible geographic routes to victory. As the General's image as a military hero was boosted back home, U.S. morale to support the war effort was enhanced. In that aspect, his inaccurate communiqués had a positive impact.

MacArthur was not the only Allied leader who played fast and loose with the truth in World War II. However, if his communiqués negatively impacted the morale of the men at the front, and if they related outright falsehoods to the American public, then it is difficult to evaluate them as anything other than a negative mark against MacArthur's record of wartime leadership. Many of the lies issued by SWPA HQ were amplified by press reports filed from the region. Correspondents were encouraged to parrot the daily communiqués, and their dispatches were heavily censored by MacArthur's staff if they did not toe the line. MacArthur used his press releases and censors as a means to promote the impression that he was often personally supervising the fighting from the frontlines even though he was usually hundreds of miles away.

An example is a photo released to U.S. newspapers of Generals MacArthur and Eichelberger riding in a jeep with a caption placing the two men "at the New Guinea Front." The photo was actually taken near Rockhampton on Australia's peaceful east coast. The fighting men of SWPA guffawed on noticing the nose of a Packard automobile in the background of the photo. As Eichelberger put it, "There weren't any Packards in the New Guinea jungle in 1944."[30]

MacArthur's public relations campaign was so effective on this point that after the end of the war, the famed historian Douglas Southall Freeman traveled to Japan and asked Eichelberger, in his superior's presence, "Just when did General MacArthur move his headquarters to Buna?" Eichelberger was sage enough to dodge the question.[31] MacArthur found he could not have it both ways: he insisted that the press focus on him and report that he was personally directing battles in his theater. But he was surprised that his subordinate commanders such as Blamey, Eichelberger, and Krueger, received little attention in American papers and magazines compared to field generals in Europe such as George Patton, Omar Bradley, and Britain's Bernard Montgomery. After Eichelberger received "too much" positive press, MacArthur became jealous and threatened to demote him, relieve him of command, and send him back to the United States. No wonder Eichelberger later told a reporter that he would rather have a rattlesnake dropped in his pants than to be mentioned in a press article.

While the General's communiqués were generally believed back in the United States and liberally used as source material for hundreds of newspaper stories, fighting men under his command in the Pacific War—from Bataan to Brisbane—were deeply offended by what they believed to be falsehoods issued by MacArthur. A parody of "The Battle Hymn of the Republic" with the following lyrics became popular:

> Mine eyes have seen MacArthur with a Bible on his knee,
> He is pounding out communiqués for guys like you and me
> And while possibly a rumor now,
> Some day 'twill be a fact
> That the Lord will hear a deep voice say
> 'Move over, God, it's Mac
> So bet your shoes that all the news that last great Judgement Day
> Will go to press in nothing less than
> DOUG'S COMMUNIQUÉ![32]

Soldiers are known to poke fun at upper-level brass, and this rarely impacts morale and fighting ability at the front. However, antipathy toward MacArthur rose to extreme levels and was clearly not helpful to the U.S. war effort. Republican senator Arthur Vandenberg hoped to have the General run as his party's nominee against FDR in 1944. Reports of disgruntlement with MacArthur were so widespread and one-sided among wounded men returning from SWPA that the senator wondered if the Roosevelt White House had engineered "some sort of diabolical arrangement to see to it that only anti-MacArthur veterans are furloughed home."[33] Sadly, this was not the case.

CHAPTER 7

The Advance Accelerates

After the successful conclusion of the battles of Guadalcanal and Buna, the United States seized the strategic initiative and moved on to the offensive across the Pacific with a rising tide of men, warships, and aircraft that allowed for multiple and shifting attacks on Tokyo's defense perimeter. The Japanese found themselves at growing quantitative and qualitative disadvantages in the air and on the sea, which reduced their field armies to ill-supplied static garrisons that could only fulfill their mission of inflicting unacceptable casualties on the Allies if the latter chose to attack them. However, the government in Tokyo often did not get the battles of attrition it desired, as the JCS in Washington, DC, urged its Pacific commanders to bypass enemy strongpoints when possible and focus on destruction of enemy shipping so as to weaken and isolate the forces defending positions that were required to support the Allied advance.

MacArthur pushed for an offensive across New Guinea and then a return to the Philippines. In contrast, Adm. King advocated a movement west from Hawaii through the Gilbert and Marshall Islands to take the Mariana archipelago, which he argued was the most strategic geographic feature of the Pacific War. MacArthur's refusal to serve under an admiral and the navy's refusal to subordinate itself to a general who had repeatedly insulted its actions led to a divided command structure, which resulted in both advances taking place. While MacArthur argued against the drive taking place in the Central Pacific, King accepted this two-pronged offensive as a "whipsaw" that would keep the Japanese off balance.

In MacArthur's area of operations, Allied forces proceeded northwest up the back of New Guinea to seize the Huon Peninsula in preparation for an assault on Rabaul. The Australians supplied multiple, mostly veteran divisions to the effort, which was supported by a U.S. airborne regiment and Kenney's 5th Air Force. The Japanese attempted to reinforce their bases at Lae, Salamaua,

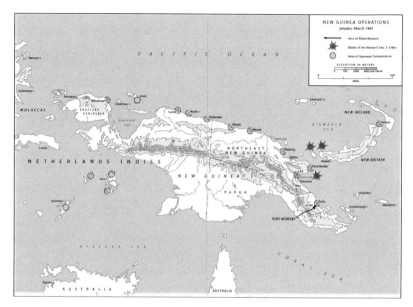

and Wewak with convoys sailing from Rabaul. These plans were detected by
Ultra, confirmed by scout planes, and attacked by SWPA aircraft. The Allies
were successful in interdicting many of the enemy's transports, culminating in
the March 1943 Battle of the Bismarck Sea, in which several Japanese ships
were sunk by land-based air attack. Thousands of enemy soldiers drowned, and
tons of supplies, weapons, and ammunition were sent to the bottom of the sea.

The Australian ground forces pushed forward and took Lae and Salamaua. The Diggers then launched follow-on attacks into the Huon Peninsula
in September, relentlessly driving back the Japanese until the port of Madang
on the Bismarck Sea was taken in April 1944. The Australians performed well
in these actions, advancing hundreds of miles in mountainous jungle terrain.
Kenney's air force was also particularly effective in utilizing the tactics of skip
bombing of naval targets and parachute fragmentation-bombing attacks on
Japanese air bases.

To the east, Adm. Halsey's U.S. Army and Marine divisions, along with a
brigade of New Zealanders, advanced northwest in the Solomons, taking New
Georgia and then landing on Bougainville before moving on to capture Cape
Gloucester on New Britain. American cryptographers became ever more adapt
at reading JN25 and deciphered the exact time and place that Adm. Yamamoto would be landing at a base in the Solomons in April 1943. On April
18, his transport plane was ambushed by American long-range P-38 Lightning

fighters, and the architect of the attack on Pearl Harbor perished in a fiery crash in the jungle. As after Midway, Milne Bay, and Bismarck Sea, the Japanese found reasons to convince themselves that their main communication codes had not been compromised.

In the north, the U.S. Navy advanced through the Gilbert and Marshall Islands, with its marines and army units seizing the atolls of Tarawa, Makin, Kwajalein, Eniwetok, and Majuro. These amphibious attacks protected MacArthur's right flank, isolated Rabaul, and took Adm. Nimitz's forces to within striking range of the Marianas. As in New Guinea and the Solomons, the fighting was fierce; Japanese defenders generally fought until killed, and very few surrendered. Rabaul was brought under relentless air attack from multiple directions, and the Japanese withdrew most of their naval and aviation assets from the base. The Tojo government reverted to its original plan of holding a defensive perimeter and attempting to inflict high levels of casualties that the American public would not be able to tolerate The IJN and IJA were ordered to retreat to a new Absolute Zone of National Defense and increased the pace of reinforcing and fortifying the Marianas and Palau Islands.

The Tokyo government miscalculated, failing to recognize that even the fraction of surging U.S. military strength directed to the Pacific was sufficient to overwhelm the output of the Japanese economy. In short, the Americans could replace lost ships, aircraft, and fighting men much more quickly. Japan's decision to advance beyond its planned defensive perimeter resulted in a rapid loss of men and equipment that could not be replaced. Of course, the Australians and Americans on the frontlines knew quite well that, even in defeat, the Japanese were not driven back easily toward Rabaul, and Allied losses were heavy in Papua and the Solomons. Admiral Halsey later wrote, "When I look back on 'Elkton,' the smoke of charred reputations still makes me cough."[1]

During this period of slow but steady victories, MacArthur had set his sights on an amphibious assault on Rabaul to seize its excellent harbor and airfields, which he believed to be essential for a continued advance toward the Philippines. However, a combination of the large number of troops the enemy had concentrated there and the growing dominance of the U.S. Navy's fleet carriers at sea made such a conquest unnecessary. The JCS ordered that Rabaul be neutralized by air attack and bypassed rather than assaulted as MacArthur demanded.[2] While the General opposed this decision at the time, he was actually quite lucky: the 100,000 Japanese defending Rabaul were well prepared, and an assault would have been costly both in time and casualties. Of course, MacArthur told his staff and field commanders with great braggadocio that bypassing the Japanese base and incapacitating it via aerial attack and blockade had been his idea. This was simply not true. Or as William Manchester put it, "The notion that isolation of Rabaul was the General's inspiration just won't wash."[3]

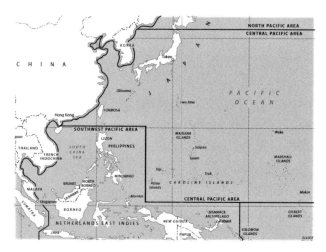

MacArthur attempted to continue promoting his version of events after the war. In his memoirs he relates that just before he revealed his plan to bypass Rabaul to his staff, one of his officers stated, "General, I know your peculiar genius for slaughtering large masses of the enemy at little cost in the lives of your own men, but I just don't see how we can take these strongpoints with our limited forces."[4] While it may not directly relate to an evaluation of MacArthur as a military leader in time of war, such a quote is still terribly disturbing. Could anyone on the SWPA staff conclude the recent campaign to take Buna and Gona had been accomplished with little cost in the lives of Australian and American soldiers? Did the General really surround himself with such "bootlickers," to use Dwight Eisenhower's phrase?

A great deal of evidence supports the assertion that MacArthur oversaw a command culture of sycophants, where senior staff members would be unwilling to disagree with the theater commander or point out a potential plan flaw that needed reconsideration. A successful military leader needs to receive honest reports from his staff. When considering MacArthur's leadership, the best we can hope for is that the General invented this quote years after the event. Of course, if we conclude that this anonymous statement was simply a blatant lie by the General, what parts of his writings can we believe? Again, as Richard Frank concluded, "The first rule of writing about Douglas MacArthur is that he is a tempting resource for color, but for facts one should often look elsewhere."[5]

After MacArthur was ordered not to land his armies at Rabaul, he argued that the concept of bypassing selected enemy forces was the fruit of his "peculiar" genius. Of course, the Japanese had engaged in the exact same tactic in

1942 as they left American forces on Luzon in their rear during their advance to seize British Sarawak and the Dutch East Indies. MacArthur put out a press release on September 21, 1943, in which he claimed that he had come up with a much better way to conduct the war than what Nimitz was up to in the POA. MacArthur called his strategy "leapfrogging" to differentiate it from the "island hopping" of the navy's operations in the Solomons and the Central Pacific.[6]

> My strategic conception for the Pacific Theater, which I outlined after the Papuan Campaign and have since consistently advocated, contemplates massive strokes against only main strategic objectives, utilizing surprise and air-ground striking power supported and assisted by the fleet. This is the very opposite of what is termed "island hopping" which is the gradual pushing back of the enemy by direct frontal pressure with the consequent heavy casualties which will certainly be involved. Key points must of course be taken but a wise choice of such will obviate the need for storming the mass of islands now in enemy possession. "Island hopping" with extravagant losses and slow process . . . is not my idea of how to end the war as soon and as cheaply as possible.[7]

It is difficult to understand how such a public statement denigrating the U.S. Navy's "island hopping" campaign, even if factual, could have been positive to the war effort. In any event, MacArthur's assertions were simply not true. First, as already noted, SWPA casualties at Buna and Gona were more severe than those suffered by U.S. land forces in the fight for Guadalcanal and were characterized by at least as much "direct frontal pressure" and "consequent heavy casualties." It is true that overall American losses in the Solomon Islands campaign, which took place under POA command, were particularly bloody and cost the Allies 7,100 men versus 31,000 lost by the enemy.[8] However, the Japanese emphasized the Guadalcanal battle over that for Papua. Most American casualties in the campaign took place at sea in the several naval engagements around the Solomons that paved the way for the ground victory won by U.S. Marine and Army troops ashore. One can fault the navy for the tactics utilized in these bloody battles of attrition in which the Japanese navy was driven back toward Tokyo, but they had nothing to do with a failure to "leapfrog" the enemy or avoid frontal attacks on land.

The navy does deserve criticism for the high casualties suffered in the Battle of Tarawa, which took place soon after MacArthur issued his "leapfrogging" press release. An absence of hydrological maps and physical reconnaissance led to U.S. landing craft running aground hundreds of yards offshore and marines having to wade to the beach through murderous fire. Even so, while errors were clearly made, American casualties of 3,281 (of which 990 were killed in action) were still lower than the 4,700 Japanese who died in the battle.[9] Most importantly, the navy made a conscious effort to rectify mistakes made at Tarawa. These efforts paid off in the subsequent amphibious operations in the Marshall Islands in which the United States inflicted a 4:1 casualty ratio on the Japanese. In that campaign, the United States suffered 3,262 casualties (661 dead) while killing more than 12,500 Japanese and taking an additional 400 prisoners of war.[10]

MacArthur's accusation that the navy did not engage in "leapfrogging'" the enemy is incorrect. When Nimitz seized the Gilberts and Marshalls, he bypassed more than 13,000 Japanese troops garrisoning the atolls of Jaluit, Mille, Maloelap, Wotje, and Kusrae, as well as Wake and Nauru Islands.[11] Nimitz also had his forces bomb and neutralize the great Japanese base on Truk Atoll rather than storm the "Gibraltar of the Pacific." By the end of the war in August 1945, both the POA and SWPA commands had bypassed a similar number of Japanese. In the POA areas, 131,000 Japanese soldiers and sailors still stubbornly held their posts in the Marshalls, Carolinas, Gilberts, and Marianas, and 62,000 more were in the Volcano and Bonin Islands. This compares to a very similar figure in SWPA of 137,000 Japanese in eastern New Guinea and the Bismarck archipelago, plus 16,000 in the Dutch East Indies.[12]

Finally, the truth was that MacArthur's SWPA battles were more costly in Allied lives than those that took place under Nimitz in the POA. There is no logical reason to omit losses suffered by Australian units fighting in New Guinea from the final body counts. As Richard Frank calculates the data, "MacArthur's forces sustained higher total casualties in combat ashore than the forces advancing under Adm Chester Nimitz in the Central Pacific. (MacArthur's casualties totaled 196,661 including 67,149 deaths, while Nimitz's casualties ashore totaled 108,906 with 28,859 deaths.)"[13]

As the forces under Nimitz began landing in the Marshalls with the start of 1944, MacArthur risked being left behind. He urgently needed to accelerate the SWPA advance to the western end of New Guinea or find a way to shut down the POA's offensive toward the Marianas. The JCS had already determined that the intermediate goal of the U.S. Pacific offensive was to land forces in the triangle formed by Luzon, Formosa, and the coast of mainland China. If the POA drive conquered the Marianas before SWPA's armies could arrive within striking range of the southern Philippines, a decision would quite possibly be made to "leapfrog" the Philippines entirely to assault Formosa or even move directly to stage landings on the Japanese islands of Okinawa or Kyushu. This was a risk MacArthur did not want to take.

With the harbor at Rabaul ruled out, MacArthur needed to secure a forward fleet base to continue his advance. A potential alternative was identified in Seeadler Harbor, formed at the confluence of the islands of Manus and Los

Negros in the Admiralties. The JCS had already authorized an assault on the Admiralty Islands in June 1944. But that was the same month the navy was planning to carry out its landings in the Marianas. Thus, on February 2, 1943, MacArthur wired Washington arguing that Nimitz end his offensive and shift all POA forces to support the army's drive toward the Philippines:

> There are now large forces available in the Pacific which, with accretions scheduled for the current year, would permit the execution of an offensive which would place us in the Philippines in December if the forces were employed in effective combination. . . . All available ground, air, and assault forces in the Pacific should be combined in a drive along the New Guinea–Mindanao axis supported by the main fleet based at Manus Island [planned for a later operation] and other facilities readily available in these waters. I propose that on completion of operations in the Marshalls, the maximum force from all sources in the Pacific be concentrated in my drive up the New Guinea coast, to be coordinated with a Central Pacific operation against the Palaus and the support by combatant elements of the Pacific Fleet with orders to contain or destroy the Japanese Fleet. Time presses.[14]

Unsurprisingly, King opposed such a change in strategy: after all, the Marianas were north of the Marshalls and on the way toward Japan, while MacArthur was urging that POA forces turn to the south toward New Guinea. The Marianas were also well situated to provide naval bases that would allow the U.S. Navy's submarine and surface fleet to interdict Japan's critical supply lines. King was not the only JCS member strongly opposed to MacArthur's proposal. Gen. Arnold wanted to take the Marianas as soon as possible. His new long-range bomber, the B-29, was proving to be relatively ineffective at striking Japan from bases in China as fuel, parts, and munitions had to be ferried over the Himalayas at enormous cost. Airbases in the Marianas would allow large-scale raids against the cities and industrial heartland of the Japanese Home Islands. Fortunately for the Allied war effort, the Marianas operation was allowed to move forward.

MacArthur was clearly worried by the possibility that a rapid Central Pacific offensive might eliminate the need to recapture the Philippines. He began to warn that to "leapfrog" the archipelago would be to abandon the people of the American colony and resorted to what sounds suspiciously like blackmail. In a cable to George Marshall in February 1944, the SWPA commander wrote,

> It is quite evident that the ultimate issue in question is the control of the campaign in the Pacific, and immediately, that for the initial major objective, the Philippine islands which have always been in my area. This has been entrusted to me from the very beginning and has been reiterated in directives

from the Joint Chiefs of Staff and the Secretary of War. While I do not for a moment believe that this will be changed, my professional integrity, indeed my personal honor would be so involved that, if otherwise, I request that I be given early opportunity personally to present the case to the Secretary of War and to the President before finally determining my own personal action in the matter.[15]

In other words, MacArthur was stating that if his superiors at the JCS did not allow him to lead an offensive to retake the Philippines, he should be allowed to go over their heads, not just to the secretary of war but to the president of the United States himself. And even then, if MacArthur did not get his way, he would consider his honor so impugned that he would resign. Of course, he would then take his case to the American public in the run-up to a presidential election, when the General was being discussed in Republican circles as their possible nominee to block Franklin Roosevelt from winning a fourth term in office. If such direct insubordination and threats to refuse to carry out orders had been allowed to take place throughout the ranks of the U.S. military during World War II, the conflict's conclusion might have been dramatically different.

It is a wonder that General Marshall did not choose to maneuver MacArthur right out of his command after receipt of such a message. The chief of staff was no pushover, and his forbearance in dealing with his former superior was exemplary. Marshall only directly replied to the SWPA commander's demand months later in a lengthy note that, with great politeness, pointed out just how out of line MacArthur's actions were. This June cable to MacArthur contained the following:

There is little doubt in my mind, however, that after a crushing blow is delivered against the Japanese Fleet that we should go as close to Japan as quickly as possible in order to shorten the war, which means the reconquest of the Philippines. With regards to the last, it seems to me that you are allowing your personal feelings and Philippine political considerations to override our great objective which is the early conclusion of the war with Japan. Also that you confuse the word "by-pass" with "abandonment," the two are in no way synonymous in my view.[16]

In any event, during the period of negotiation with the JCS as to the direction of the war in the Pacific, MacArthur realized the need to accelerate the capture of the Admiralty Islands. His staff complied by organizing a plan for a large landing of 45,000 men centered on the U.S. Army's 1st Cavalry Division along with attached marine, navy, and Australian forces. The operation, codenamed "Brewer," was to take place in early April. However, this was still not soon enough for MacArthur if he wanted to keep up with the POA's advance toward Japan. The 5th Air Force soon offered a solution. Overflights by U.S. medium bombers seemed to indicate no enemy presence at all in the Admiralties. Kenney brought this information to his commander and suggested a daring landing by a small force to seize the islands before their defenses could be built up by the enemy. MacArthur jumped on the idea and proposed a "reconnaissance-in-force" of slightly more than 1,000 men of the 1st Cavalry.

General Willoughby disagreed with the conclusions gleaned from aerial reconnaissance and passed along Ultra intelligence that the Japanese had a strong garrison on Manus/Los Negros of approximately 4,000 men. In reality, this estimate was almost exactly correct, and the Japanese were intentionally keeping a low profile: their commander had ordered no movement or obvious activity during daylight hours so as not to give away their positions. Later, a small contingent of American scouts slipped onto the south shore of the island and reported back that it was "lousy with Japs."[17] MacArthur chose to ignore his intelligence chief and ordered the attack to take place on February 29. However, in case strong opposition was encountered, a follow-on force was prepared on the Huon Peninsula, which could arrive two days after the initial landing. MacArthur also decided to personally travel with the invasion flotilla and observe the battle from the cruiser USS *Phoenix*. He stated that he would order a withdrawal if Japanese defenders were too numerous to be overcome.

The initial landing wave made it to the beach unscathed on Los Negros, but subsequent troops heading toward the shore came under withering fire. The cavalrymen were able to set up an improvised perimeter, and MacArthur decided against an evacuation, telling the landing force's commander, "Hold what you have taken, no matter against what odds. You have your teeth in him now—don't let go."[18] The SWPA commander sailed back to his headquarters and immediately issued a communiqué that the battle was effectively over and the United States was victorious.[19] Of course, the issue was still very much in doubt on Los Negros. Japanese probes were able to penetrate the cavalry's lines and brought the force's command post under fire. The Americans pulled back the perimeter to a small area around the landing beach; naval gunfire and close air support were instrumental in stabilizing the situation. The Japanese massed for a general counterattack but were not able to launch it before additional units of the 1st Cavalry began landing to stiffen the American frontlines. By March 5 the cavalrymen were able to break out of their perimeter, and on March 11 they moved across Seeadler Harbor to Manus Island.

The Japanese continued their stubborn resistance but were relentlessly pushed back, and 3,300 members of the garrison were killed. In turn, the Americans suffered 1,500 casualties. However, by the end of the month both

Manus and Los Negros had been conquered except for "mopping up," which continued until the middle of May. MacArthur's rushed, piecemeal landing operation was a gamble that paid off through the use of America's growing dominance of air and naval power. Still, it was a close-run thing. Admiral William Fechteler, commander of the operation's amphibious assault flotilla, commented, "Actually we're damn lucky we didn't get run off the island."[20]

The capture of the Admiralties and Madang on the New Guinea coast closed a major chapter in MacArthur's quest to return to the Philippines. Rabaul was no longer a barrier: surrounded and repeatedly bombed, it effectively became an open-air POW camp for the 100,000 Japanese soldiers and sailors remaining on the island of New Britain. MacArthur could now turn his attention to moving as rapidly as possible westward across the north coast of New Guinea against a Japanese enemy that was increasingly unable to supply its troops by sea or to resist the 5th Air Force in the skies.

The fall of Madang also marked the end of utilizing Australian forces in the vanguard of the Allied advance. American men, ships, and planes were flowing into the Pacific theater at such a rate that MacArthur no longer needed to rely on his allies and could now proudly direct his beloved U.S. Army in a campaign to reconquer the Philippines. As historian John McManus put it, "Like a bicycle cast aside for an automobile, MacArthur intended to make little more use of his Australian allies beyond the incorporation of a few ships into his fleet, now that he had access to the prodigious largesse of his own nation."[21] Australia's soldiers spent most of the remainder of the war besieging bypassed Japanese garrisons that were trapped further and further behind the frontlines of the American advance.

The question can be asked as to why the Joint Chiefs allowed MacArthur's subsequent drive along more than 1,000 miles of New Guinea's undeveloped coastline to the Philippines. After all, any imminent threat to Australia had been extinguished, and there was little strategic value in defeating the Japanese divisions entrenched in western New Guinea. After taking the Admiralties, why didn't U.S. forces in the area head directly north toward Japan? After all, Seeadler Harbor is significantly closer to the Marianas than it is to the Philippines.

At the Quadrant Conference of the Joint Chiefs of Staff in Quebec in late 1943, Britain's Sir Alan Brooke posed just this question: Why did the United States need to continue two separate advances in the Pacific after Rabaul had been neutralized? Why not restrict operations in New Guinea to feints so as to free up forces for the planned invasion of France? Marshall answered obliquely that the troops for MacArthur's offensive had already arrived in the Southwest Pacific or were enroute, so it was too late to divert these forces to England in time for D-Day. King agreed that while much of SWPA's strength could be transferred to the Central Pacific offensive, the two advances were complementary and forced the Japanese off balance so that the enemy could not concentrate efforts in one area.[22] Neither U.S. officer mentioned the political reality that there was a presidential election coming up in November 1944 and the open secret that MacArthur had been flirting with senior GOP politicians about becoming the party's nominee.[23] FDR was interested in keeping a happy MacArthur far away in the South Pacific, focused on returning to the Philippines, rather than a disgruntled one in the United States running against him for the nation's highest office.

Historian John Miller Jr., author of *Cartwheel: The Reduction of Rabaul*, published by the U.S. Army's Center of Military History, described the reason for the multiple advances as follows: "The Joint Chiefs decided on the two axes, rather than the Central Pacific alone, because the Japanese conquests in the first phase of the war had compelled the establishment of comparatively large Allied forces in the South and Southwest Pacific Areas: to shift all these to the Central Pacific would take too much time and too many ships, and would probably intensify the already strong and almost open disagreement between MacArthur and King over Pacific strategy."[24]

The argument that SWPA forces were not moved up to Nimitz's POA due to excessive distance is fatally undermined when one considers that the distance between Port Moresby and Guam in the Marianas is only one-quarter that from Guam to the closest U.S. West Coast port of San Diego. Thus, even the U.S. Army's own histories admit that MacArthur was allowed to continue to push west across New Guinea because of his disagreement with Admiral King regarding the proper strategy for defeating Japan. That a theater commander was allowed to impose his will on the Joint Chiefs in Washington is a shocking abdication of that body's command and control and a signal of how America's top military leaders chose to shy away from potentially suffering the wrath of MacArthur's supporters on the home front.

King chose to speak approvingly of the two-offensive "whipsaw" strategy in the Pacific, but in light of his focus on taking the Marianas and his later support of an attack on Formosa over the Philippines, he was likely making a virtue of necessity.[25] Had MacArthur's drive been restricted by the JCS after the capture of Manus Island, Tokyo may not have detected such a change for months. Even if the enemy did pick up on such a change in SWPA activities, it is unlikely that Japanese forces entrenched in Palau and New Guinea could have been safely repositioned in time to reinforce garrisons in the Central Pacific. The fact of the matter was that the Japanese were rapidly losing the ability to shift infantry divisions around the empire's defensive perimeter.

In contrast, the U.S. Navy and its carrier air arm were increasingly dominant, allowing for rapid repositioning of ground forces across the Pacific.

SWPA forces could have been sent north, and the addition of the 6th Army's offensive strength to the force that landed in the Marianas in June would have accelerated the capture of those islands. After that, a single reinforced American drive across the Central Pacific could have struck anywhere in a huge arc stretching from Mindanao through Luzon, Formosa, Okinawa, and Iwo Jima as its subsequent target. In such a scenario, the Japanese would have been forced to guess where the next blow would fall and still would have needed to maintain their garrisons in New Guinea and Palau to guard against an advance by the Australian military. Nevertheless, whether due to reasoned military strategy or FDR's cold-blooded political calculation, MacArthur continued to receive reinforcements and a free hand to strike westward to conquer western New Guinea despite the territory having questionable strategic value.

RACING TO SANSAPOR

The capture of the Admiralties solidified MacArthur's confidence in the veracity of the Ultra communication intelligence he was receiving. After all, it had just correctly reported the number of troops holding the islands of Manus and Los Negros in contrast to Kenney's overhead reconnaissance, which seemed to show that they were undefended. Having such accurate intelligence and increasingly overwhelming qualitative and quantitative advantages over the enemy encouraged MacArthur to take more risk. His subordinates had been able to land multiple waves of troops and resupply them through the course of a lengthy fight on the Admiralties while maintaining decisive air and naval superiority over the battle area. He also had a growing force of U.S. Army divisions to deploy and a rising number of naval vessels to carry them across the sea to targets of his choosing. Allied forces in SWPA were now large enough that consecutive amphibious operations could be staged only a few weeks apart. These advantages allowed him to achieve his most impressive military victory of World War II at Hollandia.

The Japanese expected MacArthur to follow a set pattern and launch an amphibious assault along a discrete stretch of the northern New Guinea coast from Hansa Bay to the town of Wewak. These were all within round-trip flying distance of the 5th Air Force's tactical fighters. In response the IJA's 18th Army deployed two divisions, the bulk of its combat power, along this stretch of coast. Several airbases to support these troops in the expected battle against the advancing Allied forces were developed further west in areas inland from the port of Hollandia on Humboldt Bay. U.S. intelligence had recently begun breaking Japanese army ciphers to complement those of the Japanese navy and were able to give MacArthur a detailed description of enemy dispositions and intentions in New Guinea: the heavily fortified coast at the front with weakly defended airbases in the rear, where large numbers of aircraft were assembling.

Thus, the Allies had a clear opportunity to "leapfrog" past two full IJA field divisions and seize the landing strips needed to support a continued Allied westward advance. As Edward Drea concluded, "ULTRA supplied MacArthur's luck because the break into the Japanese army's mainline codes came at the most advantageous time in the New Guinea campaigns. A year earlier MacArthur's forces would have been too weak to exploit such a windfall. A month later and he might have been considering how to evacuate two divisions trapped at Hansa Bay. Instead, MacArthur learned Imperial Headquarters' most secret plans at the exact moment he was most prepared to exploit its weakness."[26]

Kenney made effective use of the Ultra intelligence that the Japanese were surging combat aircraft to the airfields around Hollandia. The Japanese did not expect their bases in that area to come under sustained air attack as they believed them to be out of range of the fighters needed to protect Allied bomber squadrons. However, the 5th Air Force had amassed more than 100 P-38 fighters with aviation fuel drop tanks, which gave these planes a range of over 1,000 miles. Kenney made sure not to send these P-38s on any long missions to tip off the enemy to the 5th Air Force's new capability. Then, over several days beginning March 30, 1944, hundreds of American planes repeatedly attacked the Japanese air bases around Hollandia and destroyed most of the enemy aircraft there—the great bulk of these on the ground.

On April 22, more than 200 ships of the 7th Fleet began landing Eichelberger's I Corps of Krueger's 6th Army at both Humboldt Bay and Tanahmerah Bay further to the west as part of Operation Reckless. The invaders brushed aside Japanese forces in the area and began a two-pronged advance inland to seize the enemy airbases. Including a secondary landing, which took place to the east at Aitape to seize yet another airstrip, more than 75,000 men were landed from the 41st and 32nd infantry divisions along with support units. The size of this amphibious force emphasized the overwhelming strength that had been allotted to MacArthur's command: the Hollandia landings took place just as Madang was falling to Australian forces, fighting was still taking place on Manus Island, and the fresh U.S. 40th Division was arriving in southern New Britain to Adm. Halsey's marines and soldiers already there. The Hollandia invasion was supported by airstrikes from Nimitz's Task Force 58 of large fleet carriers, as well as by a detachment of eight of his smaller escort carriers, which provided air cover for the amphibious force.

While there were more than 10,000 Japanese in the Hollandia area, few were trained combat soldiers, and resistance crumbled quickly. The two wings of the American advance linked up five days after the initial landing, and 5th Air Force planes were soon operating from the airstrips in the area. As even MacArthur's field generals were not privy to Ultra intercepts, most in the landing force were shocked by how easily they had overcome enemy resistance and achieved their objectives. To them, the SWPA commander increasingly appeared to be a prescient gambler with uncanny instincts. MacArthur did his best to encourage such beliefs.

By landing at Hollandia, MacArthur had advanced his frontlines more than 300 miles, seized significant facilities along with mountains of supplies, and cut off more than 20,000 combat soldiers of the Japanese 18th Army. To come to grips with the American forces, these Japanese began marching westward through almost 100 miles of intervening jungle, during which time they became weaker due to disease and lack of food. The 18th Army was eventually broken as a force in July and August when it attempted to storm the U.S. lines near Aitape along the Drinuimor River. Of course, by then, American forces had already moved significantly further west toward the Philippines. Hollandia was arguably MacArthur's greatest victory of the war: he successfully utilized military intelligence and deployed his overwhelming forces where the enemy did not expect him to land. At a low cost in casualties, he was able to quicken the Allied advance while cutting off a large Japanese force that had deployed to stop him.

By this point, Ultra had become so effective at vectoring U.S. submarines to intercept Japanese transport vessels that enemy reinforcements could no longer be sent to western New Guinea. For example, the "Take Ichi" convoy left Shanghai for Manila in April 1944 with the mission of delivering the IJA's 32nd Division to the Philippines and then taking the 35th Division on to New Guinea. Guided by Ultra intercepts, a U.S. submarine torpedoed the SS *Yoshida Maru No. 1*, which sank along with an entire regiment of the 32nd Division.[27] After reaching Manila, the reduced convoy of eight transports with armed escorts, carrying more than 20,000 troops of the 35th Division of the IJA, left Manila heading south on May 1. Its location again given away by decrypted radio signals, the convoy lost three transports to U.S. submarine attack, resulting in heavy losses in both men and equipment. The remaining Take Ichi ships were diverted to Halmahera Island, and Imperial Headquarters decided to make no more attempts to reinforce its garrisons in New Guinea.[28]

With Tokyo effectively writing off New Guinea, MacArthur was able to advance rapidly and concentrate devastating force against selected lightly defended Japanese positions. Less than a month after the landings at Hollandia, American forces leapfrogged westward another 125 miles to take the airstrip on Insoemoar Island. American casualties of 150 were quite light compared to more than 750 Japanese killed, and the island was soon operating as a major airbase for the 5th Air Force. Concurrent landings just to the south along the New Guinea coast resulted in prolonged fighting around Lone Tree Hill, but loss rates from this battle were similarly uneven.

Only ten days after the landing on Insoemoar, MacArthur ordered another 150-mile jump forward to take Biak Island on May 27. However, Willoughby and his staff significantly underestimated the size of the garrison, believing that intercepted Ultra messages of 10,000 defenders referenced planned rather than actual strength. The 41st Infantry Division's landing on the island initially met with limited resistance, and MacArthur released a victorious communiqué the next day: *"We have landed on Biak Island. . . . The capture of this stronghold will give us command domination of Dutch New Guinea except for isolated enemy positions. For strategic purposes this marks the practical end of the New Guinea campaign."*[29] Unfortunately, the Japanese had other ideas. Just as the Americans were getting better at offensive amphibious operations, the IJA was learning to improve its defensive tactics. On Biak, as was increasingly experienced by U.S. forces landing on other islands throughout the remainder of the Pacific War, the defenders of the garrison chose not to contest the invasion along the shoreline. Instead, the Japanese had pulled back to higher ground and established well-camouflaged and mutually supporting positions dug into caves in the island's interior.

The Japanese waited on the hillsides overlooking Biak's main air base, which they knew would be the Americans' primary objective. As the GIs marched forward, the defenders sprang an ambush that inflicted severe casualties in fighting that soon deteriorated into a grinding battle of attrition. Biak was to be used to provide air support for the navy's imminent invasion of the Marianas, and the defenders' refusal to yield ground interfered with that timetable. MacArthur was embarrassed that the 41st Division's stalled advance meant that his planes would not be able to support Nimitz's forces as promised, and the General made his displeasure abundantly clear to Krueger. Once again General Eichelberger was rushed to the front to salvage the situation. As at Buna, he relieved the commanding general on the scene, reorganized the offensive, and brought in reinforcements.

The Japanese cave positions began to fall to American assaults supported by heavy artillery and air strikes. Weeks after the initial landing the invaders finally shattered the garrison's major points of resistance overlooking the airstrip, which began operating Allied aircraft on June 22. However, fighting continued, and "mopping up" took another month. Eichelberger got to the core of U.S. ability in 1944 and 1945 to achieve victory in battle against the Japanese when he wrote, "Our casualties at Biak were kept at a reasonable minimum because we were willing to shoot away tons of ammunition (undoubtedly at great cost to the American taxpayer) when a direct attack promised punishing casualties."[30] By 1944, American industrial output was such that huge weights of artillery ordnance could be expended against enemy formations that were often forced to operate with dwindling supplies of ammunition.

While Eichelberger's forces were still fighting to secure Biak's main airbase, Admiral Nimitz launched the invasion of the Marianas. After massive shore bombardments, three marine and two army divisions landed on the islands of Saipan, Guam, and Tinian between June 15 and July 24. In savage fighting that lasted until early August, more than 65,000 defenders died, which represented more than eight Japanese dead for every American killed. In a chilling indication of the fighting to come as battles took place closer to Tokyo, thousands of Japanese civilians on Saipan and Tinian chose suicide rather than surrender. Many jumped from high cliffs as Americans looked on in bewilderment.

In addition to success on land, the American navy guarding the invasion flotilla inflicted a crushing defeat on the IJN's remaining carrier air arm in the Battle of the Philippine Sea. Finally, Ultra intercepts guided American ships to specific locations to ambush the Japanese submarine force positioned in a picket line to detect the approaching U.S. invasion fleet. Seventeen of thirty-five enemy boats deployed along this line were sunk. Five were dispatched by the single destroyer USS *England* in just six days at the end of May. The U.S. military had clearly become a juggernaut. That it could mount the invasion of the Marianas less than two weeks after the massive D-Day operation, while yet other American armies were on the offensive in both Italy and New Guinea, speaks to the awesome power that had been mobilized to defeat the Axis.

With the fall of the Marianas, Japan's perimeter had been decisively breached, American B-29s would soon begin wholesale bombing of the Japanese Home Islands, and the U.S. Navy acquired advanced bases for its submarines to stalk enemy shipping all the way to the Japanese, Chinese, and Korean coasts. Many senior politicians and military officers in Tokyo accepted that they had lost the war, and Tojo's government fell from power. However, in light of FDR's "unconditional surrender" policy toward the Axis powers, the Japanese fought on, unwilling to accept defeat and hoping that somehow enough casualties could be inflicted on the Americans to trigger a negotiated settlement.

As Nimitz was taking the Marianas, MacArthur continued his westward advance. Forces under his command overpowered the small garrison on the island of Noemfoor and then landed unopposed at Sansapor at the far western end of New Guinea on June 30. While fighting against isolated garrisons continued, this effectively concluded MacArthur's conquest of the island. The General's staff then began planning a landing on the island of Morotai as a final staging point to provide air cover for an assault on the southern Philippine island of Mindanao.

By taking advantage of Ultra intelligence, surging American reinforcements, and the decimation of Japanese shipping, MacArthur had been able to dramatically accelerate the pace of his forces' advance. Vast distances, entire Japanese armies, and terrible jungle diseases had been overcome in the campaign from Milne Bay to Sansapor. While still much further away from Tokyo than POA units in the Marianas, MacArthur was now close enough to the Philippines that he could make the case that the American colony should be the next target of the advance across the Pacific. The question was if he would be able to fulfill his quest or decision makers in Washington would instead decide to leapfrog the Philippines and strike further north on the way to Tokyo.

The young General MacArthur
in France, 1918. NARA.

On the eve of war: MacArthur, commander of the U.S. Army Forces Far East (USAFFE),
in Luzon on August 15, 1941. His chief of staff, Gen. Richard Sutherland, stands behind
him on the far left. U.S. ARMY.

The M3 Stuart light tank. MacArthur had more than 100 on hand for his defense of Luzon. LIBRARY OF CONGRESS.

MacArthur with Gen. Jonathan Wainwright. U.S. ARMY.

The Japanese Mitsubishi A6M "Zero" was the longest-ranged single-engine fighter of World War II which was able to reach central Luzon from bases in Formosa and wreak havoc in the days after the attack on Pearl Harbor. IJN/WIKIMEDIA COMMONS/ PUBLIC DOMAIN.

MacArthur declared Manila an "open city" on December 26, 1941, to spare the population from Japanese attack. However, this placed tons of critical supplies, food, and ammunition off limits to his forces. U.S. ARMY.

MacArthur and Gen. Richard Sutherland on Corregidor before their escape to Australia. U.S. ARMY.

The garrison of Corregidor surrenders to join the tens of thousands of POWs from Bataan. U.S. Army.

An A-20 bomber of the 5th Air Force attacks a Japanese merchant vessel during the Battle of the Bismarck Sea, March 1943.

U.S. Army/Wikimedia Commons/Public Domain.

Admiral Isoruku Yamamoto, commander in chief of the Imperial Japanese Navy, saluting naval pilots at Rabaul on April 18, 1943, just hours before he was killed in an aerial ambush over the Solomon Islands by sixteen American P-38 fighters. Wikimedia Commons/Public Domain.

From left to right, Lt. Gen. Walter Krueger, commander of the 6th Army, MacArthur, and Chief of Staff Gen. George Marshall in late 1943. U.S. Navy.

MacArthur with commander of the 7th Fleet, Vice Adm. Thomas Kinkaid (left), on board the light cruiser USS *Phoenix* in February 1944 during the preinvasion bombardment of Los Negros Island. U.S. Navy.

Honolulu, July 28, 1944. From left to right: MacArthur, President Franklin Roosevelt, Adm. William Leahy, and Adm. Chester Nimitz (standing) discuss how to finish the war against Japan. U.S. Navy/Wikimedia Commons/Public Domain.

The Philippine capital and its residents suffered terribly during the Battle of Manila. This photo from May 1945 shows the destruction visited on the 400-year-old Intramuros district of the city. U.S. Army/Wikimedia Commons/Public Domain.

The famous photo from Tokyo in September 1945 shows the first meeting of MacArthur and Emperor Hirohito after the Japanese surrender. U.S. Army/Wikimedia Commons/Public Domain.

A new war: men of the 25th Division, firing from defensive positions along the Pusan Perimeter, in early September 1950. U.S. Army.

"I realize that Inchon is a 5,000 to 1 gamble, but I am used to taking such odds." MacArthur watches the amphibious assault with his chief of staff, Maj. Gen. Edward Almond (right), and Brig. Gen. Courtney Whitney (left) on the USS *Mount McKinley*. U.S. Army.

U.S. marines advance to retake a battered Seoul in September 1950. U.S. Army/Wikimedia Commons/Public Domain.

MacArthur greets President Harry Truman with a handshake rather than a salute on Wake Island. U.S. Department of State/Wikimedia Commons/Public Domain.

A unit of the Chinese People's Volunteer Army assaulting UN positions during the Second Phase Offensive, which threw MacArthur's larger force into headlong retreat. Chinese Military Science Academy/Wikimedia Commons/ Public Domain.

Lt. Gen. Mathew Ridgway (center) arrived in Korea to take over the 8th Army and soon stabilized the UN lines. U.S. Army.

"There is no substitute for victory." MacArthur addressing an audience of 50,000 at Soldier's Field in Chicago on April 25, 1951, after his relief by President Harry Truman. NARA/ Wikimedia Commons/ Public Domain.

SECOND ADVANCE

Honolulu to Tokyo

"This is the voice of freedom, General MacArthur speaking. People of the Philippines: I have returned."[1]

—General of the Army Douglas MacArthur, 1880–1964

CHAPTER 8

Leyte

In March 1944, Adm. Nimitz traveled to Brisbane to meet with General MacArthur and discuss the upcoming landings at Hollandia. The conversation was proceeding smoothly until the admiral mentioned that the JCS believed that after taking New Guinea and the Marianas, it might make strategic sense to seize Mindanao and then bypass Luzon so as to leapfrog to Formosa or the Chinese coast. Nimitz related that MacArthur

> blew up and made an oration of some length on the impossibility of bypassing the Philippines, his sacred obligation there—redemption of the 17 million people—blood on his soul—deserted by American people—etc., etc.—and then a criticism of "those gentlemen in Washington, who, far from the scene, and having never heard the whistle of the pellets, etc., endeavor to set the strategy of the Pacific War"—etc. When I could break in I replied that, while I believed I understood his point of view, I could not go along with him, and then—believe it or not—I launched forth in a defense of "those gentlemen in Washington" and told him that the J.C.S. were people like himself and myself, who, with more information, were trying to do their best for the country and, to my mind, were succeeding admirably.[1]

Clearly, MacArthur was not going to allow Manila to be bypassed without a fight.

In contrast, Adm. King very much favored bypassing at least Luzon, if not all of the Philippines. He believed the best course of action was for American amphibious forces to sail directly from the Marianas to Formosa. His reasoning was based on several strategic points that ignored items such as America's sacred obligations to the people of the Philippines. As he put it in his memoirs,

The Navy favored a direct attack on Formosa without reference to the Philippine Islands, feeling that this position would dominate the sea lanes by which Japan received essential supplies of oil, rice and other commodities from her recently conquered southern empire. The Navy had no interest in fighting the Japanese on land in their home islands, feeling that a blockade exercised by sea and air power was sufficient to win. General MacArthur, on the other hand, was strongly in favor of a return to the Philippines. There were difficulties in both plans. The Navy knew that an assault on Formosa would involve a hard struggle because the Japanese had sent heavy reinforcements of planes and troops to the island. On the other hand, a return to the Philippines would involve United States troops, planes and ships on a greater scale starting from Morotai and plugging through the entire length of the Philippines archipelago. The only merit to this plan, in King's view, was a political one, since the United States had a definite interest in aiding those Filipinos who had been fighting the Japanese.[2]

The admiral also worried that landing in the Philippines might represent a two-edged sword for the people of the colony: once U.S. forces arrived in the islands, the Japanese military could be counted on to conduct itself with a

COURTESY OF THE U.S. ARMY CENTER OF MILITARY HISTORY.

barbarism and fight-to-the-death mind-set that would result in terrible damage to the inhabitants and infrastructure of the American colony. This thinking was summed up when King argued with Adm. Halsey's chief of staff, Vice Adm. Robert Carney, who wanted to invade the Philippines rather than Formosa. "'Do you want to make a London out of Manila?' King demanded. Carney's reply was, 'No sir, I want to make an England out of Luzon.'"[3]

Of the Joint Chiefs, King, Marshall, and Arnold were in favor of jumping directly to Formosa, while Adm. William Leahy supported an initial capture of Luzon. In contrast, a majority of the senior generals and admirals in the Pacific wanted to seize bases in the Philippines first.[4] Thus, a major debate ensued and had not been resolved by July 1944. This is when Franklin Roosevelt decided to wade into the argument. The president, running for an unprecedented fourth term in office, decided that he would discuss how to finish the war with Japan with his two Pacific theater commanders at a meeting in Honolulu.

He also had ulterior motives for making the trip. Despite accepting the Democratic Party's nomination, FDR was a terribly weak and ill man unlikely to survive another term in office. He collapsed and became unresponsive for a time in his private train car soon after receiving the nomination; he often appeared cyanotic, and his blood pressure was recorded as being 185/105 or higher.[5] A lengthy ship voyage to and from Hawaii would allow the president time to rest and recover out of the public eye. He also liked the idea of being photographed by the press performing his commander in chief role while seated alongside the two popular military leaders MacArthur and Nimitz. Unlike his other wartime overseas trips, FDR did not take the Joint Chiefs with him: King, Marshall, and Arnold were pointedly not invited to the meeting in Honolulu. In fact, King was in Oahu with Nimitz and was obliged to fly back to the mainland immediately before the president's arrival.

MacArthur did not want to go to what he called a "damned photo op" but made sure to fly in early in the *Bataan*. When the president's ship pulled into dock, members of the press corps along with a large number of generals and admirals, including Nimitz, were there in full dress uniform to meet him. MacArthur was finishing up a hot bath at the time and arrived late in an open-topped convertible complete with police escort with wailing sirens. The General stood out even more that July day in Pearl Harbor in his heavy leather flying jacket, which he claimed he was wearing because it was cold up at flying altitude and he had just landed.

When FDR sat down to discuss strategy with his two theater commanders later that evening, MacArthur entered the debate on how U.S. forces should advance with two significant advantages. First, Nimitz had been delegated to argue King's case for a jump to Formosa. However, the POA commander was not wholly behind such a strategy and was willing to consider first capturing a naval and air base in the Philippines. Second, FDR knew that the sixty-five-year-old MacArthur could elect to resign and return to the United States if the Philippines were leapfrogged and his "honor was irretrievably damaged." The General was closely allied with the GOP and could be an influential surrogate for the Republican nominee on the campaign trail in the upcoming election.

MacArthur emphasized this second point and highlighted the moral and political imperatives of a return to the Philippines. As when he had been chief of staff of the army, the General spoke to the president as an equal and in a contentious manner. He highlighted the plight of the thousands of American civilians interned in Manila and demanded to know if FDR was "willing to accept responsibility for breaking a solemn promise to eighteen million Christian Filipinos that the Americans would return?"[6] If the Philippines were bypassed, MacArthur predicted, "I daresay that the American people would be so aroused that they would register most complete resentment against you at the polls this fall."

In reply, FDR related that military intelligence indicated a very large and growing Japanese garrison in the Philippines and stated his concern: "'Douglas, to take Luzon would demand heavier losses than we can stand.' MacArthur disagreed and replied, 'Mr. President, my losses would not be heavy, any more than they have been in the past. The days of the frontal attack should be over. Modern infantry weapons are too deadly and frontal assault is only for mediocre commanders. Good commanders do not turn in heavy losses.'"[7] He also promised that Luzon could be completely captured in six weeks or less.[8] This was not the only time MacArthur downplayed the ease of taking the Philippines. In December 1944 Marshall went as far as to tell Secretary of War Henry Stimson that in regard to his planned return, MacArthur was "so prone to exaggerate and so influenced by his own desires that it is difficult to trust his judgement."[9]

The SWPA commander went on to emphasize that Formosa was defended by a very large number of enemy soldiers and disputed FDR's assertion that the Philippines were protected by a huge garrison. In reality, the Philippines were held by a massive force that swelled to half a million Japanese by the time of the American landings. In contrast, Formosa's garrison was a substantial but smaller 170,000 men.[10] MacArthur also argued that assaulting Formosa was terribly risky as it would be out of range of U.S. ground-based air cover. In contrast, MacArthur described his plan for a progression of south-to-north Philippine landings (Mindanao, then Leyte, then Luzon), which would eventually retake Manila under a consistent and necessary protective umbrella of ground-based fighter protection.

After the meeting broke up for the evening, an exhausted FDR retired to his quarters and complained to his personal physician, "Give me an aspirin.

In fact, give me another aspirin to take in the morning. In all my life nobody has ever talked to me the way MacArthur did."[11] After a few final moments of discussion on the matter with the president the next day, the SWPA commander took his leave and departed in *Bataan* flying southward away from Honolulu (and Tokyo). He was exuberant and believed that he had won approval to return to the Philippines. While there is no record of the president issuing a direct order mandating an invasion of the Philippines, it was no surprise that Roosevelt's preference won out in the ongoing debate at the Pentagon. After all, in his memoirs, King titles the section concerning FDR's visit to Honolulu "President Roosevelt Intervenes in Pacific Strategy."[12] Finally, the JCS authorized an assault on the islands of Morotai and Peleliu on September 15 in preparation for a subsequent landing in Mindanao.

More than 55,000 men landed on Morotai, which was to be developed as an air base to support the Mindanao invasion. The invasion force overwhelmed the island's 500 defenders, and the Americans had a heavy bomber field operating there by the first week of October. The JCS assigned Nimitz the task of taking Peleliu to the east of Mindanao and Morotai to protect MacArthur's right flank. However, the Japanese had heavily reinforced the island, which was defended by more than 10,000 Japanese in well-prepared positions similar to those encountered on Biak. Unlike the rapid conquest of Morotai, the 1st Marine Division and the 81st Infantry Division sustained almost 10,000 casualties out of 47,000 men put ashore. These casualties can be counted as the first losses of the Philippine campaign, as Peleliu would have been bypassed had the decision been made to leapfrog directly to Formosa.

While the two amphibious forces were sailing for their objectives in mid-September, the fleet carriers of the U.S. Navy raided the central and southern Philippines to ensure that Japanese naval and aviation units were unable to interfere with the landings. U.S. carrier aircraft flew hundreds of sorties and encountered little opposition in the skies. This led Admiral Halsey to recommend that Mindanao be bypassed and that landings take place on Leyte in October before the Japanese could organize their defenses there. MacArthur endorsed this acceleration of the advance, and the JCS agreed to the change of plans.

There were significant problems with this decision. First, a leapfrog past Mindanao to Leyte meant SWPA forces would land in the Philippines too far north to be supported by ground-based air cover. This of course had been one of the General's major points in his argument against attacking Formosa when meeting with FDR just weeks earlier. Still, this would not have been a major issue if suitable landing strips could be developed quickly while the navy's carrier force provided temporary air support for the invasion. However, MacArthur's senior engineering officers warned him that poor drainage and soil conditions during Leyte's monsoon season, with its torrential rains, would preclude the timely development of sufficient airfield capacity on the island.

An inability to gain air superiority over Leyte after the U.S. carrier force was forced to retire from the area to refuel and rearm would offer the Japanese the opportunity to feed reinforcements and supplies into Leyte across the narrow straits from adjoining islands to the south (Mindanao), north (Luzon), and west (Visayas).[13] Finally, there was the possibility that the overhead reconnaissance conducted by American fliers was flawed and that Japanese ground and air units in the Philippines were intentionally keeping a low profile to conserve their strength and obscure their positions.

MacArthur had already encountered such enemy tactics in the Admiralties, and indeed the Japanese in the Philippines were lying low while they waited for an opportunity to attack an American landing force. Ultra intelligence indicated a large enemy military buildup in the archipelago, though, as already evident in his discussions with FDR, MacArthur chose to discount this information. Instead, he hoped that his return to the Philippines would only encounter limited Japanese resistance, allowing for a rapid reconquest, few civilian casualties, and little in the way of damage to the islands' infrastructure. Indeed, he seemed to believe his invading forces represented the greatest threat to the Filipinos. He issued the following message to his subordinates soon before the landing on Leyte commenced: "One of the purposes of the Philippine campaign is to liberate the Filipinos; they will not understand liberation if accomplished by indiscriminate destruction of their homes, their possessions, their civilization and their own lives; humanity and our moral standing throughout the Far East dictate that the destruction of lives and property in the Philippines be held to a minimum, compatible with the assurance of a successful military campaign."[14]

On "A-Day," October 17, four divisions of Gen. Krueger's 6th Army began landing on eastern Leyte supported by a massive fleet of 300 ships, which included more than 30 aircraft carriers and 12 battleships. MacArthur's advance into the Philippines was completely different from that of the earlier SWPA offensive in eastern New Guinea. The United States had seized complete strategic initiative and gained both quantitative and qualitative superiority over the Japanese in the air, at sea, and in artillery and armor ashore. MacArthur eventually landed seventeen divisions in the Philippines, utilizing both the 6th Army and the new 8th Army commanded by Gen. Eichelberger. Importantly for the SWPA commander, all the ground troops coming ashore to liberate the Philippines were Americans. While the government in Canberra offered a full corps of seasoned Australian troops for the Leyte operation, MacArthur refused to use them. He decided that the islands of the Philippines were to be liberated only by the U.S. Army.[15] The Australians could do their fighting and dying to retake Dutch and British territory.

The SWPA commander watched the shore bombardment and initial landing from the cruiser USS *Nashville*. After a few hours he could wait no more:

> At 1 p.m., he and his staff left the cruiser to take the two-mile landing craft ride to Red Beach. MacArthur intended to step out onto dry land, but soon realized their vessel was too large to advance through the shallow depths near the coastline. An aide radioed the navy beachmaster and asked that a smaller craft be sent to bring them in. The beachmaster, whose word was law on the invasion beach, was too busy with the chaos of the overall invasion to be bothered with a general, no matter how many stars he wore. "Walk in—the water's fine," he growled.[16]

The photographed image of the scowling MacArthur, angry yet again with the navy, appeared in newspapers across the United States. To the American public the General's expression of seemingly intense determination as he waded onto the shore became one of the most famous images of the war.

Japanese defenders from the 16th Division along the shore had been pushed back by the massive American invasion force, which was landing tanks, artillery, and supplies. After a quick walk along the beach reviewing the advance of his men, MacArthur approached a hastily prepared radio microphone to address those he had come to save. His speech began, "This is the Voice of Freedom, General MacArthur speaking. People of the Philippines: I have returned."[17] Truly this must be one of the most egocentric orations in American history. Was Gen. Douglas MacArthur himself the actual embodiment of "the voice of freedom"? Should Senator Arthur Vandenberg really have been surprised that so many American soldiers assigned to SWPA found reason to take offense with their commander's words and actions?

Over the next few days, the 6th Army pushed inland and jumped across the San Juanico Strait to land on the nearby island of Samar. The small airfields at Dulag and Tacloban were also captured, and more than fifty planes of the 5th Air Force flew in to operate out of these new bases. The Japanese commander of the Philippine garrison, Gen. Tomoyuki Yamashita, wanted to husband his forces to fight a lengthy delaying action in Luzon, which would tie down large numbers of American forces. However, he was overruled and ordered to make the defense of Leyte a priority, and four additional divisions were ordered to converge from the south and the north to concentrate forces on the island. U.S. planes and naval craft interdicted much of this shipping, but more than 30,000 Japanese soldiers were transported to the west side of the island and moved inland to oppose the Americans approaching from the east.

THE BATTLE OF LEYTE GULF AND DIVIDED COMMAND

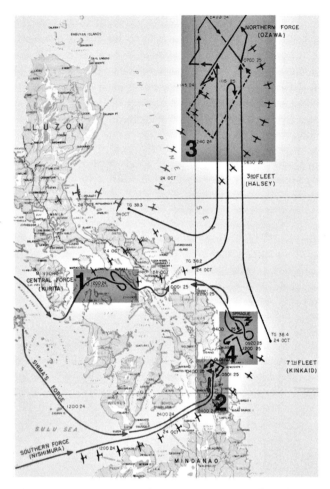

The four main actions in the Battle of Leyte Gulf: (1) Battle of the Sibuyan Sea, (2) Battle of Surigao Strait, (3) Battle off Cape Engaño, and (4) Battle off Samar.

While the 6th Army advanced inland, the IJN activated Operation Sho-Go to launch an all-out attack on the U.S. Navy in hopes of winning a decisive battle at sea and cripple the resupply of the invasion force. This led to a series of engagements, known today as the Battle of Leyte Gulf, which together constitute the largest naval battle in history. The result was the destruction of much of the Japanese fleet. The fighting began as a large formation of IJN ships under Vice Adm. Takeo Kurita, sighted approaching from the west of the Philippines, was attacked by two American submarines, which sank a heavy cruiser and heavily damaged another. U.S. Navy fliers from Adm. Halsey's 3rd Fleet of fast carriers and battleships then attacked the Japanese force as it headed for San Bernadino Strait to the north of Leyte. In the resulting Battle of the Sibuyan Sea, several Japanese ships were hit with a battleship sunk and a cruiser heavily damaged. Kurita then reversed course and fled to the west, leading Halsey to believe the Japanese squadron had been defeated and no longer constituted a threat. The U.S admiral then took the 3rd Fleet northward to attack Vice Adm. Jisaburo Ozawa's force of Japanese carriers, which had been sighted by patrol aircraft. This enemy force was acting as "bait," hoping to lure the main U.S. naval force away from Leyte. Kinkaid, off Tacloban, incorrectly believed that the 3rd Fleet had left a strong force behind to guard the exit of the San Bernadino Strait based on intercepted radio messages between Halsey and his subordinate commanders.

At the same time another Japanese squadron of two battleships, a heavy cruiser, and three destroyers under Vice Adm. Shoji Nishumara was detected steaming west for Surigao Strait to the south of Leyte. To deal with this threat, Adm. Thomas Kinkaid of the 7th Fleet sent Rear Adm. Jesse Oldendorf, with six older battleships, eight cruisers, and twenty-eight destroyers, to block this exit into Leyte Gulf. In the resulting Battle of Surigao Strait during the night of October 24–25, the Japanese force was virtually wiped out with almost no American losses.

The divided command structure of the American force at Leyte, which had been so successful to this point, now began to show strain. For more than two years the SWPA and POA forces had advanced across the Pacific under separate commanders. However, the two offensives were now merging in the central Philippines. The General would not accept a subordinate role to Admiral Nimitz, and the navy was opposed to MacArthur being in charge of the fleet of new battleships and carriers in an operation dominated by great, empty swaths of ocean. FDR declined to intervene. Thus, at Leyte, Kinkaid and his 7th Fleet took orders from the SWPA commander, while Halsey and the more powerful 3rd Fleet reported to Nimitz and received a dual mission of both defending the amphibious force and destroying Japan's remaining carriers if they approached the area.

Frustrated by this arrangement, MacArthur refused to allow Halsey and Nimitz to communicate with Kinkaid and "his navy" directly. Instead, all encrypted communication between the two fleets had to be routed via the SWPA radio hub on Manus Island. However, MacArthur failed to ensure that staffing at this location was expanded sufficiently to handle an operation of significantly larger size and scope than any he had previously commanded. Subsequently, the base at Manus Island soon became a communications bottleneck. As historian Evan Thomas relates, "Theoretically, messages marked 'urgent' had priority, but before long, there were so many messages marked 'urgent' that they began to pile up. Messages could take up to four hours to wind their way between Kinkaid and Halsey, and often arrived out of sequence, further adding to the confusion and delay. It was an atrocious form of communication. At crucial moments, the fleets might as well have been signaling each other with flags."[18] While it made sense for MacArthur to want a central communications center for the naval forces landing his men and laying down a shore bombardment, it is difficult to craft a logical rationale for placing impediments in the way of admirals coordinating their fleets in the face of likely sorties to the area by the bulk of the Japanese navy.[19]

After the American airstrikes ended, Kurita reformed his fleet, reversed course, and headed east again. His battleships and attending cruisers and destroyers slipped through the San Bernadino Strait during the night of October 24 and emerged into the northern end of Leyte Gulf the following morning. Halsey was to the north with the main U.S. battle fleet, and Oldendorf was at the southern end of the gulf with his force of older battleships and escorts. Kurita found only Taffy 3, a squadron of small escort carriers with a few destroyers and destroyer escorts, in his path. His orders gave him some latitude: He was either to engage the amphibious force's supply ships and sink them at the harbor off the Leyte landing beaches or to destroy U.S. carriers if they could be brought under fire. Thinking that he had found the main American carrier force, he ordered his ships into battle. Taffy 3, commanded by Adm. Clifton Sprague, fled east as it launched its planes while producing smokescreens in what became known as the Battle off Samar.

Kinkaid, with the remaining transport shipping off Leyte's eastern shore, urgently requested aid from Oldendorf's and Halsey's battle groups. While the Japanese squadron massively outgunned Taffy 3, it had to take evasive action as the U.S. carriers' small escort ships charged the enemy, launching suicidal torpedo attacks. In addition, more than 400 planes from Taffy 3 and the two other escort carrier squadrons in the area (Taffy 1 and Taffy 2) attacked relentlessly and even made repeated "dummy" bomb and torpedo runs at Kurita's ships after their ordnance had been expended. In the resulting melee, the Japanese had three heavy cruisers sunk and three others damaged, while the U.S. Navy lost two escort carriers, two destroyers, and one destroyer escort. As the escort carriers of Taffy 3 began to take damage, many of their planes were forced to touch down on the overcrowded airstrips at Tacloban and Dulag to refuel and rearm. Fearing a massive wave of attacks from both Leyte-based and carrier aircraft, and with reports of more U.S. flattops to the north of him, Kurita ordered his ships to withdraw. The Japanese force headed westward again through the San Bernadino Strait, losing one additional destroyer in the process.

While this was taking place, Halsey's carriers had sailed into striking range of the enemy force to the north. The IJN's "decoy" operation to draw off the main U.S. battle fleet had been successful. The Japanese had not recovered from the terrible defeat suffered in the air battle off the Marianas months earlier, and the four carriers approaching from the north with their escort vessels only had about 100 planes left aboard. This left these Japanese ships that much more vulnerable to U.S. air attacks in the Battle off Cape Engaño, in which three carriers and a destroyer were sunk before Halsey turned south to respond to the frantic pleas for help coming from Kinkaid.

As the crippled remains of the Japanese fleet retreated away from the Philippines, the U.S. Navy was left triumphant and in control of Leyte Gulf. The IJN had lost twenty-eight ships (three battleships, one fleet carrier, three light carriers, ten cruisers, and eleven destroyers). American losses of six ships were dramatically smaller (one light carrier, two escort carriers, two destroyers, and one destroyer escort), and the U.S. Navy was never again seriously challenged on the seas during the Pacific War.

Despite the overwhelming naval victory, MacArthur found reason to criticize his superiors and Nimitz. His official take on the event was that the landing force was put in the gravest danger by Nimitz's being in charge of the 3rd Fleet:

> Through a series of fatal misunderstandings directly attributable to divided command, ambiguous messages, and poor communications between the U.S. 3rd and 7th Fleets, neither Admiral Kinkaid at Leyte Gulf, nor Admiral Sprague off Samar, realized that the exit from San Bernadino Strait had been left unguarded. . . . Should the enemy gain entrance to Leyte Gulf, his powerful naval guns could pulverize any of the eggshell transports still present in the area and destroy vitally needed supplies on the beachhead. The thousands of U.S. troops already ashore would be isolated and pinned down helplessly between enemy fire from ground and sea. . . . The battleships and cruisers of the 7th Fleet were over 100 miles away in Surigao Strait with their stock of armor-piercing ammunition virtually exhausted by the pre-landing shore bombardment and the decisive early morning battle with the Japanese Southern Force. . . . Shore positions and troop installations could have been bombarded almost at leisure . . . and the ammunition-depleted battleships of the 7th Fleet could have offered only relatively minor opposition.[20]

Later, in his memoirs, MacArthur again used similar language and added the following conclusion regarding the divided command structure off Leyte:

"The near disaster can be placed squarely at the door of Washington."[21] Many have accepted as fact these dire statements that the Japanese almost won a crushing victory, but the General's counterfactual statements contain several significant inaccuracies. A review of the situation places the conclusion of a "near disaster" in serious dispute.

First, it was never likely that Kurita would ignore the six carriers of Taffy 3 when he surprised them that fateful morning. The Japanese admiral believed he was engaging fleet carriers protected by cruisers and destroyers, not smaller escort carriers protected by only destroyers and destroyer escorts.[22] It would have been difficult to turn away from such valuable targets. Next, had Kurita steamed past Taffy 3 and headed for the Leyte landing beaches, his force would have been attacked immediately by repeated sorties from the 400 planes launched by the three Taffy carrier squadrons. In addition, Adm. John McCain, commanding a powerful squadron of 2 fleet carriers, 4 light carriers, 3 cruisers and 15 destroyers was approaching from the east at high speed. His strike force of attack aircraft began launching at 10:30 a.m. and arrived over the battle area starting around 1 p.m.[23] Thus, the Japanese ships would have been constantly taking evasive action to avoid torpedo and dive-bomb attacks as they headed for the Leyte landing beaches and required to continue the same after their arrival there rather than "bombarding almost at leisure."

Second, the landings on Leyte began on October 20, and within twenty-four hours, 100,000 men and 200,000 tons of equipment had been landed; a day later only 28 Liberty ships and 25 landing craft were left in Leyte Gulf.[24] Kurita and his fleet did not arrive until three days later, on October 25, by which time the 6th Army had pushed several miles inland. This additional elapsed time also allowed for further unloading of transport vessels and for supplies to be dispersed, moved off the beach, and placed under camouflage netting to defend against ongoing enemy air attacks. Thus, few obvious targets of opportunity would have been left on the beaches for the guns of Japanese battleships.

Next, MacArthur was correct that Oldendorf was indeed approximately 100 miles away from Taffy 3 when that escort carrier squadron came under attack. However, the battle fleet was only about 65 miles from Dulag and Tacloban—about the same distance away as Kurita's ships were from those same 6th Army landing areas. Kinkaid first heard that the escort carriers were threatened at 7:01 a.m. soon after the first shots of the Battle off Samar were fired, and he ordered Oldendorf to steam north at 7:24 a.m.[25]

What would have happened had Kurita sailed right past Taffy 3 and raced for the landing beaches along Leyte's shoreline? The Japanese ships were faster and, if steaming in a direct course, would have arrived in the area before

Oldendorf's fleet came into view from the south. However, the Japanese speed advantage would have been negated as Kurita's ships engaged in evasive maneuvers to avoid constant torpedo and dive-bomb attacks from the hundreds of planes launched by the American escort carriers in the vicinity followed by those from Admiral McCain's carrier force. If the Japanese admiral had been able to beat the 7th Fleet's battle group to the waters off the landing beaches, he likely would have found few American supply and transport ships remaining at the anchorage. Liberty ships and landing craft were not fast, but they would have had a couple of hours' radio warning from Taffy 3. They could have either sailed northward past Tacloban to shelter under the 6th Army's artillery in the narrow San Juanico Strait that separates the islands of Leyte and Samar or run south toward the safety of Oldendorf's ships heading to the rescue. There were also several U.S. destroyers and destroyer escorts screening the transports and they would have likely produced smoke screens and launched torpedo attacks utilizing similar tactics to the ones that protected the escort carriers of Taffy 3.

Finally, it is not correct that the battleships and cruisers of the 7th Fleet had "virtually exhausted" their armor-piercing ammunition and could only offer "minor opposition." Admiral Oldendorf's battleships had more than 1,300 armor-piercing shells left for their main guns on the morning of October 25. This ranged from 107 rounds for the USS *West Virginia* to 360 for the USS *Pennsylvania*.[26] This compares to only 285 main battery shells fired by these same ships in total in the Battle of Surigao Strait. Oldendorf's cruisers were indeed quite low on armor-piercing shells, but they still had a large supply of high-explosive rounds, which would have been more than deadly against Kurita's cruisers and destroyers.

Had the two forces clashed off Leyte, the Japanese advantage of having newer and faster battleships would have been offset by raw numbers. Prior to losses suffered engaging Taffy 3, Kurita had twenty-three ships (four battleships, six heavy cruisers, two light cruisers, and eleven destroyers). In contrast, Oldendorf commanded forty-two ships (six battleships, four heavy cruisers, four light cruisers, and twenty-eight destroyers). To be effective in such a gunnery engagement, Kurita would have had to form and hold his squadron in formation. This would have precluded taking evasive action to evade air attack. The American planes from the three Taffy squadrons would then have had an easier time scoring hits with their torpedo and bombing attacks as they bore down on the Japanese ships with their distinctive "pagoda" superstructures.

Thus, in contrast to MacArthur's dire scenario, a Japanese naval force arriving off the Leyte landing beaches on the morning of October 25 would have likely found little in the way of transport shipping to attack and few obvious masses of supplies and men on the shore to target. Instead, Kurita would have had a choice: reverse course and try to get back through the San Bernadino

Strait or engage in a gun battle with the battleships and cruisers of the 7th Fleet. If he chose to stay and fight, keeping his ships in formation would have been terribly difficult. Th Japanese would have had to deal with upward of 100 torpedoes launched from Oldendorf's score of destroyers which each had approximately five torpedoes left after expending around half their "fish" in the Battle of Surigao Strait.[27] At the same time, aircraft from the undamaged escort carriers would have continued their attacks. Even the 6th Army ashore might have joined the fight. If the U.S. Army excelled in one area in 1945, it was in its use of heavy artillery. Any Japanese ships loitering off eastern Leyte would soon have had to contend with fire from American 155mm "Long Tom" guns.

The longer Kurita remained in Leyte Gulf fighting the 7th Fleet, the greater the threat to his force. Japanese losses would have been significant after hours of repeated air attack by Taffy 1, 2, and 3, the shell fire from Oldendorf's battleships, torpedo runs from more than a score of destroyers and attacks from McCain's carrier strikes. Then, if he waited too long, he would not have been able to escape as Halsey's fast battleships closed in from the north to seal off the San Bernadino Strait. Finally, bereft of much air cover, Kurita's ships, now low on antiaircraft ammunition, would then have been at the mercy of concentrated airstrikes from the 3rd Fleet's carriers as they steamed south into striking range.

In conclusion, a Japanese attempt to shell the Leyte shore along Dulag and Tacloban would likely have led to an even greater American naval victory than actually occurred. Similarly, had Kurita ignored the Leyte Gulf landing beaches and pressed his attack on Taffy 3, he could have sunk all six of its escort carriers. But after such an extended running battle to the east, the Japanese force, now having expended significant ammunition, would have found itself trapped on the wrong side of the San Bernadino Strait by the battleships and cruisers of either the 7th Fleet, the 3rd Fleet, or both. In such a scenario, American losses would have been far higher, but undoubtedly Japanese ones would have been as well.

After the offshore battle, MacArthur's staff, primed by their boss to denigrate the U.S. Navy, began complaining about Admiral Halsey and his decision to take his force north to sink Japan's carriers. The General ordered his men not to say anything negative about Halsey as he was a "fighter."[28] MacArthur preferred to have complaints directed at Nimitz and the JCS in Washington for not granting him overall command of everything in the Pacific. Of course, he never mentioned the fact that the communication failures that led to the events of October 25 were due to his own resistance to Halsey and Kinkaid's sending radio messages directly to each other and the failure to properly staff the communications station on Manus Island. MacArthur also took no responsibility for the naval forces under his command being surprised by Kurita's attack.

King accurately pointed out in his memoirs that Admiral Kinkaid and his 7th Fleet were most to blame for allowing a Japanese force to sail undiscovered through the San Bernadino Strait. MacArthur's navy had the responsibility—as well as the planes from its eighteen escort carriers and floatplanes from several cruisers and battleships—to patrol the northern approaches to Leyte Gulf. Such air reconnaissance became that much more pressing after Halsey announced that he was heading north to hunt a Japanese carrier force.[29]

THE WRONG ISLAND

With the naval supply lines secured, the 6th Army focused on advancing west across Leyte. While Halsey had detected little in the way of Japanese activity on the island and MacArthur had promised a rapid reconquest of the Philippines, the soldiers on the frontlines experienced a very different reality. Late 1944 brought a particularly wet monsoon season to the central Philippines, and American troops found themselves bogged down in sodden mountain terrain lashed by multiple typhoons and fighting rising numbers of Japanese reinforcements. Things were even worse for 5th Air Force operations on the island. Again, MacArthur had been warned by his engineers as early as August 1944 that airfield construction efforts on Leyte during the rainy season would not be able to support more than small numbers of SWPA aircraft. Sadly, these predictions were quite accurate.

The General chose to discount such advice and focused on the earliest possible return to the Philippines regardless of the impact on his men. Historian Max Hastings minced no words on this point:

> It is a shocking indictment of MacArthur and his staff that they chose to ignore forecasts of these difficulties, submitted long before the landings. . . . The rejection of prudent professional advice about the shortcomings of Leyte as a forward air base reflected reckless irresponsibility by the supreme commander. . . . MacArthur had allowed the geographical convenience of the island to blind him to its unsuitability for every important strategic purpose. . . . Only senior American officers, privy to the airfields fiasco, understood that MacArthur had landed 6th Army on the wrong island.[30]

The Japanese took advantage of the 5th Air Force's difficulties and chose the U.S. return to the Philippines as the moment to begin launching the new tactic of kamikaze airplane strikes on American shipping. These suicide attacks negated at least some of the hard-earned qualitative advantages the United States had achieved in the effectiveness of its pilots and technological superiority of its aircraft. The dearth of usable runway capacity meant the 5th Air Force was unable to provide much close air support for the troops or hold off incessant Japanese air raids. A frustrated and chagrinned MacArthur finally begged Nimitz to send his fleet carriers back to the Philippines in November. The POA commander cancelled planned strikes on the Japanese Home Islands. Instead, the 3rd Fleet returned to Leyte for two additional weeks conducting air support missions.[31]

Despite all of MacArthur's shortcomings on Leyte, many historians have concluded that the Japanese made even greater mistakes there. By choosing to fight a decisive battle on that island rather than conserving their forces for the defense of Luzon, the IJA suffered huge losses both on the sea and defending from unprepared positions on land. Ultra codebreaking continued its success and vectored U.S. submarines and aircraft to intercept enemy shipping sailing to western Leyte. Most notably, much of two full Japanese infantry divisions destined for Leyte's western port of Ormoc, the 23rd and 26th, were lost at sea in attacks on convoys Hi-71 and Hi-81.

Significant additional shipping was also sunk on its way to Leyte. In all, the Japanese lost twenty-four ships loaded with tens of thousands of soldiers and major amounts of ammunition, fuel, rations, and medical supplies.[32] Despite these losses, the Japanese were able to land large quantities of supplies and reinforcements on Leyte, including the elite 1st Infantry Division. A counteroffensive was even launched in early December by the IJA supported by a paratrooper assault to retake airfields in eastern Leyte. While the effort was defeated, the airborne landing of Japanese soldiers temporarily disrupted the American advance.

MacArthur needed to get his offensive back on schedule and required airstrips that were not vast expanses of mud. As the solution was not on Leyte, he decided to land elements of Krueger's 6th Army on the island of Mindoro just south of Luzon, which Ultra decrypts indicated had few enemy soldiers guarding its airfields. The plan called for a landing of the 24th Division's 19th Regiment supported by the 503rd Parachute Infantry Regiment, which would be dropped on the island. However, the airborne assault had to be scrapped as Gen. Kenney was chagrined to admit that his Leyte airfields were not even adequate to provide air cover for the invasion flotilla.[33] Once again, the carriers of Nimitz's 3rd Fleet were requested to cover MacArthur's amphibious operation, and the 503rd was pressed into service as traditional infantry in a beach assault.

The Joint Chiefs were wary of the General's plan as it would force Kinkaid's fleet to transport an amphibious force through the Surigao Strait and the island-constrained Sulu Sea, where it would be difficult for ships to take evasive action against land-based air attack. In *American Caesar*, William Manchester notes, "The Pentagon had advised the General that the operation was 'too daring in scope, too risky in execution' but MacArthur, though no one noticed it at the time, was beginning to disregard cables from Washington, even when, as in this instance, doubts there found echoes in his own staff."[34] Nevertheless, the invasion went ahead on December 15, and MacArthur was lucky that he did not travel to observe it. Had he done so, he likely would have been back on board the USS *Nashville*, which was struck by a kamikaze, killing 133 and wounding 190 others. The 19th and 503rd Regiments successfully landed on the southern end of Mindoro and quickly moved to overcome the island's small garrison. The IJN attempted to contest the invasion by sending two cruisers and three destroyers into the area. The enemy flotilla was able to shell the 503rd for about fifteen minutes, and torpedo attacks were launched on anchored U.S. shipping, but the Japanese were driven off by concerted American air attacks.

Landing strips on Mindoro were soon operating American fighter planes, which could cover amphibious operations from Manila to the Lingayen Gulf. MacArthur's gamble had paid off, and conditions were now ripe for the 6th Army to land in Luzon—except the 6th Army was still heavily engaged in fighting on Leyte. Luckily for MacArthur, he now had significant non-Australian reserve forces to utilize in addition to the troops recently put ashore on Mindoro. The 77th Infantry Division had been training for the invasion of Luzon but was instead pressed into service in an amphibious landing on Leyte's west coast to speed up the U.S. advance. MacArthur then decided to give a Christmas present to the American public. On December 26 (December 25 back in the United States), SWPA Headquarters announced that the battle was over and turned remaining operations on the island over to Eichelberger's 8th Army: "The LEYTE-SAMAR campaign can now be regarded as closed except for minor mopping up. The enemy's ground forces participating in the campaign have been practically annihilated. . . . The completeness of this destruction has seldom been paralleled in the history of warfare. General Yamashita has sustained perhaps the greatest defeat in the military annals of the Japanese Army."[35]

Of course, the fighting was by no means over, the Japanese on Leyte had not been "annihilated," and the battle for the island was much more than "minor mopping up." Eichelberger's units eventually reported that they killed over 20,000 Japanese in 1945 on the island, and by the end of the war the U.S. military incurred 15,500 casualties on Leyte, of which 3,500 were killed in action. The official historian of the 11th Airborne Division reports that the formation was engaged in "bitter, exhausting, rugged fighting—physically, the most terrible we were ever to know."[36] Men in the ranks were certainly not pleased to know they were killing and dying in a battle that was supposedly already over. Lt. Gage Rodman of the 17th Infantry expressed the outrage of many GIs in a letter to his parents: "MacArthur's communiques are inaccurate to a disgusting degree. We who were on the spot knew we were only beginning to fight when he made his ridiculous announcement that our objective was secured."[37]

CHAPTER 9

Redemption and Destruction

Douglas MacArthur's promise to President Roosevelt that recapturing Luzon would be quick and easy began to look increasingly unlikely as Ultra intelligence updated estimates of the enemy garrison. While Gen. Willoughby estimated only 137,000 Japanese on the island, 6th Army's staff and the War Department in Washington, DC, believed the total to be a much larger 235,000, which was still lower than the true figure of 267,000. When confronted with 6th Army's numbers, the General exclaimed, "Bunk!" and "There aren't that many Japanese there."[1] Several months later the SWPA communiqué announcing the end of the Battle of Luzon—long, of course, before fighting had ended—stated that over 200,000 Japanese had been killed. The final army count tallied 539,000 Japanese defenders across all of the Philippines.

MacArthur did not share Adm. King's concerns regarding how a campaign to reconquer Luzon would take place. The SWPA commander expected that Gen. Tomoyuki Yamashita and his men would conduct their defense of Luzon in a manner that paralleled the American defense of the island in 1941 and 1942. This included sparing Manila, moving forces away from major population concentrations, and leaving civilians with reasonable supplies of food. Such an expectation was not logical. After all, MacArthur wrote himself that the Japanese had not expected him to evacuate Manila early in the war.[2] Also, taking actions to spare enemy civilians the horrors of war differed dramatically from how the Japanese had fought over the previous decade, with examples ranging from the "Rape of Nanking" to Yamashita's soldiers using Allied prisoners of war for live-fire target practice after the fall of Singapore, from the mutilated bodies at Milne Bay to Japanese soldiers encouraging the mass suicide of civilians on Saipan. Somehow the man who claimed to know the "Oriental mind" believed he confronted a much more chivalrous enemy than the one arrayed against him.

On January 9, 1945, a massive force of more than 700 ships arrived off Luzon's Lingayen Gulf. After a lengthy shore bombardment, 175,000 men of the 6th Army poured onto the beaches and quickly pushed inland. The most notable opposition was from kamikaze air attacks, which damaged scores of naval vessels. This time a dock was prepared for MacArthur's landing after the beachhead had been secured. However, always keen to maximize his public image, the General chose to again wade in through shin-high surf in front of the press cameras, the same look of intense determination on his face. SWPA Headquarters proclaimed, "Our forces have landed in Luzon. In a far-flung amphibious penetration our troops have seized four beachheads in Lingayen Gulf. . . . General MacArthur is in personal command at the front and landed with his assault troops."[3]

General Krueger's divisions moved south across the Luzon Central Plain toward Manila, but he kept large formations positioned on his east flank. He was concerned that if he moved south too quickly, Yamashita's soldiers in the hills to the east would counterattack and threaten to sever his supply lines. While this tactical positioning was sound, such an attack did not take place, as the Japanese commander had split his force into three main groups with orders to dig in on high ground and force the Americans to storm these positions. The 6th Army's lack of speed infuriated MacArthur, who planned to give himself the present of a grand military parade through a liberated Manila on his birthday of January 26. To pressure Krueger, Gen. Sutherland paid him a visit and threatened his firing if the offensive was not accelerated. MacArthur also tried to embarrass his subordinate into moving faster when he moved his own headquarters twenty-five miles closer to Manila than that of the 6th Army.

Regarding the rush to take the capital city, Edward Drea concluded,

> The Southwest Pacific commander did have sound strategic reasons for insisting that Krueger accelerate his methodical advance to the south, but these did not necessarily apply to rushing to Manila. For instance, Kenney needed Clark Field's airdromes for his expanding air arm, which had already outgrown the stopgap fields cut near Lingayen Gulf. Only Clark Field's paved runways and maintenance facilities could house the heavy bombers that MacArthur promised to have flying to support the Iwo Jima and Okinawa invasions set for February and March, respectively. Manila he wanted for his own satisfaction.[4]

Clark was retaken in the last week of January, but American troops did not penetrate into the northern precincts of the capital until early February. However, MacArthur still hoped to hold his delayed parade.

Tragically for the people of the Philippines, the Japanese chose not to cooperate. While Yamashita had withdrawn the bulk of his forces into the mountains in northern Luzon, more than 15,000 Japanese sailors and soldiers remained in Manila under the command of Rear Adm. Sanji Iwabuchi. While Yamashita ordered this force to move into the hill country south and east of the capital, the withdrawal never happened. First, MacArthur had Gen. Eichelberger land units of his 8th Army to the south of the capital and cut off any chance for Iwabuchi's force to escape. It is unlikely the admiral intended to retreat as he had already instructed his men to fortify the inner core of the city, set up roadblocks, improvise booby traps, and stockpile food and ammunition. The garrison also refused to allow civilians to flee so as to hold them in place as human shields. Reports flowed into SWPA HQ that Yamashita had decided against declaring Manila an open city, and Filipino guerillas communicated detailed reports of how Iwabuchi's men were preparing for a building-to-building siege.[5] However, MacArthur continued to focus on the fastest possible offensive push to reach the capital. On January 27 he exhorted Maj. Gen. Verne Mudge, of the 1st Cavalry Division, "Go to Manila! Go around the Nips, bounce off the Nips, but go to Manila!"[6]

American cavalrymen raced south and liberated the civilian internment camp at Manila's Santo Tomas University on February 5. Thousands of American civilians had been imprisoned there since early 1942, slowly wasting away on ever diminishing supplies of food. Among those freed were the prewar elite of the colony and personal friends of MacArthur. The General had lobbied FDR on their behalf the year before in Honolulu, and he duly paid them a visit soon after their liberation. Jubilant but emaciated, these Americans surrounded MacArthur, waving, cheering, shaking his hand, and hugging him. The Japanese, knowing that the campus was no longer in their control and quite aware of the location's coordinates, began shelling the university.[7] For reasons not well explained, the General returned to his headquarters outside the city but did not have the "rescued" internees evacuated from Santo Tomas. Many were killed there in enemy artillery barrages over the next few days, an ironic end after they had successfully survived years of imprisonment.

Back at his command post on February 6, MacArthur declared the Battle of Manila to be over except for some "mopping up." His communiqué for that day began, "Our forces are rapidly cleaning the enemy from Manila. Our converging columns of the 1st Cavalry Division from the east, the 37th Infantry Division from the north and the 11th Airborne Division from the south after an overnight 35 miles advance from Tagaytay simultaneously entered the city and surrounded the Japanese defenders. Their complete destruction is imminent."[8] Reporters at the press briefing that day, who had recently returned from the intense fighting in Manila, were shocked to hear that the battle would be over presently and that a military parade would take place in a few days. Sadly, this was not to be.

As U.S. forces pushed into the central core of the city, Iwabuchi's men began to set great swaths of the metropolis alight. Approaching from the south, Eichelberger related, "I could see the city of Manila gleaming whitely in the sunshine. . . . It was strangely like a homecoming. But soon tall plumes of smoke began to rise in Manila, and at evening the tropical sky was crimsoned by many fires. The Japanese were deliberately destroying the magical town which had been traditionally called 'The Pearl of the Orient.'"[9] The Japanese also began to rape, torture, and slaughter tens of thousands of the civilians in the city. By February 10, MacArthur's headquarters was forced to admit, "In the south Manila area, where the enemy is making a final stand, the 37th and 11th Divisions are engaged in house to house and street combat, the fighting is of the fiercest."[10] The next day the communiqué described that in the city "houses and public buildings have been converted by the enemy into pillboxes and fortified strongpoints with artillery emplacements." However, SWPA HQ also assured the press, "The spirit and morale of the civilian population remain at the highest. There is ample food and relief agencies are active and efficient. Order is maintained."[11]

Ten days later, on February 21, MacArthur's communiqué announced, "In south Manila the bitterest fighting continues as our troops slowly compress the enemy's lines. . . . He is acting with the greatest savagery in his treatment of non-combatants and private property."[12] The next day's communiqué described an "enemy whose savage barbarism has seldom been displayed in a more repulsive form."[13] MacArthur had forbidden the launching of tactical airstrikes and indirect artillery barrages due to fears of causing widespread collateral damage to both property and civilians. However, as American casualties mounted and the advance slowed, field generals appealed to headquarters for the green light to begin employing their heavy guns.

MacArthur relented, and as the 37th Infantry Division's history of the campaign relates, "Every effort had been made to spare the civilian population known to be held in captivity somewhere in the area, but as the tactical need for heavy fire power increased permission was sought and obtained to place area artillery fire in front of our advancing lines without regard to pinpoint targets."[14] By the time the Battle of Manila was over, U.S. forces had fired off more than 42,000 shells, of which more than half were from the army's heavy 105mm and 155mm guns.[15] Such profligate use of artillery produced massive destruction and shockingly high numbers of civilian deaths. "One post-war estimate suggests that for every six Manileros murdered by the Japanese defenders, another four died beneath the gunfire of their American liberators. Some historians would even reverse that ratio."[16]

Regardless of the cause, more than 100,000 Filipinos died in the fighting. According to William Manchester, MacArthur "had been unprepared for the fanatical defense of the blazing, crumbling capital, and he was in anguish. Taking Manila had become a fixation with him. When the embattled enemy disregarded his repeated appeals to them to surrender, he became further distraught."[17] King's fears were more than realized as the destruction in Manila greatly exceeded that which befell London. Of all the cities ravaged in World War II, only Warsaw suffered more damage in percentage terms than the Philippine capital.

Finally, by early March, Iwabuchi and his men were dead and the Battle of Manila was over. The devastation of the "liberated" city was redolent of Calgacus's description of the Romans in Briton—"where they make a wasteland, they call it peace"—or a later comment by an American officer in the Vietnam War: "It became necessary to destroy the town to save it." The pomp and ceremony of a military parade along the waterfront was cancelled. At a subdued ceremony at Manila's Malacañan Palace commemorating the transfer of power to civilian authority, MacArthur became overcome by emotion and was unable to complete his prepared remarks.

Aid to those in need in Manila was slow in arriving. Admiral Iwabuchi had made sure that no docks survived, and the harbor was littered with scuttled wrecks in which snipers waited to kill before they themselves died. Despite MacArthur's assurances to FDR, the port facilities in Manila were not available to assist in the follow-on assaults on either Iwo Jima or Okinawa. The destruction along the waterfront was highlighted when Mrs. MacArthur arrived by ship on March 6 to succor her husband and the General had to ride out on a small Higgins boat to ferry her to shore. American military commanders in war zones were not allowed to have their wives and children in attendance. However, as usual for MacArthur, rules were for other people.

The Philippines lost much in the Battle of Manila: art, architecture, literature, files, and records were destroyed along with great amounts of infrastructure. Many of the nation's cadre of trained bureaucrats and professionals were killed by Japanese bayonettes or American artillery. Yet the dying was not yet complete. Yamashita's forces still controlled much of the archipelago, and as American forces advanced to the far corners of the colony, Filipino civilians continued to be caught in the crossfire until the very end of the war.

It is not clear how, once MacArthur decided to storm Manila, he could have ameliorated the barbaric scorched-earth policy employed by the Japanese. However, the blatant error of promises made to FDR that a reconquest of the Philippines would be quick, easy, and low in casualties must be laid at the General's feet. As historian Max Hastings concluded,

> In all a million Filipinos are estimated to have died by violence in the Second World War, most of them in its last months. There was intense debate about whether MacArthur should have bypassed Manila, rather than storm it. What

is certain is that he was mistaken in his belief that he could serve the best interests of the Philippine people by committing an army to liberate them. Whatever Filipinos might have suffered at the hands of the Japanese if the Americans had contented themselves with seizing air bases for their advance on Tokyo, and held back from reoccupying the entire Philippines archipelago, would have been less grievous than the catastrophe they suffered when MacArthur made their country a battlefield.[18]

VICTOR AND NORTHERN LUZON

With the capture of Manila, MacArthur and his headquarters staff pivoted to focus on planning the largest amphibious landing in history: the invasion of Japan. However, there was still a great deal of fighting to take place in the Philippines. Krueger's 6th Army was tasked with "mopping up" Yamashita's large force in northern Luzon. At the same time MacArthur directed the 8th Army to finish off the enemy in Leyte and southern Luzon and to dispatch units to liberate the rest of the Philippines.

This latter offensive, in what became known as Operations Victor I through V, routed enemy garrisons on every other major island left in Japanese hands. While MacArthur remained in Manila with his family, Eichelberger was given free rein to retake Palawan, the Visayas, and Mindanao. Amphibious assaults took place at a rate of one per week and utilized four American infantry divisions (24th, 31st, 40th, and 41st). Many of MacArthur's supporters like to depict his field generals as plodders who held back their commander's brilliance on the field of battle. Such accusations seem particularly unfair, at least regarding Eichelberger, when one considers the speed and scale of the Victor landings across the southern and central Philippines, along with the low cost of casualties taken versus dramatically larger ones inflicted on the enemy. MacArthur was suitably impressed and sent Eichelberger a congratulatory message calling his subordinate's efforts a "model of what a light but aggressive campaign can accomplish in rapid exploitation."[19]

Why are the Victor operations so unknown? The answer is likely twofold: first, the liberation of the central, western, and southern Philippines was not authorized by the JCS, and second, the invasions had effectively zero strategic significance in the defeat of Japan. In fact, not only did the army chief of staff not plan to utilize American troops to free bypassed Philippine islands south of Luzon, but he told his British counterparts at the Yalta Conference in February that this would not happen. While in these meetings on the shore of the Black Sea, "George Marshall said he assumed that 'Filipino guerrillas and the newly activated Army of the Philippine Commonwealth' could 'take care of the rest of their country.'"[20] MacArthur, Marshall's subordinate, failed to obtain permission prior to the launch of the Victor operations, which engaged much of the

U.S. 8th Army and the 7th Fleet. Historian Samuel Eliot Morrison wrote, "It is still somewhat of a mystery how and whence, in view of these wishes of the J.C.S., General of the Army Douglas MacArthur derived his authority to use United States Forces to liberate one Philippine island after another. He had no specific directive for anything subsequent to Luzon."[21]

The JCS retroactively chose to approve MacArthur's offensive. However, the seeds of MacArthur's blatant insubordination in 1950 and 1951 had clearly sprouted prior to the Mindoro invasion and were allowed to grow in Victor I through V. They would not ripen fully until five years later in Korea. MacArthur's staff justified the offensive "to assure complete domination of the shipping lanes of the southern and central Philippines and unquestioned control of the entire archipelago."[22] A history published by the U.S. Army was blunter:

> On the morning of 28 February 1945 with an assault on the long, narrow, westernmost Philippine Island of Palawan, 8th Army began a campaign to capture the bypassed islands south of Luzon and Leyte. MacArthur wanted air bases on Palawan, on the Zamboanga Peninsula of Mindanao, and on the Sulu Archipelago to support a reoccupation of North Borneo. The rest of the islands—the central group of Panay, Negros, Cebu and Bohol, and southernmost Mindanao—he wanted for political considerations, to complete his return to the Philippines.[23]

Back on Luzon, even after the Battle of Manila had concluded, the fighting was by no means over. MacArthur had promised FDR that the island would be conquered in a maximum of six weeks. However, the Japanese refused to conform to this prediction. General Yamashita's forces fell back slowly into the mountainous northeast. Of more than 10,000 members of the U.S. Army killed and 36,550 wounded retaking the Philippines, more than 8,000 died in Luzon, and 29,560 were wounded there.[24] Krueger's 6th Army was occupied for months blasting apart one Japanese prepared position after another. Starting in late February and continuing through the end of June, Krueger employed four divisions (25th, 32nd, 33rd, and 37th) to methodically reduce the defending Japanese forces in northern Luzon. Yamashita's 14th Area Army was larger than the 6th Army units attacking it, but the Japanese had no air cover, were relatively poorly supplied and dramatically outclassed by American artillery. Nevertheless, the Japanese resistance slowed Krueger's advance to a crawl.

Whenever possible, the enemy fought from mutually supporting cave or subterranean positions in steep terrain that could not be detected until engaged by GIs advancing on foot. After suffering casualties detecting these strongpoints, the Americans would call in overwhelming air and artillery strikes and then advance to finish off any remaining defenders with flamethrowers and explosive charges. MacArthur chafed at the slow advance of the

6th Army in the north, but the SWPA commander had determined that every last square mile of the colony must be liberated at the earliest possible date to restore American honor.

While the result of any individual engagement in the northern Luzon campaign was not in doubt, the Japanese fought until they were killed in place or grudgingly gave ground. This was dangerous, time-consuming, and exhausting work for the Americans. *Triumph in the Philippines*, published by the U.S. Army after the war, described the fighting as "a knock-down, drag-out slug fest. The spectacular could hardly happen—there wasn't room enough. Troops would become tired and dispirited; nonbattle casualties would exceed those injured in combat. Supply would be very difficult, the evacuation of the sick and wounded an even greater problem. This was combined mountain and tropical warfare at its worst."[25]

Like Eichelberger's Victor operations in the south, Krueger's conquest of northern Luzon is relatively unknown. While the JCS had at least authorized the conquest of the island, the battles to take Baguio, the Villa Verde Pass, and the mountains of the Cordillera Central have received little notice in the historical record. This is because these victories had no obvious strategic importance to the winning of the war. The Japanese soldiers dug in across northern Luzon represented no threat to the main air and naval bases on Luzon and in no way could hinder the U.S. landings on Iwo Jima and Okinawa or the planned invasion of the Japanese Home Islands. However, MacArthur found it intolerable that the enemy would continue to control any territory of the Philippines. Thus, the offensive ground on into the least populated, remote mountainous terrain in Luzon. The main result of the fighting was dead Japanese, dead Filipinos, dead Americans, destroyed towns, and jungle that reverted to U.S. control.

Yamashita's strategy in Luzon in 1945 was to maintain a viable force that could tie down the largest number of American troops who could not be employed elsewhere. In this he was quite successful. Eventually, on June 28, 6th Army's headquarters was reassigned to prepare for the invasion of Japan. MacArthur announced the end of the supposed "mopping up" in a communiqué that proclaimed,

> Except for isolated operations this closes the major phases of the Northern Luzon Campaign, one of the most savage and bitterly fought in American history. No terrain has ever presented greater logistical difficulties and none has ever provided an adversary with more naturally impregnable strongholds. . . . Our troops comprised the I Corps and the north Luzon guerrillas, all of the 6th Army, closely and most effectively supported by the Far Eastern Air Force and the 7th Fleet. The entire island of Luzon, embracing 40,420 square miles and a population of 8,000,000, is now liberated.[26]

In truth, the "entire island of Luzon" was not yet liberated, and the 8th Army took over operations in northern Luzon. Over the next month and a half of heavy fighting, three U.S. divisions suffered an additional 1,600 casualties trying to break into Yamashita's redoubt in the remote Asin Valley. This pointless bloodletting only ceased with the end of the war. Upon news of the emperor's capitulation in August 1945, Yamashita marched out of the jungle and surrendered along with more than 50,000 of his men.

DOWNFALL

At the Argonaut Conference of the Combined Chiefs of Staff on Malta in February 1945, it was decided to move ahead with planning for Operation Downfall to force Japan's surrender. The operation was to commence with multiple simultaneous landings across the beaches of the southern island of Kyushu in late 1945 (Operation Olympic). This would be followed in 1946 by an even larger assault on the island of Honshu targeting the capture of Tokyo (Operation Coronet).[27] MacArthur, the senior military commander in the Pacific with experience fighting the Japanese, was the obvious choice to command Downfall. If it went forward, the invasion would be the largest amphibious operation in human history and significantly greater in size than the one overseen by General Eisenhower in Normandy.

MacArthur was certainly keen to command such a major historical event, which would allow him to become arguably America's greatest-ever military leader. However, he once again found himself up against Admiral King. Both the navy chief and Adm. Nimitz believed that an invasion of the Home Islands should be avoided.[28] Their concern was that an invasion would lead to massive American casualties and that the Japanese could instead be forced to surrender under the pressure of blockade and bombardment. As 1945 progressed, it certainly seemed that having hundreds of thousands of U.S. troops storm ashore in Kyushu and Honshu would not be necessary.

The Japanese had very few transport vessels left afloat, and U.S. submarines increasingly roamed at will in the seas around the Home Islands. Ultra intelligence identified the locations of enemy minefields, allowing for ambushes to be sprung in supposedly safe channels. Despite initial resistance, Nimitz convinced the USAAF to utilize about 5 percent of its B-29s based in the Marianas to lay mines around Japanese ports in the appropriately named Operation Starvation. Starting in April 1945, this effort led to the sinking of more than 650 enemy ships, and Japan was increasingly cut off from the outside world—except for the nightly firebombing of its cities from the sky. Most of the IJN's ships were at the bottom of the Pacific, which was dominated by the U.S. Navy (with an astounding 100 aircraft carriers in operation by the end of the war). Food was increasingly scarce on the Home Islands; the Japanese were beginning to starve, and the end of the war was in sight.

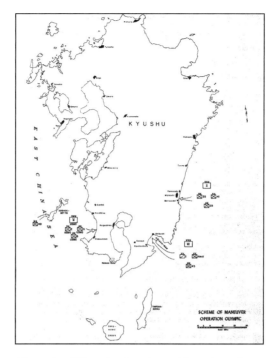

Operation Olympic, the planned invasion of southern Kyushu.

Courtesy of the U.S. Marine Corps.

Despite this, MacArthur urged the earliest possible invasion of Kyushu. In April, he wrote to Marshall that blockade and bombardment by the U.S. Navy and the USAAF could not succeed as these efforts "would fail to utilize our resources for amphibious offensive movement assume success of air power alone to conquer a people in spite of its demonstrated failure in Europe, where Germany was subject to more intensive bombardment than can be brought to bear against Japan, and where all the available resources in ground troops of the United States, the United Kingdom, and Russia had to be committed in order to force a decision." Thus, an invasion was necessary as it "would permit application of full power of our combined resources, ground, naval, and air, on the decisive objective; would deliver an attack against an area which probably will be more lightly defended this year than next."[29]

MacArthur proposed that he command the Kyushu landing of an enlarged 6th Army with attached marine divisions on "X-Day" in November 1945. While King certainly wanted a rapid conclusion to the war, he was in no way swayed by MacArthur's arguments that a ground-based slug fest was necessary. Still, an invasion might become necessary, and contingency planning needed to take place. Nimitz sent members of his staff to Manila in May to work out details of the amphibious operation with their counterparts at MacArthur's headquarters. Of course, King wanted Nimitz to be in command, while MacArthur coveted that role. A compromise was worked out that was similar to what had prevailed during the Leyte invasion, with MacArthur being in command of army air and land units and Nimitz continuing to have authority over naval operations.

It is surprising that President Harry S. Truman allowed MacArthur to be named commander of Olympic. The new president had a poor opinion of MacArthur and wrote in his diary,

> He is worse than Cabot and Lodge families—at least they talked to each other before telling God what they will do. Mc [sic] is telling God directly. It is a shame that we have such haughty people in key positions. I can't understand why the hell Roosevelt didn't order Wainwright to return home and didn't leave McArthur to be a martyr. . . . We could have had a real general and a fighting man if we had Wainwright and not an actor and a cheater as we have now. . . . I must decide the Japanese Strategy—will we invade Japan properly or lock it and bombard it? This is the hardest decision ever. But I will take it after I have all the information.[30]

Of course, it would have been politically difficult for Truman to place any general besides MacArthur in command of the Kyushu invasion ground forces. Of other American leaders, only Eisenhower was a credible candidate after his successful role in charge of the Normandy landings and subsequent drive across western Europe into Germany. However, he had no experience fighting the Japanese and no established working relationship with U.S. Navy and U.S. Army Air Force commanders in the Pacific.

Both those in favor of an invasion of Japan and those opposed, who preferred to wait for bombardment and blockade to force a surrender, had strong arguments in their favor. Okinawa, considered one of the Home Islands by the Japanese, was invaded in April, and the fighting was some of the most savage of the war. In excess of 100,000 Japanese soldiers and Okinawan conscripts were killed, as was upward of 50 percent of the civilian population of 300,000. However, the Americans suffered more than 50,000 casualties there, of which 12,000 were killed in action. President Truman was concerned that Japanese resistance to an invasion in Kyushu and Honshu would be just as fierce but on a vastly larger scale, considering the nation's population of seventy million. On the other hand, the collapse of the Japanese empire's seaborne merchant fleet had crippled its ability to move food supplies to population centers not only in Japan but also in occupied cities in China, Korea, Indochina, and the Dutch East Indies. Starvation was becoming a scourge across the region, and estimates were that upward of 100,000 would die due to lack of nutrition per month by late in 1945.

Time was not on the side of those in favor of an invasion of Kyushu. A rapid military buildup took place on the island as the Japanese correctly determined where the Americans would land based on distances from Okinawan airfields and the locations of appropriate beaches for amphibious assaults. American planning assumed that there would be no more than six Japanese divisions and 2,500 aircraft on Kyushu by November to oppose the 6th Army's landing force of fifteen divisions and 2,700 aircraft.[31] However, Ultra intelligence revealed a rapid enemy buildup around the proposed invasion beaches. The Japanese soon had fourteen divisions and seven additional brigades on the island, with ten of those divisions and four brigades adjacent to where the invaders were to land. Almost as bad was the startling increase in enemy airpower in the region with upward of 10,000 dispersed warplanes along with local aviation fuel stores.

Military intelligence also made clear that the Japanese did not plan to fight only a conventional battle on Kyushu. Millions of male and female civilians, ranging in age from fifteen to sixty, were recruited into the Volunteer Fighting Corps (Kokumin Giyu Sentotai). They were equipped with anything from obsolete rifles to bamboo spears and trained to make banzai charges on American lines. Nimitz's staff believed that most of these former civilians would indeed fight to the death, just as many did in the Battle of Okinawa. While U.S. machine gun and artillery fire would mow down the ranks of these suicidal charges, a percentage could be counted upon to break into the invaders' battle lines and run up the American casualty count.

The Japanese military also planned to vastly increase the use of "special attack units"—in other words, kamikazes. Thousands of kamikaze speedboats (shinyo), kamikaze manned torpedoes (kaiten), kamikaze midget submarines (kairyou), kamikaze rocket-powered flying bombs (ohka), and even kamikaze divers walking along the seafloor (fukuryu) were positioned along the coast of Kyushu to attack the American invasion fleet. Most concerning to the U.S. Navy was the large number of light trainer aircraft made primarily of wood and fabric and carrying one or two bombs being prepared to act as kamikazes. The dearth of metal in these planes made them difficult to detect using radar, and for the same reason American variable-timed proximity-fused antiaircraft shells often failed when used against them. On the night of July 9, the destroyer USS Callaghan on radar picket duty off the coast of Okinawa was attacked by such a kamikaze. The mostly wood and fabric Yokosuka K5Y was able to avoid both early radar detection and antiaircraft fire before crashing into the destroyer and sinking it.

Nimitz's staff expressed concern that it had no effective defense against such kamikazes, especially if they launched from a multitude of small airstrips close to the proposed landing beaches, providing less time for combat air patrol units to shoot them down. The navy also took note of the rising concentration of Japanese forces in Kyushu with great alarm. On May 25, Nimitz formally informed King that he no longer supported the invasion operation.[32] Leapfrogging ahead of ground-based tactical aircraft support to land directly on the Kanto Plain around Tokyo appeared just as unappealing. One armored and eight enemy infantry divisions, along with three "depot" (less effective reserve) divisions, were already in that area. The Japanese were also raising additional units and moving them to the region.

This Ultra intelligence caused great concern not only among upper-level navy circles but also in the White House. Marshall passed along to MacArthur that Truman was becoming alarmed at the likelihood of massive American casualties in an invasion of Kyushu. In a June 18 meeting at the White House with the JCS, the president expressed his concern that fanatical resistance would create "an Okinawa from one end of Japan to the other."[33] Marshall presented MacArthur's prepared comments regarding the risks of the invasion:

> I believe the operation presents less [sic] hazards of excessive loss than any other that has been suggested and that its decisive effect will eventually save lives by eliminating wasteful operations of non-decisive character. I regard the operation as the most economical one in effort and lives that is possible. In this respect it must be remembered that the several preceding months will involve practically no losses in ground troops and that sooner or later a decisive ground attack must be made. . . . I most earnestly recommend no change in OLYMPIC.[34]

The meeting participants then discussed the likely numbers of U.S. losses in the operation. Adm. William D. Leahy pointed out that if the 35 percent casualty rate suffered by American forces on Okinawa was applied to the 750,000 men earmarked to land on Kyushu, U.S. casualties could exceed 250,000. In contrast, Marshall offered a much lower number and applied the percentage suffered by the Luzon invasion force to the 750,000 figure, which yielded 31,000 total U.S. casualties. "Left unsaid was that any change to OLYMPIC would deny MacArthur his role in history as the commander of the greatest invasion force ever assembled."[35]

Of course, the invasion did not take place, so we will never know exactly how large American losses would have been on Kyushu and if the higher Okinawa or lower Luzon casualty ratio would have been experienced. Logic tells us that the fighting on the Home Islands would have been just as savage as what American forces encountered at Buna, Saipan, Biak, Iwo Jima, Manila, and Okinawa. The Japanese dug in along the coast of Kyushu would have fought in the belief that they were defending sacred soil and that it was an honor to sacrifice their lives to protect their nation.

In addition, a battle for Kyushu would have resulted in vastly more kamikaze activity than what MacArthur had encountered in the Philippines. Instead of a few hundred such attacks in that campaign, the invaders of Kyushu likely would have had to suffer through multiples of the 1,500 aerial suicide attacks mounted during the Battle of Okinawa. Such kamikazes also likely would have been more successful. Off Okinawa, U.S. Navy ships were able to use their radar to detect incoming enemy aircraft at significant distances as they flew south from bases in the Japanese Home Islands. This allowed the Americans more time to direct carrier fighter aircraft on intercept missions and to ready antiaircraft guns for firing at maximum range. During an invasion of Kyushu, kamikazes would have been flying shorter distances to their targets while screened by intervening mountainous terrain from radar detection as they approached the coastline. Other suicide craft to be employed on Kyushu, especially kamikaze speedboats attacking at night and rocket-powered flying bombs launching during the day, could have caused mass casualties among the invaders.

Inflicting at least Admiral Leahy's 250,000 casualty figure in southern Kyushu was the explicit goal of the Japanese leadership, which did indeed wish to create an "Okinawa from one end of Japan to the other." They believed that such large attritional losses would force the United States to negotiate a conditional surrender. The emperor's generals and admirals accepted that the totals of dead Japanese soldiers and civilians could easily have run into the millions during the fighting on Kyushu. Major General Graves Erskine, commander of the 3rd Marine Division, summed up the American conundrum accurately: "Victory was never in doubt. Its cost was. . . . What was in doubt, in all our minds, was whether there would be any of us left to dedicate our cemetery at the end, or whether the last Marine would die knocking out the last Japanese gun and gunner."[36]

As the United States built up its forces in the Pacific with troops shipped into the region from Europe after Germany's surrender, Japanese military strength in Kyushu continued to grow. Marshall sounded out MacArthur on August 7 as to whether an alternative landing on Honshu or Hokkaido should be considered. MacArthur sent his unequivocal reply within forty-eight hours that the invasion must go forward as planned:

I am certain that the Japanese Air potential reported to you as accumulating to counter our OLYMPIC operation is greatly exaggerated. We have recently seen the 3rd Fleet approach the northern and central shorelines of Japan close enough for gunfire bombardment and yet no reaction from the Japanese air has taken place. Our air forces are daily flying throughout APN and provoke no reaction. . . . I further doubt the often repeated reports that large numbers of aircraft are still being manufactured in JAPAN. As to the movement of ground forces, the Japanese are reported to be trying to concentrate in the few areas in which landings can be effected from TOKYO southward, and it is possible that some strength may have been drawn from the areas of northern HONSHU. I do not credit, however, the heavy strengths reported to you in southern KYUSHU. . . . In my opinion, there should not be the slightest thought of changing the OLYMPIC operation. . . . Throughout the Southwest Pacific Area campaigns, as we have neared an operation intelligence has invariably pointed to greatly increased enemy forces. Without exception, this build-up has been found to be erroneous. In this particular case, the destruction that is going on in JAPAN would seem to indicate that it is very probable that the enemy is resorting to deception.[37]

Historian Richard Frank declared that this cable to Marshall "contained an extraordinarily brazen lie."[38] While intelligence estimates of Japanese strength on individual islands were not generally overstated, MacArthur had often incorrectly downplayed enemy concentrations when Ultra intercepts did not conform to his desires. Frank goes on to state, "It is almost impossible not to believe that MacArthur's resort to falsehood was motivated in large measure by his personal interest in commanding the greatest amphibious assault in history."[39] After the war, U.S. forces validated Ultra intelligence regarding the increase in Japanese forces in southern Kyushu, and American military officers who visited the coastline were shocked by the strength of the fortifications built there to repel a landing.

Despite MacArthur's assurances to Marshall that the Japanese were engaged in massive deception efforts to cover up a terribly weakened military, he never mentioned this in his later writings; nor was it mentioned in the reports written by his staff in Tokyo after the war. In fact, in his memoirs, the General stated that in August there were a full twenty-two enemy divisions of well-trained fighting soldiers based just in the Tokyo region.[40] This suggests that MacArthur knew the truth about the enemy's remaining strength, did not want to acknowledge it, and was willing to lie about it not only to his direct superior in the army but to President Truman as well.

Would the invasion have gone forward in the absence of Truman's authorization of the use of the atomic bomb? The answer can never be known with clarity, but King planned to trigger a debate before the end of August urging a cancellation of Olympic.[41] What would have happened if Truman been confronted by his top admiral and the Pacific naval commander, both strongly opposed to an invasion of Kyushu? Amid warnings of hundreds of thousands of American casualties, the president would have been under great pressure to consider other options.

While some revisionists now dispute the need to drop the atomic bomb on Hiroshima and Nagasaki to end the war, it is quite clear that the Japanese military was committed to waging a great battle on Kyushu. These generals and admirals were willing to accept millions of dead Japanese civilians, along with hundreds of thousands of military casualties, in the hope that concurrent high American losses would result in a negotiated peace that avoided Japan's unconditional surrender. Certainly, the threat of a U.S. invasion and the entry of the Soviet Union into the war in the Far East strengthened the emperor's call to end the fighting, but the fact is that the Japanese military only accepted surrender when faced with the demonstrated otherworldly force of atomic weapons.

While upward of 200,000 Japanese died in the two atomic bombings, many more would have perished in the next few months due to starvation and bombing had the war continued. Japanese losses would have been dramatically greater still had the invasion of Kyushu gone forward. In addition, similarly large masses would have starved to death across Tokyo's remaining empire had the atom bombs not been used and Japan not surrendered in 1945. We will never know how long the Japanese would have continued to fight in the absence of the atomic bomb, and there is no way to know for sure if King and Nimitz would have been able to block the Kyushu landings. What is clear is that Operation Olympic, had it taken place, would have resulted in massive casualty counts on both sides. The United States suffered 111,000 killed and missing in four years of fighting in the Pacific. An invasion of Kyushu could have easily doubled that figure.

Of course, the war did end without a contested invasion, and MacArthur was made commander of the occupation force of Japan. In his memoirs MacArthur makes a great deal of his courage in landing at Atsugi airfield outside Tokyo: "For the supreme commander, a handful of his staff, and a small advance party to land unarmed and unescorted where they would be outnumbered by thousands to one was foolhardy. But years of overseas duty had schooled me well in the lessons of the Orient and, what was probably more important, had taught the Far East that I was its friend."[42] Many of the General's admirers believe this was his bravest moment.

Once again, the truth was quite a bit different. The "small advance party" that preceded MacArthur to Atsugi actually consisted of General Eichelberger and more than 1,000 elite veteran paratroopers. Eichelberger's was one of the first planes to land, and for the next two hours a C-47 full of heavily armed

11th Airborne Division troops touched down every three minutes and disgorged its passengers to take up an expanding perimeter around the airstrip. By the time the *Bataan* landed, even the division's band was assembled on the tarmac to provide a proper martial musical greeting for MacArthur.[43]

In addition, the 4th Marine Regiment was landing at the same time in Tokyo's harbor. A veteran marine officer related with some hyperbole, "Our first wave was made up entirely of admirals trying to get ashore before MacArthur."[44] Certainly, all the Americans disembarking at Atsugi that day were dramatically outnumbered, and if there had been trouble, every one of them would have been at risk. However, by the time MacArthur landed, any Japanese who wished the General harm would have had to fight his way through more than a battalion's worth of veteran U.S. troops, during which time the *Bataan* likely would have had time to fly away, carrying America's highest-ranking military officer. Thankfully, all was calm and the terrible fighting was finally over.

SECOND RETREAT

Seoul to the Naktong

"MacArthur was not a strategist; he was a politician. In fact, he was the finest politician ever to wear the Army uniform."[1]

—Lt. Gen. Victor Krulak, U.S. Marine Corps, 1913–2008

CHAPTER 10

A New War

At the conclusion of World War II, Douglas MacArthur settled into his new role as Supreme Commander for the Allied Powers (SCAP) in Tokyo for what became a tenure that lasted five years. Many consider his service as the omnipotent leader of a defeated Japan as his greatest success. However, an evaluation of the General's performance in this role is beyond the scope of this book, which focuses on MacArthur's strengths and weaknesses as a military leader in time of war. While he was quite effective in his new role, it should be noted that the major initiatives instituted by the SCAP did not spring to life from his own personal intellect, as he often claimed. Rather, he followed specific guidelines transmitted to him from Washington. "Initial Post-Surrender Policy for Japan" (a document officially known as SWNCC 150/4/A and approved by President Truman on September 6, 1945) and "Basic Directive for the Post-Surrender Military Government in Japan Proper" (JCS 1380/5, issued by the Joint Chiefs of Staff on November 3) laid out the reform and reconstruction agenda undertaken in Tokyo after the conclusion of World War II.[1]

It also bears mention that few who applaud MacArthur for his time rebuilding Japan compare his performance to that of the U.S. generals and high commissioners who acted in comparable capacities in occupied Germany and Austria in the years after 1945. Somehow those two European nations also recovered to become similarly peaceful, democratic societies without the benefit of MacArthur's genius. General Joseph McNarney, Gen. Lucius Clay, and High Commissioner John McCloy are not exactly famous names in the United States; nor are they revered as near-gods in Germany the way many look up to MacArthur in Japan. The same is true for Gen. Mark Clark and Gen. Geoffrey Keyes in Austria. Might MacArthur's massive ego and his tight control of message and public persona in the press explain at least some of this differential?

Regardless of the SCAP's abilities as "shogun of Japan" in rebuilding the nation, one of his primary roles was to act as the military commander of U.S. armed forces in the country and the adjacent territory of Korea south of the 38th parallel, which had been occupied by the United States at the end of the war. As Michael Schaller has painstakingly documented in *The American Occupation of Japan*, the U.S. State Department increasingly usurped the SCAP's power regarding domestic management of Japan's economy and political structure after 1947. This meant that MacArthur's primary remaining responsibility became the training and readiness of the American military under his command.

This change in focus was put in writing in April 1949, when SCAP Headquarters issued a policy directive announcing that U.S. forces in Japan would now be relieved of the great bulk of their occupation duties. In June, MacArthur announced that the U.S. military stationed in Japan would begin training for combined-arms offensive operations against a potential opposing military force. By 1950, four army divisions of the 8th Army were left in Japan, along with navy and air force assets.[2] As local police forces were able to maintain the peace in a rapidly recovering economy, MacArthur had the opportunity to prepare his men for what was becoming an increasingly dangerous world.

There were many reasons the 8th Army could have been brought to an acceptable level of combat readiness by 1950. While its divisions were understrength, a significant percentage of its officers and noncoms had served in World War II and knew what was needed to prepare a force to fight. MacArthur certainly had been sent a fighting man to lead his ground forces in Lt. Gen. Walton Walker, who arrived in Japan in late 1948 to assume command of the 8th Army. The pugnacious five-foot, five-inch Walker had fought with distinction in France in 1918 and had risen in World War II to command first an armored division and then a corps as the Allied front moved from Normandy through Germany to victory. General Sutherland had retired after the Japanese surrender and been replaced by Maj. Gen. Edward "Ned" Almond as chief of staff. The two-star Almond often acted domineeringly toward the three-star 8th Army commander, and friction between the two men was constant. MacArthur did not much like Walker either, perhaps because he was a protégé of Marshall and Eisenhower, whom the SCAP saw as rivals.

Next, American forces in Japan, while lightly equipped, were armed with weapons that had proven their effectiveness in the later stages of World War II. The 8th Army could also depend upon the support of U.S. air and naval power, which were both unmatched in the world. Finally, the peaceful situation in Japan allowed for complete focus on training to fight a conventional campaign. Unfortunately, in light of the army's experience in the early months of the Korean conflict, this job was done poorly.

First, the excuse was used that large-scale war-gaming exercises could not take place in densely populated Japan, so the occupation force only practiced small-unit operations. This ignores the fact that the majority of the population of the island of Honshu resides in an area from the city of Osaka in the south up through Nagoya and then on to the Kanto Plain centered on Tokyo. Much of the rest of the island is covered by mountainous forest areas with limited road networks and low population densities. Having soldiers train in such steep terrain is not easy, but of course a military commander's job is to make sure that his solders' drill is rigorous.

With a rebellion in Japan doubtful, a look at the map showed the areas most likely to involve the United States in a shooting war in East Asia in 1950: a Soviet incursion into the Japanese island of Hokkaido, an attack into South Korea by the North Korean Communists, a defense of the island of Formosa against a landing by the People's Republic of China (PRC), or possibly even a landing to support the French in northern Indochina. All of these areas contain large swaths of mountainous terrain often covered by dense forest. Thus, Japan represented an excellent place to prepare the 8th Army for whatever U.S. foreign policy required. As the supreme commander, MacArthur clearly had the power to ensure proper space and time for his men to train for large combined operations. This did not take place.

Once again, MacArthur took little interest in the training of his troops. As in Manila before the bombing of Pearl Harbor, he isolated himself in an office complex in the capital city, rarely met with his divisional commanders, and almost never traveled to the field to take an interest in military exercises. The occupation forces generally lived easy lives, were allowed to hire household servants, and spent a good deal of time drunk and sleeping with Japanese women. William Manchester, the admiring biographer, relates that the General told an aide,

> He knew his occupation troops were "unprepared to fight a war on such short notice," that soft duty had "taken its toll." Characteristically, he assumed no responsibility for this, blaming "frills and fancies" inspired in the Pentagon which "militated against producing good soldiers." He had told Major Bowers that "a soldier's first duty is to keep fit," but he had let his men grow flabby. Somebody else had blundered. MacArthur didn't make mistakes. Other men did, undermining him, making his tasks harder.[3]

So, for multiple reasons, when the Korean War broke out, the 8th Army was not appropriately prepared to fight. While MacArthur might blame the Defense Department, President Truman, or others for the poor readiness level of the men under his command, the fact is that they were the men under his command.[4] Historian Robert Smith places most of the responsibility for the situation on MacArthur's "indolence" and writes of the troops,

They never learned how to act in battle. They learned nothing about night fighting or about fighting in mountainous terrain like that in Korea and Japan. Instead, they were employed, (according to reports in *Time* magazine) in "putting down Communist agitators, collecting taxes, and chasing smugglers." Many of them, if they had no soft noncombat-type jobs in the Army, sought civilian jobs that helped fatten their incomes and widen their ranges among the bars and beer parlors, where friendly companions and complaisant ladies were always in good supply.[5]

Finally, MacArthur believed the chances of the United States being pulled into a Far Eastern conflict in the final years of his career to be quite low. This despite the strident anti-American rhetoric of the PRC, the French flailing in their war with the Communist Viet Minh, and the deteriorating border situation between the two Koreas. Certainly, Washington seemed lukewarm about aiding the French in maintaining their Asian empire, and the Truman administration had written off the forces of the Chinese Nationalists, who had retreated to Formosa, and expected the island to fall to Mao Zedong's PRC in the near future. Similarly, in Washington it was decided that "from a military point of view, it is the opinion of the Joint Chiefs of Staff . . . that the U.S. has little strategic interest in maintaining its present troops and bases in Korea."[6] MacArthur made this policy public when he gave an interview to the *New York Times* on March 1, 1949, in which he described a U.S. defense perimeter in Asia that clearly excluded Formosa and Korea.[7] Secretary of State Dean Acheson followed this up with a speech in January 1950 that made the same point.

The Communists paid notice that the Republic of Korea (ROK) and Formosa were not geographies the United States would fight to protect. While MacArthur spent his days in Tokyo expecting that it was only a matter of time until a peace treaty was signed with Japan and he could retire from the army with honor, possibly to run for president in 1952.[8] It seems that little was done at SCAP HQ to improve the training of the South Korean military or prepare contingency plans to utilize U.S. forces to intervene in the peninsula if a change in policy took place in Washington. As the Cold War intensified, policy did indeed change with Truman's adoption, in the spring of 1950, of the NSC-68 policy paper, which called for military confrontation against Communist aggression anywhere it took place in the world.

Even if MacArthur had focused his time training the 8th Army for war, the weakening of the readiness of American forces would have been difficult to halt. After the end of the world war, the United States rapidly demilitarized and dramatically cut back the defense budget, and a dearth of voluntary enlistments led to a deterioration in the caliber of the average soldier in the ranks.

However, as the combat efficiency of the U.S. divisions in Japan declined, a question begged to be asked: If these tens of thousands of soldiers had not been deployed all the way across the Pacific to be ready to fight, why exactly were they there? The same question could have been asked about MacArthur himself. Sixty-eight years old in 1948, he was well past the army's mandatory retirement age, and no immediate national emergency required his continued presence in command. He also held his occupation post significantly longer than his counterparts in Germany and Austria. Nevertheless, MacArthur told his political supporters back in the United States that he could not retire just yet and was committed to remain in Japan until a formal peace treaty was signed. Of course, how long he remained in his post was supposed to be not his decision but rather that of his military and civilian superiors.

In the run-up to the 1948 elections, the GOP once again courted the General to be its presidential nominee. In contrast to 1944, MacArthur leaked that he was now ready to accept the party's nomination if it was offered to him. By delaying the signing of a peace treaty with Japan, a Democratic president once again made sure that MacArthur remained far away in Asia during an election campaign. Still, President Truman was so concerned that MacArthur would win the GOP nomination and "make a Roman triumphal return to the U.S. a short time before the Republican convention meets in Philadelphia" that he secretly offered a deal to Eisenhower: if Ike would seek the Democratic nomination, Truman would take the second spot on the ticket as his vice presidential candidate.[9]

The president's worries were overwrought. MacArthur's failure to travel to the United States in person and utilize his remarkable rhetorical skills in front of crowds of voters was a huge impediment to his campaign. He garnered few votes in the primaries, and Thomas Dewey once again secured the GOP nomination. Eisenhower declined to run for the nation's highest office, and Truman remained the Democrat's standard bearer in 1948. The president's surprise victory in November represented one of the great upsets of American electoral history.

With the election out of the way, MacArthur remained in Tokyo. Relative calm in Japan contrasted with deteriorating relations with the Soviet Union, Mao's forces rapidly completing their conquest of the Chinese mainland, the French fighting a Communist insurgency in Indochina, and a deteriorating situation along the "temporary" Korean border. Rising tensions in the region should have signaled to MacArthur the imperative to be ready to fight an armed conflict with a Communist opponent in East Asia. To do so successfully, he needed to maximize the readiness of the men remaining under his command, but he spent little time ensuring this and rarely left downtown Tokyo.

STALIN ROLLS THE DICE

After the Japanese surrender in 1945, the Soviets had occupied Korea north of the 38th parallel and installed Kim Il-sung as the head of the Communist government of the Democratic People's Republic of Korea (DPRK). The Americans had supported the competing government of the Republic of Korea (ROK) in the south headed by the elected president, Syngman Rhee. Military forces there were commanded by Gen. John Hodge, who reported to MacArthur in Tokyo. Hopes that the peninsula could be peacefully reunited diminished as relations between not only the two Koreas but also the United States and the Soviet Union deteriorated.

As the United States declared the ROK outside its strategic perimeter, the Communist Korean People's Army (KPA), or Inmun Gun, grew rapidly to upward of 200,000 men. They were equipped by the USSR with significant offensive weapons, including more than 100 T-34 tanks and a similar number of modern tactical aircraft. At the same time, the United States was in the process of withdrawing its ground forces except the 500 soldiers assigned to the Korean Military Advisory Group (KMAG) charged with assisting the ROK military, which was lightly equipped with American armaments. SCAP Headquarters noted the growth of the KPA's size and its new military equipment but discounted the potential fighting prowess of the North Koreans. As the United States declared the ROK not worth fighting for, the Communists expanded the military pressure on the south and tested American resolve.

Kim sent guerilla fighters south of the 38th parallel in a largely unsuccessful attempt to spark an insurgency against the ROK. The KPA also temporarily invaded the Ongin Peninsula northwest of Seoul and later brought the south's city of Kaesong under heavy artillery fire. The U.S. response, both diplomatic and miliary, was muted. At the same time, despite the American men stationed in the KMAG, there was little concern or focus in Tokyo on the capabilities of the KPA. As Matthew Ridgway, the American general brought in to salvage a rapidly deteriorating military situation in 1951, later wrote, "What is truly inexcusable, I believe, and what cost us dearly in blood, was a failure to assess properly the high level of combat effectiveness that the North Korean People's Army had attained."[10]

Reports emanating from the offices of the newly formed CIA office in Tokyo were direr than those from MacArthur's headquarters, and on March 10, 1950, the agency predicted that "North Korea will attack South Korea in June 1950."[11] This was extremely accurate: in fact, it was not until the following month that Kim traveled to Moscow and received final permission from Joseph Stalin to invade the ROK.[12] In contrast, MacArthur gave an interview to the *New York Times* in which he prophesized that war in Korea was not imminent.[13] In May, the U.S. Department of the Army's G-2 in Washington, DC, noted the concentration of heavy Communist forces along the 38th parallel and that war could break out at any time.[14] Finally, the CIA issued a report:

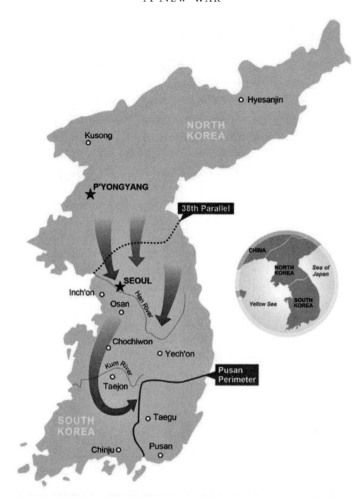

The North Korean invasion and the establishment of the Pusan Perimeter.
COURTESY OF THE U.S. ARMY SPECIAL OPERATIONS FORCES.

Forwarded routinely on 19 June 1950, six days before the North Korean assault, provided Washington with strong evidence of an imminent enemy offensive—extensive troop movements along the 38th Parallel; evacuation of
all civilians north of the parallel for two kilometers; suspension of civilian
freight service from Wonsan to Ch'orwon and the transportation of military
supplies only; concentration of armored units in the border area; and the arrival of large shipments of weapons and ammunition.[15]

   Col. Charles Willoughby, still acting as MacArthur's G-2, had consistently
downplayed the potential of an offensive by the KPA. On the same day as the
CIA report of June 19, he transmitted his conclusion to Washington that the

DPRK was only interested in overthrowing the ROK government by nonmilitary means.[16] Ridgway later wrote of the CIA cable, "How anyone could have read this report and not anticipated an attack is hard to fathom. This report was not used as a basis for *any* conclusions by G-2 at General Headquarters in Tokyo and it was forwarded to Washington in routine fashion with no indication of urgency."[17]

Whether or not MacArthur read the CIA's warning, he certainly did not anticipate the invasion, which was launched on June 25, 1950. Despite all the intelligence warnings that war in Korea was imminent, he later wrote,

> The Communists showed great shrewdness in masking their preparations for attack. Along the 38th parallel itself they deployed only a lightly armored force similar to that of their neighbors to the south. But this was only a screen for the purpose of deception. Back of this first line of offense, they concentrated a powerful striking army fully equipped with heavy weapons, including the latest model of Soviet tanks. The thrust across the border was launched by the lightly armed first line which then swung right and left, while the heavy main force charged through the gap.[18]

Once again, at the start of yet another war, MacArthur chose to play fast and loose with the truth. First, as already noted, U.S. intelligence had clearly detected a large concentration of KPA armor and artillery near the border. Second, in contrast to MacArthur's narrative, the offensive began with a heavy artillery barrage and T-34 tanks leading the invasion force across the 38th parallel.[19] Finally, while a minor point, the General must have known that the T-34 was not the Soviets' latest model. The USSR already had thousands of them in service along its western border areas when the Germans attacked in 1941. The T-54 went into production in 1946 and was the "latest model of Soviet tank" in 1950.

Regardless of these details, while the SCAP was not the only one surprised by the North Korean invasion, he was the senior U.S. military commander in the region. As in Manila on December 8, 1941, it was his job not to be surprised and to ensure that the men under his command were ready for any likely eventuality. Somehow, less than a decade later, MacArthur and the forces under his command were unprepared for a war that he had been warned was about to commence. The General initially misread the situation, announcing that the fighting in Korea was only "a border incident" and the ROK forces would be able to halt the KPA attack with little if any American assistance.[20]

However, the head of KMAG informed MacArthur later in the day of the seriousness of the invasion and that the ROK would be out of ammunition within ten days. The General, with no authority to do so, immediately decided that the United States would resupply the South Koreans. He ordered that hundreds of thousands of artillery rounds and millions of bullets be rushed to the port of Pusan (also written in English as Busan) on the southern tip of the Korean Peninsula. As in the Victor operations five years earlier, MacArthur decided to make U.S. military policy on his own and waited for the JCS to approve his decision afterward. He wired Washington that he planned "to supply ROK all needed supplies as long as they show ability to use same."[21]

Upon hearing of the invasion, President Truman met with his advisors and decided the Communist offensive must be stopped and rolled back. He authorized the already in-process resupply of the South Korean military, ordered an advisory group of officers be sent to Seoul to coordinate assistance efforts with the ROK government, and directed that air and naval forces be used to help hold the capital, along with its main airfield at Kimpo and port at Inchon, for as long as possible. This meant that U.S. aircraft would soon be engaging with those of the DPRK over the skies of southern Korea. However, Truman wanted to move very carefully and not allow the fighting in Korea to grow in geographic scope and involve the USSR and the PRC. As part of this strategy, he ordered that units of the Seventh Fleet take up positions between Formosa and the Chinese mainland so as to "neutralize" the island.

The USSR was boycotting the United Nations at the time to protest that the PRC had not been given China's seat on the Security Council. This allowed the United States to avoid a Soviet veto as it pushed a resolution through the body calling on UN members to engage in armed action to protect the ROK and placing the United States in charge of the multinational UN military force. While this may have seemed an American diplomatic victory, Stalin claimed in a confidential August 1950 letter that the UN boycott was specifically timed so that the United States could obtain its resolution. The Soviet leader wrote that such a Security Council authorization would increase the chance of the United States being pulled into a conflict in Korea. This would distract the United States from Europe and either lead to a rapid and embarrassing U.S. defeat in Korea or tie down his global opponent in the Far East in an extended war between the United States and China.[22] Whether or not this postevent explanation by the Soviet leader is true, he did know about the invasion in advance and it is difficult to deny that Stalin obtained the goals he described as the Korean War progressed.

MacArthur boarded the *Bataan* on June 29 for a visit to meet with President Rhee and U.S. officers on the ground in Korea for the day. Approaching the Suwon airbase, his B-17 was intercepted by a North Korean Yak-9, which was chased away by escorting American Mustang fighters.[23] As the *Bataan* prepared to land, MacArthur decided on his own not only that the United States should shoot down North Korean planes over the ROK but that the opposing force's bases should be destroyed. Thus, he authorized U.S. aircraft to cross into

DPRK airspace and begin bombing military landing strips in that country. The
order sent out via radio from the B-17 to headquarters in Tokyo read, "Take
out North Korean airfields immediately. No Publicity. MacArthur approves."[24]
The president and the Joint Chiefs were actually preparing such an order, but it
was not received in Tokyo until June 30. Once again MacArthur had acted on
his own to make America's foreign policy. And again, he was not reprimanded.

After landing, the General met with President Rhee along with senior
ROK and KMAG officers. The situation was grim, and it was not clear if more
than 25,000 ROK soldiers still remained with their units.[25] MacArthur then
rode north in a jeep to a bluff where he could look across the Han River into
Seoul. He later wrote,

> Below me, and streaming by both sides of the hill, were the retreating, pant-
> ing columns of disorganized troops, the drab color of their weaving lines in-
> terspersed here and there with the bright red crosses of ambulances filled
> with broken, groaning men. . . . In that brief interval on the blood-soaked
> hill, I formulated my plans. They were desperate plans indeed, but I could
> see no other way except to accept a defeat which would include not only
> Korea, but all of continental Asia. That scene along the Han was enough to
> convince me that the defensive potential of South Korea had already been
> exhausted. There was nothing to stop the Communists from rushing their
> tank columns straight down the few good roads from Seoul to Pusan at the
> end of the peninsula.[26]

The orders MacArthur received the next day approved the ongoing air
attacks on North Korea as long as they only struck military targets. The Joint
Chiefs also directed that a regimental combat team be rushed to Pusan to secure that port and its surrounding airfields. MacArthur had been alarmed by
the situation he had seen on the ground in Korea and believed that the ROK
military had collapsed. He sent a reply communicating this fear and argued
that a larger American force, which included two additional divisions, would
be required to hold Pusan. Washington agreed and authorized MacArthur to
transfer to Korea whatever units of the 8th Army he deemed necessary. He also
asked that additional reinforcements be sent to his command and was appalled
when the JCS replied that most of the requested units were needed for the
defense of Europe.

The obvious course of action was for Gen. Walton Walker to position
his divisions on a defensive line anchored along the Naktong River to the
west and the Taebaek Mountains to the north. This "Pusan Perimeter" would
enclose a rectangular area roughly 100 miles north to south and 50 miles
across.[27] While the 8th Army rushed to this line, embedded U.S. advisors
could simultaneously coordinate a fighting withdrawal by the South Korean

military to this new perimeter. As the ROK forces retreated, the KPA invaders would be forced to advance while exposed to U.S. Air Force (USAF) attacks that also targeted supply nodes such as bridges, roads, and railroad lines. Such a strategy would conform with the instructions transmitted to Tokyo by the Joint Chiefs.

Even though it is more than 200 mostly mountainous miles from Suwon to Pusan and both cities and the territory between them were still under control of the ROK military, MacArthur believed that Washington's orders were unsound. In that hour on the hill overlooking the Han River, he had concluded that the South Korean military had been routed and would not stand and fight the Communist invaders. Such an assumption led MacArthur to believe that the only chance to secure a perimeter around Pusan was to rush arriving U.S. Army units northward as quickly as possible toward Seoul to slow the North Korean advance.

Just as MacArthur underestimated the fighting qualities of the ROK army, he was also tragically unaware of the competence of the North Korean military. He soon came to realize that the Korean men fighting on both sides of the conflict were tough and determined soldiers the equal of Americans on the battlefield. MacArthur, immediately after visiting Suwon, "assured Marguerite Higgins, the correspondent for the *New York Herald Tribune,* that he could stop the North Korean advance with two American divisions. In a matter of six days or less, his estimate and his requests to the Pentagon began to skyrocket, for if anyone had been 'fooled' by his enemy, it was MacArthur himself."[28]

The General's initial assumption regarding the weakness of the KPA yielded a belief that more than 100,000 North Korean soldiers could be stopped by a third as many men in two of his understrength and undertrained U.S. Army infantry divisions based in Japan. He even decided that sending smaller American units north toward Seoul to act as blocking forces made sense. However, he soon learned that the KPA was generally better trained and better equipped than the units of the 8th Army. By the time he realized his error, thousands of GIs lay dead, many with their hands bound and a bullet in the back of the head.

MacArthur's choice did give General Walker more time to ship men and equipment of the 8th Army from Japan before the North Koreans arrived along the Naktong. The trade-off was that the unlucky American infantrymen sent north would be in fragmentary units, unsupported on their flanks, massively outnumbered, and unaccompanied by tanks or even much artillery.

It was a prescription for military defeat, terrible U.S. casualties, and plunging morale. No staff work was done to determine if this course of action was truly necessary; no discussions took place with the KMAG command staff to determine if perhaps the men of the ROK with U.S. air support could slow the

North Korean advance. Despite the obvious and now well-known consequences of MacArthur's choice, few have taken the time to even question if it was the correct decision or an error that cost thousands of American lives.

AN ARROGANT DISPLAY OF STRENGTH

Of course, sending small units of poorly equipped, poorly trained infantry to stop a much larger enemy advance supported by modern tanks was a recipe for heavy American casualties, and the frittering away of the limited U.S. Army strength available in Japan. MacArthur's choice was effectively a death sentence for many. The 24th Infantry Division had been undergoing air deployment training, and much of it was in Kyushu near Pusan; thus, it was chosen for sacrifice. Seriously understrength, it was the unit least ready to fight in the 8th Army and had recently been rated at only 65 percent combat efficiency.[29] The choice to commit the 24th, on its own, along a defensive line to act as a firebreak against the dramatically larger KPA advance spearheaded by Soviet armor, was a poor one. Fragmenting the division into even smaller contingents and shipping them off individually toward Seoul bordered on sending them on a suicide mission.

MacArthur later justified rushing troops northward as follows:

> The immediate necessity was to slow down the Red advance before it enveloped all of Korea. My only chance to do this was to commit my forces piecemeal as rapidly as I could get them to the front, relying upon the stratagem that the presence of American ground forces in the battle area would chill the enemy commander into taking precautionary and time-consuming methods. . . . I had hoped by that arrogant display of strength to fool the enemy into a belief that I had greater resources at my disposal than I did.[30]

Despite MacArthur's hopes and his later self-congratulatory statements on the matter, there is little evidence that the North Koreans were fooled or that they shied from immediately attacking the small American units that blocked their path. General Almond admitted later that the forward deployment took place in a slap-dash manner. After the war, an interview he gave contained the following: "'It was the only thing we could do.' The troops were stripped of all equipment except side arms and were carried by plane, assembled at Pusan and then moved north 'to the degree the enemy would permit.'"[31]

MacArthur's narrative and tales of heroic defense by outnumbered U.S. units in this period have dominated histories of the early stages of the war, and few have considered if perhaps MacArthur was guilty of negligence in the deployment of his forces. Some historians have at least taken the time to question if the 24th Division's devastating losses were necessary or even if its fighting retreat was the main reason the KPA's offensive was slowed. Robert Smith argues in *MacArthur in Korea* that bombing the road and rail links across the Han River, which flows east to west through Seoul, was the main impediment to a faster enemy advance: "MacArthur and his sycophants bragged often that the brilliant tactics of the Commander in Chief forced the enemy to halt at the banks of the Han and deploy his artillery, for fear the American forces might be too strong for him to overcome by tanks and infantry alone. But if anything did slow down the North Koreans it was the skill and celerity of the Air Force in taking out the bridges over the Han and in destroying much of the enemy armor."[32]

The initial American men sent north from Pusan comprised Task Force Smith, a battalion of infantry supported by an artillery battery and commanded by Lt. Col. Charles Smith. This small force of 540 men, composed primarily of nineteen- and twenty-year-olds, had little combat training, few antitank guns, only a handful of antitank artillery rounds, and field radios that often did not function. These U.S. soldiers arrived at the town of Osan, twenty-five miles south of Seoul, late in the night of July 4–5. They took up positions on two hills along the main roadway running south and were ordered to block the North Korean advance. Many of the men looking north were confident that the Communists would turn and run as soon as they realized that they were up against American troops. They would soon learn how wrong they were.

MacArthur claims in his memoirs that when the North Korean commander discovered that American soldiers were in his path, "he decided, as I had anticipated, against taking any chance. So, instead of continuing to drive his tank columns forwards, he deployed all of his forces across the difficult terrain in conventional line of battle. This was his fatal error."[33] That description of the battle contains several false statements. First of all, there was no delay as the North Korean commander "deployed all his forces in conventional line of battle." In actuality, as the sun rose, only a few hours after its arrival, Task Force Smith came under attack and was quickly defeated.

The first North Koreans the men of Task Force Smith saw were in a long line of T-34s heading south along the road. The tanks proceeded right through the American positions, and few even stopped to fire on the defenders as they rumbled off out of sight. As with the Germans in 1941, the Americans in 1950 found that the T-34 was extremely difficult to put out of action with light antitank weapons, which deflected off the tanks' sloping armor. Two of the T-34s were knocked out by a combination of artillery and bazooka fire, but the rest of the armored vehicles rumbled on to the south. Thus, the enemy did not deploy all his forces in conventional line of battle, and in contrast to MacArthur's boast, the KPA tank columns continued to drive forward.

About an hour after the T-34s had passed, a large mass of North Korean infantry accompanied by a column of trucks came into view, and the Americans opened fire. These two approaching regiments of the KPA outnumbered the American battalion on the order of ten to one, and the defensive lines were quickly penetrated in the center and flanked on both sides. The GIs were soon overrun and suffered a casualty count that approached 40 percent as the force retreated in disarray. Historian T. R. Fehrenbach summed up the engagement as follows: "Task Force Smith, designed to be an arrogant display of strength to bluff the enemy into halting his advance, had delayed the Inmun Gun exactly seven hours."[34]

Next to stand in the path of the North Koreans was the 34th Infantry Regiment, which attempted to hold a line south of Osan at Pyongtaek. It too was "understrength, untrained, undisciplined, and unprepared."[35] The regiment was quickly outflanked and defeated when it came under attack by KPA formations and forced to retreat south to Chonan. There, the rapidly shrinking American force was again overrun on July 8, leading to another retreat. The regiment's remaining GIs headed south until they reached the Kum River, where these survivors linked up with the rest of the 24th Division arriving from Pusan.

The divisional commander, Maj. Gen. William Dean, ordered his men to cross back to the south side of the river, destroy all bridges, and hold a line there. The American defense was anchored by the city of Taejon, 100 miles from Seoul and 125 north of Pusan. Of the 16,000 men of the division that had arrived in Korea in the first week of July, only about 11,500 could still man the line by this point to hold back the KPA offensive. In the battle that followed, the North Koreans committed approximately a two-to-one advantage in men and scores more tanks than the first few arriving to support the defenders. Many of General Dean's men were exhausted, morale was shaky, and supplies of ammunition were low. The KPA units had their own problems as they were at the end of a rapidly lengthening supply line and had been under constant attack from American planes for upward of two weeks. Nevertheless, the KPA forces successfully crossed the Kum River on July 14 under cover of an artillery barrage. The Americans retreated into Taejon and were soon surrounded. The North Koreans broke into the city in dual advances, and house-to-house fighting raged over the next few days.

Eventually the men of the 24th Division broke out to the south and retreated. The survivors began to reach the Naktong River on July 21 and passed through the lines of the U.S 1st Cavalry Division, which had dug in there. The Americans had suffered more than 1,000 dead, and twice as many were reported missing. Most of the latter were either killed in action or summarily bound and executed by the North Koreans soon after being captured.

General Dean was one of the lucky ones who survived as a POW until after the conclusion of the war. His men had successfully slowed the enemy advance, but at great cost. In seventeen days of fighting, the 24th Division suffered more than 30 percent casualties, lost almost all its heavy equipment, and retreated 100 miles—and the enemy had still advanced at an average of 6 miles per day.[36]

A history of the battle published by the U.S. Army found much to be lacking in the preparedness of the force sent forward to blunt the KPA advance. Many senior commanders were new to their units and did not know their men. There was an extreme shortage of ammunition, especially of armor-piercing high-explosive antitank rounds. Communication was consistently poor with radios that did not work or batteries that failed quickly. Maps were subpar and based on a Japanese survey that dated back to the end of World War I, despite the United States having been in control of southern Korea for the previous five years. Convoy discipline on roads was poor, as was the maintenance of vehicles.[37]

A history of the first six months of the Korean War published by the U.S. Army, *South to the Naktong, North to the Yalu*, draws conclusions that reflect poorly on MacArthur's preparation of his men for battle.

> There were many heroic actions by American soldiers of the 24th Division in these first weeks in Korea. But there were also many uncomplimentary and unsoldierly ones. Leadership among the officers had to be exceptional to get the men to fight, and several gave their lives in this effort. Others failed to meet the standard expected of American officers. There is no reason to suppose that any of the other three occupation divisions in Japan would have done better in Korea than did the U.S. 24th Division in July 1950. When committed to action they showed the same weaknesses. A basic fact is that the occupation divisions were not trained, equipped, or ready for battle.[38]

The North Koreans reaching the newly established Pusan Perimeter found that the UN forces holding this line were generally strong enough to withstand all attacks thrown at them. MacArthur now had under his command in Korea three U.S. divisions of the 8th Army (the 25th, the 1st Cavalry, and the battered 24th), the 5th RCT just arrived from Hawaii, and five ROK divisions that had retreated south (the 1st, 3rd, 6th and 8th, as well as the Capital Division) By the time the Battle of Taejon ended, UN forces in Korea already approximated the opposing KPA invaders in size. MacArthur's command soon grew to outnumber the North Koreans in both men and firepower over the course of August.

During this month the ROK military expanded, and additional U.S. reinforcements began to arrive in Pusan, including the 2nd Infantry Division, the

1st Provisional Marine Brigade, and four medium tank battalions (6th, 89th, 70th, and 73rd).[39] The British 27th Infantry Brigade also arrived, the first of many contingents of allied UN nations to fight in the conflict. The KPA was increasingly at a disadvantage as MacArthur had at his disposal a more mechanized force operating on interior lines, control of the air and the sea, and a steady supply of new fighting men being shipped in from overseas. By the end of August, the UN force holding the lines within the Pusan Perimeter totaled 180,000 men.[40]

Did a significant percentage of an American infantry division need to be sacrificed to achieve the successful establishment of the Pusan Perimeter? MacArthur believed it did and later wrote that his decision to send the 24th northward in a piecemeal manner "exacted a painful sacrifice from my men committed to this unequal battle, but it paid off in precious time, so essential if any tactic in the prevailing situation was to be successful."[41] However, the General's decision to make this "painful sacrifice" was of course based on his assumptions that the ROK had been shattered as an effective fighting force after the first few days of fighting, that it would not stand and fight, and that it could not slow the North Korean advance. There is a great deal of evidence that these assumptions were flawed. If so, the deaths of many U.S. troops in July 1950 were unnecessary.

What would have happened had the 24th Division instead formed up as a complete unit along the Kum River with days to prepare defensive positions and calibrate its artillery with orders to hold at first and then slowly fall back in phases? In such a scenario, the KPA would have arrived at the Naktong a week or so earlier than it did to face an additional U.S. division (1st Cavalry) along with elements of five ROK divisions. The UN line would have been buttressed by rapidly increasing air power along with reinforcements streaming to the front (25th Division, 5th RCT). Would the North Koreans have been able to cross the river in the face of this defensive force supported by armor, artillery, and airpower? Perhaps, but it seems quite likely that the rising number of ROK soldiers in the line, along with additional UN forces landing at Pusan, would have been sufficient to hold the invaders.

A major reason the 24th Division was sent north on its own, unprepared and unsupported, is that MacArthur concluded in an hour standing on a rise overlooking the Han River on June 29 that the ROK was beaten as a fighting force. Later that day he cabled Washington his impression that "the Korean Army has made no preparations for a defense in depth, for echelons of supply or for a supply system. . . . The Korean Army is entirely incapable of counter-action and there is grave danger of a further breakthrough. If the enemy continues much further it will seriously threaten the fall of the Republic."[42]

However, as already mentioned, it is a long distance from the Han to the Nak-tong. Along the narrow valleys and steep mountains of South Korea, the ROK was able to reconstitute much of its strength and recover from its initial dismal showing in the first few days of the Communist attack.

Despite suffering upward of 70,000 casualties, the ROK army began to grow as it pulled back. Starting with close to 100,000 men on the first day of the invasion, many ROK units were initially scattered by KPA forces moving south, and the defenders may have been down to 22,000 men in their units after the first week of combat.[43] However, retreating formations picked up stragglers, while new recruits from the nation's large population of 20 million took their place on the firing lines. By late July, the ROK was up to 86,000 soldiers in the ranks and grew to 91,000 by September 1.[44] Moreover, the av-erage ROK soldier was increasingly well equipped and resupplied due to the arrival of American shipments to Pusan. While the ROK's recovery could not have occurred if the United States had stayed out of the conflict, it is difficult to believe that it only took place because the 24th Division was rushed more than 100 miles north of Pusan to slow the North Korean advance. The people of South Korea were more than willing to fight for their newly independent na-tion. By the end of the war, despite taking in excess of half a million casualties, the men of the ROK's armed forces had grown to exceed 600,000 compared to the KPA, which peaked at around 250,000. Thus, in retrospect, it is difficult to conclude that the ROK was shattered beyond repair after the first few days of fighting in 1950.

As the KPA pushed south, it became quite clear that the ROK military was not "beaten as a fighting force" and would indeed stand and fight. In fact, the performance of many units of the South Korean military began to improve as fighting wore on into its second month. This was especially true when the USAF conducted close air support missions and the U.S. Navy was able to provide shore battery fire. Most histories of this period are focused on the mo-ment-to-moment travails of the U.S. 24th Division. However, an order of mag-nitude more ROK soldiers were fighting, and often dying, in desperate battles to slow the KPA advance in actions where the invaders suffered prohibitive casualties.

There were many examples of the ROK standing its ground during the retreat to the Naktong. For example, while the U.S. 24th Division was fighting the Battle of Taejon in the west, the ROK 3rd Division was able to stabilize its frontlines and counterattack to retake the town of Yongdok, from which it had just been expelled by the KPA's 5th Division. In fighting that dragged out over three weeks, the town traded hands several times. U.S. naval bombardments and USAF bombing missions were instrumental in slowing the KPA advance, but it was the ROK infantryman who had to fight and die in "a smoldering no man's land. The pounding of the artillery, naval gunfire, and air strikes had stripped the hills of all vegetation and reduced to rubble all small villages in the area."[45]

Historian Clay Blair accused MacArthur's forward deployment strategy of being "fantastical," documented the valiant defense offered by the ROK, and questioned the need for the sacrifice of the 24th Division.[46] He concluded,

> The Americans had achieved little in this piecemeal and disorganized waste of precious lives and equipment. At most they delayed the NKPA a total of three, possibly four, days. Notwithstanding Army claims to the contrary, these delays were not in any way decisive to the American forces and might well have been matched at less cost by a consolidated and cohesive defense behind the Kum River. Moreover, the collapse of these ill-trained, ill-equipped, ill-led, and thinly disposed American units in the first combat was a psychological victory of incalculable dimensions to the NKPA. In combat, as elsewhere, success breeds success.[47]

The ROK most certainly did not collapse over the course of July as per MacArthur's early dire predictions. The General even publicly commended the ROK Capital Division on July 27 for its performance fighting the KPA east of Taejon.[48] When able to utilize U.S. air or naval support, the South Koreans were increasingly able to stand against KPA units, as in the battles of P'ohang-dong and Andong in the southeast of the peninsula. The 8th Army was also becoming stronger as reinforcements arrived by sea. The UN force under MacArthur's command was now operating along interior lines, that much closer to USAF bases in Kyushu, and much of the Pusan Perimeter was within range of the U.S. Navy's gunnery support.

General Walker gave a speech to his men along the Pusan Perimeter on July 29 that became known as his "stand or die" address:

> There is no line behind us to which we can retreat. Every unit must counter-attack to keep the enemy in a state of confusion and off balance. There will be no Dunkirk, there will be no Bataan, a retreat to Pusan would be one of the greatest butcheries in history. We must fight until the end. Capture by these people is worse than death itself. We will fight as a team. If some of us must die, we will die fighting together. Any man who gives ground may be personally responsible for the death of thousands of his comrades. I want you to put this out to all the men in the Division. I want everybody to understand that we are going to hold this line. We are going to win.[49]

One can imagine that such a line would have held just as well had Walker given his address a few days earlier to a force that included a 24th Division that had not been so terribly chewed up in its defeats at Onsan, Pyongtaek, and Chonan.

MacArthur's second retreat was over. While the North Korean attacks continued, and despite moments of panic and desperate fighting along the perimeter line, the UN forces held. In addition, American military hardware superiority over the KPA was rapidly increasing. U.S. aircraft dominated the skies over the battlefield, and U.S. naval vessels ruled the seas off the coasts. American artillery on hand now outclassed what the North Koreans could ship and supply down the length of the peninsula along a single, often interdicted railway line. Most of the KPA's T-34s had been knocked out of action, while more than 1,300 Chaffee, Patton, Pershing, and Sherman tanks were deployed to the peninsula by the end of the year. The UN force could now shift over to the offensive and liberate South Korea. The question was where MacArthur would strike.

LAST ADVANCE

Inchon to the Yalu

"Fine! Fine! The more arrogant and more stubborn he is, the better. An arrogant enemy is easy to defeat."[1]

—Mao Zedong, chairman of the Communist Party
of China, 1893–1976

CHAPTER 11

Inchon

Douglas MacArthur claimed that when he stood on the hill overlooking the Han River in late June, he immediately constructed in his mind the basic strategy for defeating the KPA: retreat to an area around Pusan and then stage an amphibious landing at Seoul's port of Inchon to cut off the North Koreans in what was originally known as Operation Bluehearts. That he did not know if Inchon (also written in English as Inch'on or Incheon) was a suitable location to stage a modern landing operation from the sea was unimportant. This plan eventually led to the greatest gamble and the greatest victory of his career. Unfortunately, his gravest mistake and one of the most shocking defeats in military history soon followed.

America's Far Eastern commander initially believed that he could execute his plan solely with forces on hand in Japan using two divisions to hold Pusan and a single division transported by sea to envelop the enemy in the rear. Initially the landing was to take place on July 22. However, as MacArthur came to realize how much he had misjudged the fighting ability of the KPA, he pushed back the landing date, and his demands to the Pentagon rose dramatically. All of the ROK military, most of the 8th Army, and additional U.S. formations were required to hold the line along the Naktong River.

MacArthur subsequently decided that he needed an additional corps-sized force to seize Inchon and sever the Communists' main supply lines. The amphibious landing operation was renamed Chromite, and soon X Corps was activated to lead it. The 1st Marine Division and the 7th Infantry Division sailed to Japan and were assigned to the mission. However, while the forces for the amphibious assault had been provided, approval of MacArthur's scheme became one of significant acrimony inside the U.S. military. The issue was not whether a landing should take place behind enemy lines in Korea but whether such an operation could succeed at Inchon.

The positives of such a strategy were obvious, and amphibious attacks were an established part of American military doctrine when confronting an enemy on a peninsula: after all, the U.S. military had recently built up a great deal of institutional expertise in amphibious operations in Italy and France and across the Pacific in World War II. In addition, the United States dominated the seas and the skies in the Korean theater of operation to a level it had never achieved when it transported its forces to contested shores in battles such as those for Normandy, Saipan, Anzio, Leyte, Salerno, or Okinawa. The problem was that MacArthur wanted to land at Inchon. In theory this was an excellent place to strike as it was close to the psychologically important prize of Seoul, the action would cut the railway running to the southern end of Korea, and the KPA appeared to have concentrated its forces along the Naktong.

However, seasoned U.S. Navy amphibious operation officers saw a landing at Inchon as presenting terrible risks. As Gen. Ridgway put it,

> The doubts of the plan's success were well-founded, for a combination of perfect timing, perfect luck, precise coordination, complete surprise, and extreme gallantry were all needed to spell victory here. It would have been difficult to find, on the entire tortuous Korean coastline, a spot more difficult to assault. Inchon's natural defenses rendered it nearly immune to hostile approach by sea. The thirty-foot tides, receding, left a tight and twisting channel through mile-wide mudflats that seemed ideally fashioned to ground our LSTs and turn them into artillery targets. What seemed to me an impregnable small island dominated the channel. And the channel itself, the only approach to the port, had surely been mined, as the island was most certainly fortified. In addition, the operation was timed for the typhoon season and there was at least an even chance that a howling storm might scatter our amphibious force and lay them all open to destruction.[1]

In addition, Inchon was also an urban area where an invading force got bogged down in house-to-house fighting. MacArthur did not believe this to be a problem, and landing in city harbors had not generally been an option in the great advance of American forces in the Southwest Pacific Area between 1942 and 1945. However, U.S. military commanders stationed in the European theater of operations during World War II had learned from the failed raid on the city of Dieppe that such a target was much riskier to seize than a rural beach setting. They also knew from the landing at Salerno the danger of an armored counterattack on a shallow beachhead held primarily by infantry. These men were now in positions of authority in the Pentagon and were intensely concerned by MacArthur's plan.

Navy and marine officers were also concerned that Inchon did not actually have beaches on which to land. Instead, it had high seawalls that would have to be scaled by marines emerging from landing craft. The port also had some of the highest tidal flows in the world. This meant that ships could only remain in the channel for a short period or would become beached on Inchon's expansive mudflats. Thus, the first assault wave would be on its own for several hours until the second could arrive. U.S. Navy officers assigned to plan the Chromite operation were appalled. Comdr. Arlie Capps later wrote, "We drew up a list of every natural and geographic handicap—and Inchon had 'em all." Comdr. Monroe Kelly commented, "Make up a list of amphibious 'don'ts,' and you have an exact description of the Inchon operation."[2]

To compound navy and marine unease, MacArthur decided to name Gen. Almond as commander of X Corps even though he had never been involved in an amphibious operation, much less been in charge of one that presented numerous and potentially disastrous challenges to its success. Also concerning was that Almond was to continue serving in the full-time position as MacArthur's chief of staff while also in charge of Chromite. Almond's abrasive personality had not endeared him to officers in the Far East. His own G-3, Col. (later Maj. Gen.) John Chiles, once said of his superior, "He could precipitate a crisis on a desert island with nobody else around."[3] Of course, Almond was also "completely devoted to General MacArthur. General MacArthur didn't have anybody that was more of a disciple than Ned Almond."[4] Such a character was a danger to an operation that required excellent teamwork between the army, marines, navy, and air force. Many did not believe that Almond was qualified for the position and referred to the choice of the chief of staff to take charge of Chromite as "Operation Three Star," designed to secure a promotion to lieutenant general for MacArthur's favorite.

Even if an army general was going to lead the Inchon operation rather than one from the marines, many talented men with experience in amphibious landings could have been brought in to command X Corps. Almond's career would not have recommended him for such an important appointment. He had fought in World War I as a major and rose through the ranks to eventually lead the 93rd Infantry Division in Italy. The primarily African American soldiers of the 93rd performed poorly in combat. There were various reasons for this, and many were not Almond's fault. However, he blamed his men's race for blunting his career, and his discrimination against blacks was extreme even for a white American army officer of that era.

Almond got along poorly with Gen. O. P. Smith of the 1st Marine Division. The two were very different men. For example, MacArthur's chief of staff enjoyed his creature comforts and, when in Korea, lived in a luxurious trailer with a separate dining room and soldiers acting as waiters serving food freshly flown in from Japan. In contrast, Smith eschewed any special privileges of rank and tended to sleep in crude shelters in the field with his men and eat the same rations. Almond could have attempted to build a good relationship with Smith and learn from his subordinate who had participated in World War II amphibious operations on New Britain, Peleliu, and Okinawa. Sadly, this did not take place, and many reported that a mutual loathing developed between the two generals. Almond's character as a leader was summed up by Col. Maurice Holden, the G-3 of the U.S. Army's 2nd Division: "When it paid to be aggressive, Ned was aggressive. When it paid to be cautious, Ned was aggressive."[5] Marine Col. (later Lt. Gen.) Victor Krulak of the 1st Marine Division was not impressed by Almond's boldness and later commented, "Almond, well, he wasn't much of anything."[6]

Several officers suggested that the amphibious attack take place at more advantageous sites along Korea's west coast, including Posung-myon, thirty miles south of Inchon; Kunsan, even further south; or north of Seoul at Chinnampo. Admiral James Doyle, in charge of the amphibious naval force, recommended that the landing take place at Posung-myon, especially after "navy underwater demolition teams had made several trial landings there and had found that beach conditions were much better than at Inch'on and would not restrict the landing to a particular day or hour. The area was not built up and . . . was in striking distance of the enemy's lines of communications south of Seoul."[7] Marine general Lemuel Shepherd also met with MacArthur to argue for Posung-myon. However, all counterproposals were brushed aside. MacArthur had determined that Inchon was the only possible location for a successful invasion.[8]

The Joint Chiefs of Staff (JCS) sent two of its members, Gen. Lawton Collins, army chief of staff, and Adm. Forrest Sherman, chief of naval operations, to Tokyo to discuss Chromite's target. They attended a meeting on July 23, in which Admiral Doyle presented the navy's views on the pros and cons of landing at Inchon and concluded, "The operation is not impossible, but I do not recommend it." MacArthur then launched into a long oration arguing his case and pointed out that the difficulties at Inchon were actually positives, as the KPA would never expect the United States to land there. He then declared, in a statement full of irony, "My confidence in the Navy is complete, and in fact, I seem to have more confidence in the Navy than the Navy has in itself. The Navy has never let me down in the past, and it will not let me down this time."[9] MacArthur closed his argument by stating, "I realize that Inchon is a 5,000 to 1 gamble, but I am used to taking such odds. We shall land at Inchon and I shall crush them!"[10]

After the meeting, Gen. Walker was asked why Inchon had been chosen rather than Kusan or Posung-myon. Walker replied, "MacArthur has everyone thinking of Korea as an island and Seoul the final objective. Once it's taken, the war would be over."[11] Military leaders in Washington, hesitant to oppose

MacArthur directly, were still not convinced that the risks of landing at In-chon were worth taking. On September 7, as the men of the invasion force prepared to board their ships, the JCS formally requested that MacArthur re-consider Inchon as the target of the amphibious operation and estimate the chances that a landing there could succeed.[12]

MacArthur relates in his memoirs that this message "chilled me to the marrow of my bones" and asks rhetorically, "What could have given rise to such a query at such an hour? Had someone in authority in Washington lost his nerve? Could it be the President? Or Marshall, who had just become Secretary of Defense? Or Bradley? Or was it merely an anticipating alibi if the operation should run into trouble?"[13] MacArthur's immediate reply all but guaranteed victory, argued that Inchon was the sole point where the United States could win the war, and falsely stated that all his subordinate commanders approved of the landing operation: "There is no question in my mind as to the feasibility of the operation and I regard its chance of success as excellent. I go further and believe that it represents the only hope of wresting the initiative from the enemy and thereby presenting an opportunity for a decisive blow. . . . I repeat that I and all of my commanders and staff officers, without exception, are en-thusiastic for and confident of the success of the enveloping operation."[14] The next day the JCS approved the operation.

As the Chromite flotilla arrived in position on September 15, 1950, Almond showed just how inappropriate was his command of the operation. He was standing at a ship's rail with Colonel Krulak, who was then serving as chief of staff of the 1st Marine Division. The initial wave of the assault was forming up in heavily laden LVTs (landing vehicles, tracked). Thousands of these amphibious craft had been a key component of American shore landings all through World War II, from Guadalcanal to Leyte to Okinawa, and the men affectionately gave them nicknames like "Buffalos," "Alligators," and "Amtracs." Almond looked down and asked, "Can those things really float?"[15] Krulak stared back incredulously and excused himself to relate the story to General Shepherd. The LVTs did indeed float, and they motored off toward Inchon.

THE CHINESE PREPARE TO INTERVENE

As the United States stabilized the Pusan Perimeter and readied X Corps for Chromite, the Chinese were preparing to enter the war. Mao Zedong's armies had only recently defeated the Kuomintang (KMT) and forced its remnants to flee to Formosa. The nation was destitute after more than fifteen years of war; yet Mao was ready to attack the United States and its allies in Korea. From his vantage point in Beijing, recent U.S. actions appeared to mirror previous ones of Japan. Mao and other members of his government feared that "imperialists" based in Tokyo were once again about to attack from Korea into Manchuria and from Formosa onto China's coast.

Truman believed that by sending the U.S. Navy into the strait between Formosa and the Asian mainland in June, he was "neutralizing" the island. However, Beijing saw the action as a great provocation, as it did the U.S. intervention in Korea. China had dominated the peninsula for much of the last 1,000 years, and the new Communist government believed it was entitled to resume its control of the region. The Japanese had seized Formosa and Korea from China in 1894 as a precursor to moving into Manchuria in 1931, then invading the Chinese heartland from the north and landing forces in its central coast cities starting in 1937. Now the United States, rabidly opposed to communism and a staunch ally of the Kuomintang, appeared to be taking the exact same geographic path. Unless it was stopped, Mao believed the result would be identical: a foreign attack to conquer his nation.

The Communists became even more aroused when Chinese Nationalist leader Chiang Kai-shek offered to send tens of thousands of his troops to fight in Korea under UN command. MacArthur was initially positive about accepting the reinforcements, but the JCS and Truman refused them due to political considerations, the questionable fighting quality of such troops, and the amount of logistical support they would require. Later, the General claimed that the Nationalist Chinese forces were as "well-equipped and well-trained and of the same general quality as the soldiers of Red China. They were certainly trustworthy, free men in the Nationalist Army by choice, and would have been undoubtedly effective in battle."[16] Such a characterization was in stark contrast to the poor performance of these fighting formations from 1945 to 1949.

While not able to use KMT forces, MacArthur still made comments to the press that they should be "unleashed" in Korea and flew to Taipei at the end of July for talks with Chiang.[17] Afterward MacArthur announced, "Arrangements have been completed for effective coordination between American forces under my command and those of the Chinese government."[18] This seemed to indicate that the United States was entering into a new military alliance with the Kuomintang to either involve the Nationalist forces in Korean fighting or have the United States base forces on Formosa with the possibility that the island would be used as a launchpad to invade China's central coast.

Truman was concerned that actions taken in the Far East were precipitating a conflict with the People's Republic of China (PRC). He sent his advisor, Averell Harriman, to visit MacArthur in Tokyo on August 6 to reiterate the president's policy of keeping Taiwan out of the current conflict. Harriman reported,

In my first talk with MacArthur, I told him the President wanted me to tell him he must not permit Chiang to be the cause of starting a war with the Chinese communists on the mainland, the effect of which might drag us into a world war. He answered that he would, as a soldier, obey any orders that he received from the President. . . . For reasons which are rather difficult to explain, I did not feel that we came to a full agreement on the way we believed things should be handled on Formosa and with the Generalissimo. He accepted the President's position and will act accordingly, but without full conviction.[19]

While in Tokyo, Harriman also received a lecture from MacArthur regarding how to understand "the Oriental Mind." Harriman related, "He described the difference between the attitude towards death of Westerns and Orientals. We hate to die; only face danger out a sense of duty and through moral issues; whereas with Orientals, life begins with death. They die quietly, 'folding their arms as a dove folding his wings, relaxing, and dying.'"[20] While MacArthur considered himself a master of reading the people of the Far East, he failed to grasp that the senior leaders of the new Chinese government were terribly paranoid. In fact, Mao and his advisors were increasingly coming to believe that the United States and China were entering into a state of war—one that China could not lose, lest it be ripped apart again. Mao decided that he must attack before the Chinese heartland was invaded. He had almost no navy with which to transport his army to Formosa, and so his only option for an offensive was to fight in Korea.

On July 7, as the U.S. 24th Division was being overrun south of Seoul, Mao took action, reasoning that "in case we needed to enter the war we would be prepared."[21] The best units of the People's Liberation Army (PLA), the 38th, 39th, and 40th armies, were sent to the Korean frontier area to reinforce the 42nd Army already there. These units were soon placed under command of the newly established People's Volunteer Army (PVA), the force selected to advance south of the Yalu River if China chose to enter the conflict.

Supplies and ammunition for a potential intervention were stockpiled in the region. The PRC leadership understood that daring to attack MacArthur's force would result in a tough and bloody campaign, and field hospitals with a capacity of 100,000 men were set up near the border.[22] Beijing also began an internal propaganda campaign to prepare the people for war with the slogan "Defending the homeland and safeguarding the country."[23] Mao did not move toward war lightly. He and his advisors agreed that the PRC's intervention in Korea could lead the U.S. Air Force to bomb major Chinese cities and the U.S. Navy to blockade and shell Chinese ports.

The Chinese military leadership near the Korean border met in a conference to decide if it would be better to wait for the Americans to invade Manchuria or move into Korea and fight there. They recommended to Mao that they advance into Korea. The Chinese military thought they could win based on six main factors:

1. They could bring large forces to bear that would outnumber the Americans' ground force, and the weaker ROK military was suspect.
2. The Chinese would be able to focus on this one conflict, while the United States had military commitments in Europe and elsewhere.
3. The Chinese would be operating on interior lines much closer to its bases of supply versus the United States, which would have to project force across the entire Pacific.
4. Chinese morale would be higher as its forces would be fighting for a just cause.
5. The United States would not use atomic weapons as doing so would hurt America in world public opinion.
6. The United States' preponderance of firepower could not be used effectively if the Chinese avoided frontal assaults and instead infiltrated through gaps in the front to cut supply lines required to bring up artillery shells, fuel, and so forth.[24]

Tactically, the Chinese worked to further inspire their men to want to march into Korea and convince them that they could best the U.S. military. For example, former KMT troops who had fought with the Americans in Burma in World War II were brought in to discuss U.S. Army weaknesses. Training exercises began with the intent to blunt their army's technological military weaknesses, including practicing antiaircraft and antitank tactics.[25] Mao had made no step that committed him to war, but he watched the United States warily as his military prepared to fight.

Only a few weeks after Harriman's trip, MacArthur directly disobeyed Truman by sending a statement to the national encampment of the Veterans of Foreign Wars (VFW). The text excoriated U.S. policy and called for an aggressive defense of Taiwan:

> Should Formosa fall into the hands of a hostile power, history would repeat itself. Its military potential would again be fully exploited as the means to breach and neutralize our western Pacific defense system and mount a war of conquest against the free nations of the Pacific basin. Nothing could be more fallacious than the threadbare argument by those who advocate appeasement and defeatism in the Pacific that if we defend Formosa we alienate continental Asia. Those who speak thus do not understand the Orient. They do not

grant that it is in the pattern of the Oriental psychology to respect and follow
aggressive, resolute and dynamic leadership—to quickly turn on a leadership
characterized by timidity or vacillation—and they underestimate the oriental
mentality.[26]

MacArthur went on to state that a loss of Formosa would put at risk the people
of the Philippines, Australia, New Zealand, and the West Coast of the U.S.
mainland, as if the American military bases on the islands of Okinawa, Guam,
Luzon, Wake, and Oahu simply did not exist.

Truman was angered when this statement was released to the press as it
placed pressure on him to extend America's security umbrella to include Formosa and play an ongoing role in the Chinese civil war. The president considered demoting MacArthur immediately and confining his command to the
occupation of Japan.[27] However, Truman decided against this as it would send
a signal that the United States would not defend Formosa. Thus, he only directed MacArthur to withdraw his statement to the VFW. However, as the
New York Times reported in a front-page article, "General MacArthur's views
on Formosa have differed sharply from those of the Administration. The General has expressed his opinions to some top leaders who have visited him in
Tokyo. Because of this, State Department officials apparently were not too surprised at the new development. Some of them long have expected there would
have to be a showdown with him on the subject of Formosa."[28] In other words,
MacArthur was making American foreign policy in the Far East at odds with
that of the executive branch of the U.S. government.

Of course the statement to the VFW was studied in detail in Beijing, and
its belligerent tone helped lead Mao to precipitate a wider war in the Far East.
With his focus on the KPA, MacArthur and his staff missed that the PRC was
preparing to enter the conflict and were also unaware that the Chinese had
figured out that the Americans would soon land at Inchon. X Corps almost
sailed into a massive trap. The PLA general staff studied MacArthur's actions
in World War II and guessed correctly that he would launch a two-division
amphibious assault, with the most likely target being Inchon, as early as late
August.

The PLA didn't need to have broken any U.S. codes; coming to this conclusion only required some general intelligence gathering and logical analysis.
It knew that a marine and an army division had arrived in Japan but were not
being sent to the Pusan area. Large numbers of British and U.S. naval vessels,
especially landing craft, were moving to the region. The United States had
landed behind enemy lines on the west coast of peninsular Italy in World War
II at Salerno and Anzio, and MacArthur, supported by the navy, had engaged
in numerous amphibious attacks to cut enemy supply lines in the defeat of the
Japanese Empire.

The Chinese warned the North Koreans and the Soviets of these conclusions and suggested the KPA move forces to Inchon. Mao even personally made this suggestion to Lee-Sang-jo, a representative from the KPA who visited Beijing to brief the Chinese on the course of the war. The Soviet Union also warned the North Koreans that MacArthur was likely to stage an amphibious assault in their rear area. Inexplicably, and luckily for MacArthur and X Corps, Kim Il-sung did not heed these warnings.[29]

VICTORY AT HIGH TIDE

As the debate over the Inchon landing took place, MacArthur was akin to a gambler sitting at a blackjack table in a Las Vegas casino playing with a very large pile of chips all wagered on one hand. He has a king and a nine—a score of nineteen. He asks all those around him if he should take a hit. Those advising him beg him not to, focusing on the high odds stacked against such an action. Yet the gambler, with supreme confidence, asks the dealer for another card. There is a sharp intake of breath from all around. And the card is . . . a two of clubs. Twenty-one! A winner! Those around the table whoop and holler and believe they are looking at a hot hand, a gambling genius. Of course, winning by asking for a hit when showing nineteen doesn't make one smart, just extremely lucky. Casino owners love this type of gambler. In the end, by catering to men like MacArthur they get rich.

The landing at Inchon was the greatest victory of MacArthur's lengthy career. In the final analysis, success depended on so many things going right (they did) and so many things not going wrong (they didn't). For example, the tides had to conform to expectations, the KPA had to be unprepared to move in reserves, fewer mines needed to be floating off the port than feared, the shore batteries on the island dominating the port (Wolmido) needed to be silenced quickly, and the first wave of marines needed to find a way to knock out Soviet tanks in the city before they could threaten the beachheads.[30] Everything went according to plan in the first days of the operation, and for a time MacArthur had a reputation in the Far East and Washington as an infallible strategist.

Inchon fell almost immediately to the 1st Marine Division, which pushed inland to seize Kimpo airfield two days later on September 17. The advance then began to bog down as MacArthur ordered his men northeast and across the Han River into Seoul on September 22. The North Koreans staged a stubborn defense of the ROK's capital with the arrival of the KPA's 25th Infantry Brigade and the 78th Independent Infantry Regiment in the city immediately after the Inchon landing. In a pale reflection of Manila in 1945, Ridgway relates, "MacArthur reacted with his customary optimism, counting the victory complete before the prize was really in his grasp. On September 25 both he and General Almond announced that Seoul was 'once more in friendly hands.'

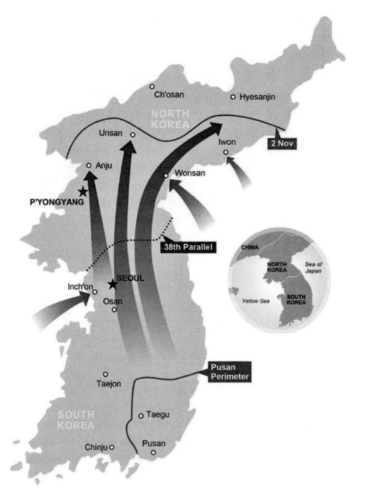

The landing at Inchon and the UN advance to the Yalu.

Courtesy of the U.S. Army Special Operations Forces.

But the 1st Marine Division could have told a different story. There was bitter street fighting ahead that lasted three days and cost added casualties among civilians as well as fighting men."[31]

Once again, MacArthur had prioritized the capture of a capital city on a specified date. This time he instructed Almond to complete the occupation of Seoul by September 25, exactly three months from the start of the North Korean invasion. This led to brutal urban combat in which the American forces had to eject the KPA from buildings that had been turned into makeshift for-tifications. As casualties mounted, much of the downtown area was brought under artillery fire, as had taken place in Manila in 1945. At times the tubes of the marines' howitzers became so hot that they had to cease firing until they cooled.[32] In Moscow, *Pravda* hyperbolically compared the heroic defense of Seoul to the Battle of Stalingrad. Eventually the city was taken, though it was now littered with destroyed buildings and dead civilians.

The Inchon landing quickly severed the KPA's rail and main road supply line. The 8th Army, now with a strength of more than 150,000 men, began a simultaneous attack in the south and began to break through enemy lines along the north and west bank of the Naktong River.[33] At first, the approximately 70,000 North Koreans along the perimeter held their lines in most areas, but the KPA divisions soon began to stream northward in retreat, with the UN forces in pursuit. Had X Corps remained on the south bank of the Han and bypassed Seoul to push east toward Korea's central mountain spine, many more North Koreans could have been killed or captured. Still, retaking the ROK capital was an important psychological victory. Only 25,000 to 30,000 KPA soldiers were able to successfully retreat from the Pusan Perimeter to north of the 38th parallel, but many other scattered survivors regrouped as guerilla bands to carry out a harassment campaign that lasted until the end of the war. The 8th Army linked up with Almond's two divisions and prepared to push into North Korea.

The great success at Inchon has precluded much analysis of the risks taken and the options discarded in the battle's planning and execution. Certainly the U.S. military establishment would not recommend that the lesson learned from the Chromite operation be that amphibious assaults should take place at the most difficult and most dangerous point on an enemy's coastline or that major operations should be mounted where the odds are 5,000 to 1. Few have asked if as great a victory, or an even greater one, might have been achieved with less risk had X Corps targeted the more southerly and less perilous targets of Kusan or Posung-myon. The answer is likely yes. Both alternative amphibious landing points were lightly defended and more attractive in terms of the shore geography; both would have cut the KPA's rail and road links to the north and placed a large American force in the enemy's rear. Without the distraction of Seoul to be captured, X Corps could have focused on pushing east as rapidly as possible and then south to more quickly link up with the 8th Army breaking out from Pusan. Tens of thousands of additional KPA soldiers might have been killed or taken captive, leaving fewer at large to retreat into North Korea or scatter into the southern hinterlands to act as guerillas.

No definitive answer can be known as to whether Inchon was the best option, but the question deserves to be asked. To repeat, on September 7 MacArthur wrote the Joint Chiefs that Inchon represented the "only hope of wresting the initiative from the enemy and thereby presenting an opportunity for a decisive blow. To do otherwise is to commit us to a war of indefinite duration, of gradual attrition, and of doubtful results." This was simply untrue. MacArthur's forces already outnumbered the KPA along the Pusan Perimeter by two to one.[34] As discussed, the U.S. military also dominated the sky and the sea and had deployed to the battle area significantly more and better artillery and armor than the enemy. In addition, the enemy had to transport everything it needed hundreds of miles south down a lengthy and limited road and rail network to the front under constant air interdiction. In contrast, the UN force's supplies and additional reinforcements were being delivered by the world's largest merchant marine fleet to an excellent nearby port facility. These advantages alone should have allowed a competent UN commander to find multiple avenues to achieve a smashing victory.

As if this were not enough, MacArthur had an additional 40,000 men of X Corps, including the elite 1st Marine Division, to deploy along with its amphibious expertise. Almost any successful descent in the enemy's rear, combined with an offensive by the 8th Army, would have unhinged the KPA lines along the Pusan Perimeter and triggered a retreat. Alternatively, the fresh X Corps could have been integrated into General Walker's force, giving him approximately the three-to-one manpower advantage that has traditionally been the preponderance of force leading to victories in offensives throughout history. The reinforced 8th Army could then break out northward using its mechanized mobility advantage to wheel to the west to create a caldron in which the KPA would be trapped. While such a decision would have left Seoul under occupation slightly longer, the trade-off could have been a more decisive victory over the enemy's ground forces. Seoul's capture might then have taken place with less damage to its infrastructure and population.

CHAPTER 12

To Destroy the Enemy

As the KPA streamed north in disarray, the decision now needed to be made if the "police action," as the Truman administration described the conflict in Korea, would end at the 38th parallel or if UN forces should advance further north. Douglas MacArthur urged the latter. As early as July 13, 1950, he told Army Chief of Staff Lawton Collins and Air Force Chief of Staff Hoyt Vandenberg that

> he believed strongly that driving back the Communists in the *de facto* war in Korea would check Communist expansion everywhere and thus obviate the necessity of our being fully prepared to meet aggression elsewhere. In vigorous and colorful language, he protested any delay of half-way measures. . . . He said he meant to destroy the KPA and not merely drive it back across the 38th Parallel. He said that in the aftermath of operations, the problem would be to "compose and unite Korea." He added that it might be necessary to occupy all of Korea, though this was speculative at that time.[1]

Many in the Pentagon and State Department agreed with such a policy. The diplomat George Kennan was the most prominent opponent of advancing into North Korea. Much of his concern stemmed from his assessment regarding MacArthur's judgment and unbound ability to set U.S. policy in East Asia.[2] Kennan was overruled, and Truman authorized the advance north of the 38th parallel. The president was cognizant that the Soviet Union or the PRC might react militarily to a UN attempt to unify all of Korea under a government based in Seoul. His orders to MacArthur transmitted through the JCS contained the following: "Your military objective is the destruction of the North Korean armed forces. In attaining this objective, you are authorized to conduct military operations, including amphibious and airborne landings or ground operations north of the 38° parallel in Korea."[3] The JCS also explicitly ordered

MacArthur to use only ROK forces in the provinces of northern Korea that bordered China and the USSR. MacArthur specifically acknowledged in writing that he would proceed in line with these directives.[4]

At the same time, the PRC made clear that it would intervene in the conflict if the U.S. military pushed above the 38th parallel. As the two nations had no official diplomatic relations at the time, other channels needed to be used. On September 25, 1950, Chinese general Nie Rongzhen told the Indian ambassador to Beijing that China would not "sit back with folded hands and let the Americans come up to the [Sino-Korean] border."[5] On October 1, PRC premier Chou Enlai also made a public pronouncement that "the Chinese people will absolutely not tolerate foreign aggression, nor will they supinely tolerate seeing their neighbors being savagely invaded by imperialists."[6] MacArthur wanted to make a dramatic announcement after his forces pushed north of the 38th parallel on October 2, but the JCS forbade such an action. This hardly mattered as the next day Chou Enlai requested that the Indian ambassador pass on to Washington that China would enter the war if non-ROK troops crossed into North Korea.[7]

As MacArthur sent his forces north, one of the most militarily questionable decisions of his career took place. Immediately after X Corps linked up with the 8th Army advancing from the south, Gen. Almond's command was ordered to turn around and withdraw through the port of Inchon. Thus, less than a fortnight after landing in Korea, two full U.S. divisions were pulled out of the pursuit of the KPA. MacArthur directed that X Corps would sail all the way around the peninsula to land at Wonsan, a port in the northeast of North Korea. This would allow Almond to retain a separate command and not have to report to Gen. Walker. The decision made little sense, was immediately controversial, and eventually cost the UN forces dearly. MacArthur later defended his decision as follows:

> The supply situation at Seoul was insufficient to maintain both the 8th Army and the X Corps, and it was essential to establish a new port of supply entrance on the east coast. Due to tide difficulties at Inchon, where only 5,000 tons a day could be landed, and the destruction of the railroad from Pusan to Seoul during the campaign, limiting overland transportation to a minimum, Wonsan was selected as the new supply base. Tactically, it could bring flank pressure if necessary, for the capture of Pyongyang.[8]

This argument is not convincing. First of all, trying to embark two divisions through the limited port facilities available in Inchon interfered with the navy's efforts to land supplies for the 8th Army there. The lack of dock space also slowed the embarkation of X Corps. In the end, the heavy equipment of the 7th Division was loaded at Inchon, while its soldiers were transported south by truck to Pusan.[9] MacArthur insisted on prioritizing loading the 1st Marine Division, and the resulting logistics snarl contributed to Walker's divisions running low on many essential items as they pushed north. The strained supply situation worsened the further from Inchon the UN lines advanced, and major airlift efforts were unable to alleviate the situation. A lack of ammunition, fuel, and other items was of little worry if the war was just about over. However, it would become a critical factor if the Chinese or the Soviets intervened in the fighting.

After the fall of Seoul and the breakout from the Pusan Perimeter, the UN advance did not encounter much sustained resistance, so there seemed little reason to expect that taking Pyongyang required another amphibious assault behind enemy's lines. If MacArthur wanted to take Wonsan, X Corps could have pushed due east over existing roads from Seoul to sieze small harbors along the coast before moving north along the paved coastal route to the objective. Or the same force could have participated in the taking of the North Korean capital of Pyongyang and then moved overland across the Korean Peninsula.[10] Either advance would have likely succeeded as the KPA was so outnumbered and in disarray by this point that it could pose little resistance to the UN offensive.

In fact, elements of ROK I Corps operating as part of the 8th Army advancing north along the east coast were able to push overland more than 250 miles to take Wonsan on October 10. This was two weeks before the amphibious force carrying Almond's command could arrive. Pyongyang also fell quickly nine days later to 8th Army units that had passed through the withdrawing X Corps. The result was that the 1st Marine Division staged an unopposed "administrative" landing in Wonsan on October 26. The men of the 7th Division, not fully loaded onto ships in Pusan until October 17, were diverted 150 road miles further north to unload at the port of Iwon after it too had been taken by South Korean forces.[11] ROK I Corps was then placed under Almond's command, as were all UN forces on the eastern side of Korea. This effectively elevated the general to the position of an army commander. "Operation Three Star" was well underway. The 8th Army and the ROK II Corps remained under Walker's control in Korea's west.

This separation of MacArthur's forces made some sense as the mountainous spine of the peninsula lent itself to separate commands. The issue was the need to coordinate the two advances pushing north and how each would support the other. If the operation was only going to be a lightly contested march to the Manchurian border with the final drives conducted solely by ROK troops, this divided force structure was reasonable for the mission. However, if MacArthur planned to push all his forces as quickly north as possible with his chief of staff focused on managing the eastern advance, the UN fighting men would be at great risk if the Chinese or Soviet armies attacked.

Against this backdrop MacArthur was again reminded to refrain from conducting air attacks on targets in the PRC and not utilize U.S. troops in the far north of Korea. Truman also requested a meeting with his Far Eastern commander.[12] MacArthur had turned down the president's requests to come to the United States in the 1945–1949 period because he was "too busy." Now, after the Inchon landing, the General decided that he could not travel even as far as Hawaii to see his commander in chief. A compromise was worked out where Truman would fly the 4,400 miles to Wake Island to confer with MacArthur.

As for the meeting with Franklin Roosevelt in Honolulu in 1944, MacArthur arrived on the island first and chose to greet his commander in chief in an outfit somewhat less formal than his dress uniform. At least this time he didn't decide to take a bath and keep his boss waiting. The famously well-dressed Truman was unhappy to look out his plane's window to see his subordinate standing on the tarmac without a tie and wearing a terribly beat-up old campaign cap. Even worse, MacArthur declined to salute the president and instead shook hands with him as if the two were equals. Of course, all the press in attendance noticed this breach of protocol.[13] Later, at the end of the meeting, which lasted only an hour and a half, MacArthur declined Truman's request that he remain on Wake Island for lunch and flew back to Tokyo. General Omar Bradley, chairman of the Joint Chiefs, who had traveled to Wake with the presidential party found this "insulting."

In the discussions on Wake, Truman was clearly concerned about the many pointed warnings the PRC had delivered through diplomatic channels. The president asked about the chances of Chinese intervention. MacArthur replied,

> Very little. Had they interfered in the first or second months it would have been decisive. We are no longer fearful of their intervention. We no longer stand hat in hand. The Chinese have 300,000 men in Manchuria. Of these probably not more than 100–115,000 are distributed along the Yalu River. Only 50–60,000 could be gotten across the Yalu River. They have no Air Force. Now that we have bases for our Air Force in Korea if the Chinese tried to get down to Pyongyang there would be the greatest slaughter.[14]

The meeting adjourned, with Truman assured that the Chinese not only would not intervene but would be handily defeated if they did and the war in Korea was all but over.

As MacArthur flew back to Tokyo, he had little idea that the analysis he had offered to the president was terribly flawed. The PLA was accustomed to fighting and winning against opponents who had air superiority (first the Japanese, then the Kuomintang). Next, the Chinese were adept at moving large numbers of men across long distances without significant mechanized supply lines. In contrast, the further north UN forces moved, the longer and more tenuous their logistics tail became as the terrain became increasingly mountainous with few roads fit for motorized transport. In contrast to MacArthur's analysis, Gen. Xie Fang, chief of staff of the PVA and other senior generals had recommended to Mao Zedong back on August 31 that "the Chinese forces not intervene until after U.S.-led forces crossed the 38th Parallel, because it would help Chinese forces both politically and militarily."[15] This thinking was based on concern that if the Chinese intervened while UN forces were pinned down around the Pusan Perimeter, the United States could mount an amphibious assault near Pyongyang or Seoul and cut off the Communist armies. The Chinese commanders also recognized that an undeveloped logistics network was one of their largest weaknesses and that the shorter their supply lines, and the longer the U.S. ones, the better.

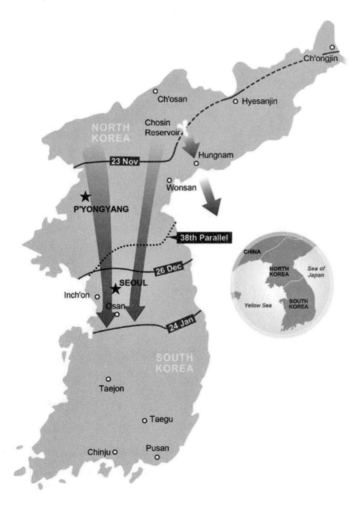

The Chinese intervention and the rout of the UN command.

Mao had asked his advisors about MacArthur's personality and been told that the General was famous for his arrogance and stubbornness. The Chinese leader replied, "Fine! Fine! The more arrogant and more stubborn he is, the better. An arrogant enemy is easy to defeat."[16] The North Koreans were begging the PRC to intervene, and on October 8 Mao decided it was time to act. He issued orders for PVA forces to begin taking up positions south of the Yalu. The Chinese informed Joseph Stalin of this and requested equipment, supplies, and Soviet air cover. Just as the meeting on Wake Island ended, a regiment of the PVA's 42nd Army slipped into Korea on the night of October 16. Many more followed, and soon four full Chinese armies had crossed the Yalu undetected.[17]

As the UN forces pushed forward, Walker and Almond's orders were changed. Up until October 17, they had been told not to utilize any non-ROK troops in the far northern portion of the peninsula near the PRC border as per the earlier JCS cables sent to Tokyo. Now, as the frontlines reached the point where U.S. troops were to be barred from advancing, MacArthur lifted the constraint, and all units were authorized to continue northward. The JCS immediately contacted their commander in the Far East demanding an explanation for the violation of their instructions.

General MacArthur's reply the next day justified lifting the restriction as a matter of military necessity. He said that the ROK forces could not handle the situation by themselves, that he felt he had enough latitude under existing directives to issue the order, and that, furthermore, the whole subject had been covered in the Wake Island Conference. While it is clear that the Joint Chiefs of Staff felt that MacArthur had violated their basic 27 September directive, they did not countermand his orders to go to the Yalu.[18]

Once again, MacArthur's superiors in Washington abdicated their responsibility when the General chose to disobey orders. General Ridgway, then the army's deputy chief of staff, related how the senior officers of the JCS viewed the Far Eastern commander in the face of this insubordination: "But in the Pentagon as well as in the field there was an almost superstitious awe of this larger-than-life military figure. . . . Then there were those who felt that it was useless to try to check a man who might react to criticism by pursuing his own way with increased stubbornness and fervor."[19]

Concern among the Joint Chiefs and their staffs increased daily as the UN units became increasingly dispersed the farther they advanced toward the Yalu. However, no official questioning of MacArthur's direction of the war was cabled to the Far East. Finally, Ridgway decided to speak up at a full JCS meeting and called on his superiors to act. He related that his demand was met with silence from the forty other men in the room. As the meeting broke up Ridgway confronted his old friend, four-star general Hoyt Vandenberg, who was then chief of staff of the U.S. Air Force:

> "Why," I asked him, "don't the Joint Chiefs send orders to MacArthur and tell him what to do?"
>
> Van shook his head.
>
> "What good would that do? He wouldn't obey the orders. What can we do?"
>
> At this I exploded.
>
> "You can relieve any commander who won't obey orders, can't you?" I exclaimed. The look on Van's face is one I shall never forget. His lips parted and he looked at me with an expression both puzzled and amazed. He walked away then without saying a word and I never afterward had occasion to discuss this with him.[20]

Despite Chinese government officials making belligerent statements and the ongoing infiltration of entire army formations from Manchuria, the tone at headquarters in Tokyo was confident. As related by Col. John Chiles, "MacArthur did not *want* the Chinese to enter the war in Korea. Anything MacArthur wanted, Gen. Willoughby produced intelligence for. . . . In this case, Willoughby falsified the intelligence reports. . . . He should have gone to jail."[21] Urged to advance quickly toward the border and told to expect little opposition from the remnants of the KPA, the poorly supplied 8th Army in the west and smaller X Corps in the east marched into increasingly mountainous territory as winter weather arrived and temperatures plunged to well below zero. Walker's men crossed the Chongchon River and headed north, where they encountered PVA forces for the first time in what the Chinese called the First Phase Offensive.

The initial major combat took place along the 8th Army's right flank from October 25 to 29 as the ROK II Corps was ambushed by a much larger force of Chinese infantry near the town of Onjong. The ROK 6th Division and an additional infantry regiment were shattered, allowing the PVA to stream southwest to strike at the center of the UN line in Unsan. On November 1 the Chinese attacked and defeated elements of the U.S. 1st Cavalry Division. Much of the fighting took place at night and featured flanking movements, which allowed the PVA to set up a series of roadblocks in the rear of the ROK and U.S. forces. Desperate defensive fighting by the recently arrived soldiers of the 27th British Commonwealth Brigade finally stopped the Chinese advance at Pakchon just north of the Chongchon. While MacArthur's headquarters disagreed, the troops at the front were quite certain that they were fighting a new enemy. As one U.S. company commander wrote in a letter home on November 4, "This is certainly no time for optimism. The enemy is well trained and organized. . . . Anyone who says they ain't Chinks is crazy!"[22]

The intensity and effectiveness of the attack was a shock to the UN units. By the time the Chinese broke off contact, two U.S. Army divisions, three ROK divisions and the recently arrived brigade of Turkish soldiers had suffered large enough losses of men and equipment that they required significant rest, replacements, and refitting before they were able to return to the frontline.[23] Walker ordered a retreat and reformed his army along the south bank of the Chongchon. He reminded MacArthur, "The advance north from Pyongyang was based on a calculated logistical risk involving supply almost entirely by airlift. Available supplies were sufficient only for bare maintenance of combat operations against light opposition, with no possibility of accumulating reserves to meet heavier opposition."[24]

In the east, X Corps came under less severe attack from elements of three PVA divisions. As in the west, Chinese prisoners disclosed the divisions and armies to which they belonged. Truman and the JCS, hearing of the fighting and highly concerned about a PRC intervention, asked for an update from Korea. MacArthur replied on November 4 that these attacks were most likely being carried out by small numbers of Chinese volunteers who would be able to offer only minimal assistance to the KPA.[25]

In keeping with his rapid change in tone after the initial North Korean invasion in June, the JCS received an urgent message from MacArthur two days later that "men and material in large forces are pouring across all bridges over the Yalu from Manchuria. . . . This movement threatens the ultimate destruction of the forces under my command."[26] MacArthur authorized the bombing of the bridges connecting North Korea and China to halt the influx of the PVA and likely to send a signal to Mao. When the Joint Chiefs discovered this, they countermanded the order and directed that no bombing missions take place within five miles of the border. MacArthur's reply to the JCS included the following:

> Under the gravest protest that I can make, I am suspending this strike and carrying out your instructions. . . . I cannot overemphasize the disastrous effect, both physical and psychological, that will result from the restrictions which you are imposing. I trust that the matter be immediately brought to the attention of the President as I believe your instructions may well result in a calamity of major proportion for which I cannot accept the responsibility without his personal and direct understanding of the situation.[27]

Despite the message's lack of respect in tone and borderline insubordination, General Bradley granted MacArthur's request and took the complaint to the president. Truman split the difference with his field commander and authorized the air strikes as long as American planes remained in the airspace on the Korean side of the border. The bombings went ahead but were less than decisive. A month later eight of the twelve major bridges crossing the Yalu were still intact. In addition, by this time the river had frozen solid so that the Chinese were able to cross at will, no longer dependent upon bridges until the spring thaw.[28]

MacArthur also issued a communiqué on November 6 stating that he had already won the Korean War and that "the defeat of the North Koreans and destruction of their armies was thereby decisive." He continued, "In the face of this victory for United Nations arms, the Communists, without any notice of belligerency, moved elements of Chinese Communist forces across the Yalu River into North Korea. . . . [A] new and fresh army faces us, backed up by a possibility of large reserves and adequate supplies within easy reach of the enemy but beyond the limits of our present sphere of military action."[29] However, no further attacks fell upon MacArthur's command. After imposing their painful defeat on UN forces, the PVA divisions ran low on supplies, broke off contact in both the east and the west, and vanished north back into the mountains. Had the Chinese left Korea, or were they just preparing an even larger attack?

As the PVA melted away, MacArthur immediately returned to a state of optimism and assured Washington on November 9 that the USAF could interdict any PVA reinforcements that might attempt to enter Korea and that he had sufficient ground strength to finish the conquest of the nation. The UN force once again had the initiative, and there was discussion as to the proper course of action. The British recommended that the frontline be pulled back to the narrow "neck" of Korea and leave the northern part of the peninsula as a buffer zone. Some in Washington agreed, but this was unacceptable to MacArthur. Nothing short of total victory was acceptable to him. He compared the "shortsightedness" of the British proposal of not occupying a sliver of what he described as the "merciless wasteland" of far northern Korea to the ceding of the Sudetenland to Germany in 1938.[30]

Soon MacArthur announced to the JCS that he would renew the offensive to reach the Yalu:

I plan to launch my attack for this purpose on or about November 15th with the mission of driving to the border and securing all of North Korea. Any program short of this would completely destroy the morale of my forces and the psychological consequences would be inestimable. . . . To give up any portion of North Korea to the aggression of the Chinese Communists would be the greatest defeat of the free world in recent times. Indeed, to yield to so immoral a proposition would bankrupt our leadership and influence in Asia and render untenable our position both politically and militarily.[31]

MacArthur's confidence held though even Willoughby was increasingly unwilling to hide the buildup of Chinese forces across the UN front. The intelligence chief warned on November 10 that the PVA was growing in strength in front of X Corps in the west, stating, "It is believed that this enemy concentration even now may be capable of seizing the initiative and launching offensive operations."[32] As Ridgway later wrote, "The wholly human failing of discounting or ignoring all unwelcome facts seemed developed beyond the average in MacArthur's nature. His own G-2, for example, had estimated that the CCF [Chinese Communist Forces] could put 200,000 troops across the Yalu per month. . . . MacArthur assured the J.C.S. that complete victory was possible and that it would be a grave miscalculation to abandon the original plan to destroy all resisting armed forces in North Korea."[33]

On November 24, MacArthur flew to Korea from Tokyo and traveled to the banks of the Chongchon at Anju to personally launch what became known as the "Home by Christmas Offensive." The General commented to some of his subordinate officers regarding the troops, "Well, if they go fast enough, maybe some of them can be home by Christmas."[34] Members of the press overheard this and reported it in major U.S. newspapers the next day. Some historians now claim that these comments were taken out of context. However, the fact remains that an offensive to the Yalu was ordered and that MacArthur also stated unequivocally at the time, "The Chinese are not coming into this war."[35] He believed the war was all but over and led the American public to believe the same.

Of course, the Chinese had already announced with the battles of Onjong and Unsan that they were indeed coming into the war. The confidence of the PVA had improved markedly with its success besting both ROK and U.S. Army units. The Chinese resupplied and waited patiently. They hoped that the UN troops would advance northward into a massive ambush.

U.S. military intelligence had credible reports that large numbers of PVA divisions had already crossed south into Korea. More than 100 Chinese prisoners had been taken by the 8th Army and X Corps by late November and divulged that they were from six different armies of the 9th Army Group. As each Chinese army comprised three divisions of about 10,000 men apiece, MacArthur should have realized that 180,000 soldiers or more could be waiting to attack his advancing UN force.[36] However, years later in his memoirs, despite significant evidence to the contrary, MacArthur only admits to the 8th Army coming into contact with a total of three Chinese divisions prior to November 24.[37] In fact, the actual number of men Mao had sent to fight in Korea was around 300,000 as the 13th Army Group had also slipped an additional twelve divisions over the Yalu.[38]

The UN forces were not prepared to fight a large-scale battle. The weather was now bitterly cold, with nighttime temperatures dropping to −20°F, yet many of the men had not yet received winter clothing or boots. The British Commonwealth Brigade was still dressed in its tropical clothing from Hong Kong.[39] The 8th Army's supply shortage was only partially alleviated by airlift efforts. Its I Corps was operating with reserves of only one day of ammunition and half a day of petrol.[40] MacArthur could have chosen to delay the offensive to allow for a sufficient stockpiling of military stores, but that would have pushed planning for the end of the offensive past Christmas. Thus the UN troops resumed their advance toward the Yalu prepared for only a "mopping up" operation.

After MacArthur's death, Ridgway published a scathing indictment of the episode:

> But MacArthur, like Custer at the Little Big Horn, had neither eyes nor ears for information that might deter him from the swift attainment of his objective—the destruction of the last remnants of the North Korean People's Army and the pacification of the entire peninsula. While MacArthur's intense eagerness to complete his mission with dispatch is understandable, it is difficult to justify his plan and orders in the face of all that was known about the enemy's strength, his own supply situation, the terrain and the manner in which his own forces were dispersed—even had they been adequately equipped and at full strength, which was far from the case.[41]

LAST RETREAT

From the Yalu to the Potomac

"I fired him [MacArthur] because he wouldn't respect the authority of the President. . . . I didn't fire him because he was a dumb son of a bitch, although he was, but that's not against the law for generals. If it was, half to three-quarters of them would be in jail."[1]

—President Harry S. Truman, 1884–1972

CHAPTER 13

There Is No Substitute for Victory!

Both Gen. Walker in the west and Gen. Smith of the 1st Marine Division in the east were wary and believed the Chinese were massing to attack. However, MacArthur and Almond anticipated a quick victory, and plans for a final offensive were prepared. As they expected an easy advance, no mobile reserve was created in case the Chinese struck at a particular point. In the west, Walker had significant misgivings and had his staff draft plans for a potential retreat. An order he passed to a subordinate commander on the frontlines directed that "if he smells Chinese chow, pull back immediately."[1] The right side of his line was still anchored by the ROK II Corps, which was now significantly weaker than in October before it had been mauled by the PVA.

In the east, the smaller X Corps advanced more slowly. Smith ordered the 1st Marine Division to proceed cautiously, taking high points for overwatch while the main force proceeded along the area's few roads by way of valley floors. He left garrison forces to protect his main supply route and established an airbase close to the frontlines. This slowed forward movement to only around a mile per day and resulted in complaints from Almond, who demanded a faster tempo of advance. The X Corps commander remained true to his aggressive reputation and told his subordinates, "The enemy who is delaying you for the moment is nothing more than remnants of Chinese divisions fleeing north. . . . We're still attacking and we're going all the way to the Yalu. Don't let a bunch of Chinese laundrymen stop you."[2]

To the north, the PVA prepared to attack. Stalin backed down from his promise of providing air support to cover the planned offensive, claiming that his forces needed significantly more time before they could intervene over the battlefield. Supplying arms and equipment to the Chinese was one thing.

Direct military conflict with the United States in the skies over Korea was an-other. He did promise weapons shipments and protection by his air force above China itself, and in the end that was enough for Mao Zedong.[3]

The PVA generals were quite heartened by the success of the First Phase Offensive. They were confident not only that they could defeat ROK forma-tions but that the road- and supply-dependent American divisions were also susceptible to the PVA's tactics of night infiltration and flanking maneuvers through broken terrain. Mao thought it possible that the Americans would send smaller units forward to perform reconnaissance but hoped that MacAr-thur would remain true to his character and be aggressive. By advancing rapidly into mountainous territory, the UN force was doing exactly what the Chinese leader had hoped. Mao's orders by radio to his senior field generals in Korea included the following: "If resistance is on a small scale, the Volunteers will surely annihilate the enemy; but if it is heavy, withdraw and suck the enemy into a trap. Then the enemy can be destroyed by our main forces."[4]

MacArthur relates in his memoirs, "On November 27th, the Red com-mander, General Lin Piao, launched his full forces across the Yalu and into battle."[5] Like his statements regarding the start of hostilities in his other cam-paigns, this one is full of inaccuracies, and for facts we must look elsewhere. First, the Chinese attack began on the evening of November 25 against the center and right side of the 8th Army's front.[6] Second, Lin Piao had declined Mao's offer to lead the PVA due to poor health and was in the Soviet Union at the time. Instead, Gen. Peng Dehuai, led the Chinese forces in Korea. Finally, the PVA had already infiltrated most of the forces it would utilize in its Sec-ond Phase Offensive south of the Yalu well before the operation was launched. That this happened without MacArthur's command detecting the movement does not mean it did not take place.

In any event, the Chinese first blow was most successful in the attack on the ROK divisions on the 8th Army's right flank. The Korean units were strung out in mountainous terrain near the peninsula's spine, where the UN command was split in two and separated by twenty or more miles. The Chinese offensive was immediately effective, and once again the ROK forces were thrown into a headlong retreat. This allowed the PVA to move forces south and west to roll up the UN line. The U.S. 2nd Infantry Division was then defeated along with the Turkish brigade. These units had their fronts smashed, were outflanked, and roadblocks were set up in the rear where many fleeing troops were killed or captured. Upward of 20 percent of the 2nd Division became casualties, and the unit abandoned much of its artillery, heavy machine guns, radios, trucks, and jeeps. With the 8th Army's right wing in tatters and no mobile reserve to plug the gap through which the Chinese were pouring south, Walker was forced to order his troops to pull back. Soon "bug-out fever" was at epidemic levels, and the UN force was in full retreat.

In the east, X Corps suffered similarly when it was attacked. The Chinese slipped past the most advanced units of the 1st Marine Division on the west side and the 7th Infantry Division on the east side of the Chosin Reservoir. The PVA set up roadblocks in the American rear along the single main supply road, while other units assaulted the American formations directly. In bitterly cold conditions, the PVA wore down the U.S. forces, inflicted significant casualties, and forced X Corps into a desperate attempt to break out of encirclement.

MacArthur believed that his command was at risk of being ejected from Korea. His cable on November 28 to the JCS contained the following: "The resulting situation presents an entirely new picture which broadens the potentialities to world embracing considerations beyond the sphere of decision by the theater commander. This command has done everything possible within its capabilities but is now faced with conditions beyond its control and strength."[7] Only a few weeks earlier, MacArthur had promised that the Chinese would be slaughtered if they tried to intervene in the conflict, argued for an immediate offensive, lectured the JCS on global strategy, and emphasized the driving moral need to conquer all of North Korea. Now he effectively passed responsibility for the deteriorating situation to his superiors in Washington.

The JCS hesitated to issue tactical orders to a field commander but believed the best course of action was as follows: (1) ensure that surrounded U.S. Marine and Army units were extricated from PVA encirclement, (2) pull back to the narrow neck of the Korean Peninsula, and (3) have the 8th Army and X Corps establish contact with each other. The UN command could then present a united front against the Chinese. On November 29 they cabled MacArthur, "Strategic and tactical considerations are now paramount. What are your plans regarding the coordination of the 8th Army and X Corps and the positioning of X Corps, the units of which appear to us to be exposed?"[8]

MacArthur replied the next day and dismissed his superiors' concerns,

Any concept of actual physical combination of the forces of the 8th Army and X Corps in a practically continuous line across the narrow neck of Korea is quite impracticable due to the length of that line, the numerical weakness of our forces, and the logistical problems due to the mountainous divide which splits such a front from north to south. The X Corps will contract its position, as enemy pressure develops, into the Hamhung-Wonsan sector. The Corps Commander has been enjoined against any possibility of piecemeal isolation and trapping of his forces. While geographically his elements seem to be well extended, the actual conditions of terrain make it extremely difficult for an enemy to take any material advantage thereof.[9]

He expanded on this a few days later when he wrote to his superiors,

> There is no practicability, nor would any benefit accrue thereby, to attempt to unite the forces of the 8th Army and the X Corps. Both forces are completely outnumbered and the junction would, therefore, not only not produce added strength, but actually jeopardize the free flow of movement that arises from the two separate logistical lines of naval supply and maneuver. . . . The Chinese troops are fresh, completely organized, splendidly trained and equipped and apparently in peak condition for actual operations.[10]

General Bradley was furious at the blasé manner in which MacArthur rejected the recommendations offered by the JCS and minimized the risk to the 1st Marine and 7th Infantry Divisions. He later complained bitterly that MacArthur treated the JCS "as if we were children."[11] He could also have complained that describing the PVA soldiers as "splendidly equipped," given that they were short of rifles and mostly wearing sneakers in winter snow, was an absurdity.

The forward units of X Corps would have strongly disagreed with MacArthur's reports to Washington regarding their situation. As the PVA chose to travel off road networks through mountainous territory, "the actual conditions of terrain" were not in fact a major impediment for "the enemy to take any material advantage thereof." Thousands of American fighting men were surrounded around the Chosin Reservoir, with miles-long roadblocks established in their rear blocking the flow of supplies while heavy attacks repeatedly struck their frontlines. The famous and ultimately successful "attacking in a different direction" withdrawal of the 1st Marine Division in brutally cold weather through PVA encirclement south and east to the port of Hungnam has probably received the most attention in the United States of the entire war.

While heroic, this retreat in no way eliminated the fact that the Chinese were victorious almost everywhere. The PVA attack was particularly devastating for the U.S. 7th Infantry Division, which broke out to the south, but only after two of its three regiments suffered 40 percent casualty rates, which included more than 2,500 dead. X Corps was evacuated by ship, and the Chinese encountered only light resistance from remaining ROK forces as they pushed south. With the PVA streaming toward the 38th parallel down the east coast, Walker chose to abandon Pyongyang and the neck of Korea and pulled his forces back toward Seoul. Almond's command was transported by sea back to Pusan, where it was loaded onto trucks, brought north to the front, and finally came under 8th Army control.

Later, MacArthur attempted to minimize the defeat through the use of weak excuses and outright prevarication. First, he tried to argue, "Our losses in the entire Yalu operation were comparatively light. In the 8th Army, the number of troops killed, wounded and missing amounted to 7,337 and in the X Corps to 5,638. This was about half the loss at Iwo Jima, less than one-fifth of that at Okinawa, and even less in comparison with the Battle of the Bulge."[12] William Manchester repeated these casualty figures almost verbatim in *American Caesar* and claimed, "MacArthur's Korean retreat was one of his most staggering feats of arms."[13] Sadly, the General's numbers were not accurate. Actual total UN losses were twice as large.[14] As with his boast of low casualties at Buna in World War II, MacArthur once again neglected to count those allied men who fell fighting and dying alongside those from the U.S. Army. South Korean casualties alone were greater than 10,000. The Turkish and British Commonwealth brigades also took serious losses. More importantly, while Iwo Jima, Okinawa, and the Battle of the Bulge were bloody attritional battles, they were ultimately American tactical and strategic victories. The withdrawal from the Yalu was nothing if not a painful defeat.

It is true that the mechanized mobility of the UN and its control of the air limited casualties during the retreat as wounded could be evacuated and enemy pursuit was not as fast as the UN forces attempting to "bug out." Still, the fact remains that the men in MacArthur's frontline fighting units suffered a significant loss of manpower and were routed. Combat effectiveness of the UN command was also gravely reduced. Weapon and equipment losses were significant, and what the Americans and South Koreans left behind, the underequipped PVA rapidly put to use. MacArthur admitted to the JCS on December 3 that his American troops were "mentally fatigued and physically battered" and that the fighting ability of ROK units at his disposal was now "negligible."[15] Such a defeat is difficult to describe as a "staggering feat of arms."

Next, MacArthur tried to convince posterity that what the press called the "Home by Christmas Offensive" was not an offensive at all and only a "reconnaissance-in-force," with forward units ordered to retreat quickly if they encountered large formations of Chinese. This is simply not true. MacArthur clearly sent the vast bulk of his combat forces forward in a full-scale offensive. He had no mobile reserve prepared to assist those in advanced positions who came under attack and encirclement in such a reconnaissance. Research by Professor Richard Ruetten and others has shown definitively that the "reconnaissance-in-force" explanation was invented by MacArthur after the launch of the offensive. After all, the JCS was not informed of such a designation, the headquarters staff in Tokyo made no plans for a retreat if the reconnaissance did not progress according to plan, and MacArthur announced the offensive on multiple occasions as one that would end the war.[16] A true reconnaissance-in-force of selected units would have discovered stiff resistance south of the Yalu by the PVA. The UN commander could then decide to advance to the attack or dig in along a defensive line.

MacArthur also attempted to portray the defeat on the Yalu as a victory with the claim that the Home by Christmas Offensive had saved his army. "I myself felt we had reached up, sprung the Red trap, and escaped it. To have saved so many thousands of lives entrusted to my care gave me a sense of comfort that, in comparison, made all the honors I had ever received pale into insignificance."[17] He argued that had he dug in on a defensive line and not pushed north, the Chinese horde would have fallen upon the UN command in the spring and destroyed it. Only by triggering the "Red trap" before it was fully prepared was a great defeat avoided.

This defense does not stand up to even cursory scrutiny. How exactly would the poorly supplied PVA troops have remained hidden and been sufficiently supplied for months in roadless mountainous country through the long and brutal Korean winter? How would this army have been able to sustain an attack in the spring as the USAF bombed the bridges crossing the Yalu after the river thawed? It is difficult to believe that the UN forces would have suffered such high levels of casualties and collapsed as quickly had they been dug in along a defensive line further south rather than strung out along tenuous supply routes and separated in unsupported attacks.

KEYS TO THE CHINESE VICTORY

How bad was the defeat suffered by MacArthur's command? While few Americans like to confront the truth, Mao achieved one of the most impressive and surprising battlefield victories in modern history. Consider that the world had just recently completed the largest war in the history of mankind, in which the tank, the airplane, and mobile artillery matured rapidly to become the dominant weapons systems on the battlefield. Linked together with fleets of trucks to move men and supplies and portable radio communication to coordinate these combined arms, the combat force America fielded in 1950 barely resembled the one that landed in France to fight in World War I just a bit more than thirty years earlier. The United States arguably led the world in military technology, and MacArthur's command in Korea had been lavished with such modern equipment.

In contrast, the attacking PVA armies were equipped in a manner more akin to forces MacArthur had faced in the jungles of New Guinea between 1942 and 1944: light infantry forced to carry much of its own ammunition and supplies on foot supported by very limited numbers of crew-served machine guns and man-portable mortars. The PVA attacked with almost no tanks, aircraft, or trucks, with little artillery and few radios. It was an amazing quantitative mismatch. Even the Chinese infantry was ill equipped, as upward of one-third of the troops had no rifles and were armed only with grenades. They were ordered to infiltrate near enemy lines at the start of a battle, throw their grenades, and eventually pick up rifles from the fallen. In contrast to American officers who relied on radio and wired field telephones, PVA leaders generally directed their forces through use of horns, whistles, gongs, flutes, and runners. This was communications technology more akin to what MacArthur's father utilized in the American Civil War in the 1860s.

The prevailing belief in the United States today is that a "horde" of Chinese soldiers swarmed over the vastly outnumbered men in the UN lines. In fact, in late November the UN force was actually larger than the combined PVA and KPA forces that attacked south of the Yalu. A U.S. Army history of the period relates that MacArthur was in charge of "a force of some 553,000 men from the Republic of Korea and thirteen members of the United Nations. Ground forces in Korea totaled 423,313 men; air forces based in both Japan and Korea around 55,000; and naval forces, ashore and afloat, about 75,000. The ground forces were predominately South Korean (223,950) and American (178,464). The American contingent included 153,536 Army and 24,928 Marine Corps troops."[18]

To oppose MacArthur's 553,000 men, the PVA's 9th and 13th army groups of thirty divisions contained slightly more than 300,000 men.[19] They were supported by fewer than 100,000 remaining members of the KPA though much of that force was operating in guerrilla bands far to the south of the battlefront. While controlling a larger force, MacArthur may have had a somewhat smaller number of infantrymen on the line than the enemy. This is because the U.S. Army had a lower "tooth-to-tail" ratio than the PVA. However, such a "tail" of men supporting B-29s bombers flying from bases in Japan, F9F Panther tactical aircraft launching from aircraft carriers off the Korean coast, mechanics ensuring that M26 Patton tanks could support infantry positions, trucks transporting a steady supply of 155mm shells to artillery batteries, and so forth, has proven itself time and time again to be of greater value than some extra soldiers with rifles (or perhaps only grenades) at the front.

Both sides had somewhat comparable levels of battlefield experience. The U.S. units were leavened with noncoms and officers who had seen a great deal of fighting against the Germans and Japanese from 1942 to 1945. While much of the rank and file were men who had missed World War II, most had become combat veterans in Korea up against the KPA, which was better equipped than the PVA. Similar comments could be made about the ROK forces. Some had seen action in World War II, and the rest had experience fighting the KPA. While not as well equipped as their American allies, the ROK military in late 1950 still possessed more firepower and mechanized mobility than the Chinese who attacked them.

On the other side of the battle, the experience of the PVA troops was primarily from fighting in the Chinese Civil War from 1945 to 1949, where the resistance of KMT units often melted away when attacked by Communist forces. Many of the Chinese soldiers had also fought against the Japanese in

World War II in actions dominated by skirmishes and ambushes rather than set-piece battles. Many of the PVA formations were composed of recent Nationalist Chinese converts who had changed sides or been captured in the civil war. Few of these men were true believers in communism, and they were not necessarily enthused about being "volunteered" to fight against their former ally (the United States) in the bitterly cold mountains of northern Korea. Almost none of the PVA soldiers had experience dealing with the sort of artillery and airstrike power of the U.S. military that was brought to bear against them.

Thus, the UN forces were arguably not only massively qualitatively superior to the PVA and quantitatively more numerous but also more experienced in the sort of fighting that took place at the end of 1950. For MacArthur, in such battles against the Japanese in World War II from 1943 to 1945, the outcome was almost always a smashing U.S. victory with exceedingly lopsided casualty counts. Yet the PVA forces were generally extremely successful everywhere they attacked. Considering the massive disadvantages they faced, how did the Chinese achieve victory?

First of all, the PVA leadership realized that its men were poorly armed with only grenades and a hodgepodge of older Japanese, Soviet, and American rifles and machine guns. This resulted in a requirement to hide during the day to avoid coming under airstrikes and artillery barrages. Then at night, the PVA divisions would close and intermingle with UN formations to negate their opponents' advantages of firepower, armor, and coordinated radio communication. This led to tactics of movement and infiltration, usually during the hours of darkness. Compact combat groups of 50 to 100 men would infiltrate as close as possible to UN lines and then rush the remaining short distance to close for battle. As many American units were overrun at night in fighting that often became hand-to-hand, demoralized survivors related inaccurate rumors of "human wave" attacks to the U.S. press, which duly reported such tactics.[20]

The Chinese military leadership also turned its lack of wheeled transport to an advantage by directing its divisions to move off roads, seize high ground, and set up roadblocks in UN rear areas. Such tactics caused a sense of panic in attacked UN units, cut off the flow of ammunition and supply heading northward, and isolated the UN frontline from reinforcement. The PVA also exploited weaknesses evident in MacArthur's command, which had advanced into large prepared ambushes. The UN supply lines were extended and tenuous. Major formations were separated by mountainous terrain and unable to support each other due to the mechanized and road-bound nature of the U.S. military. The Chinese movement off major road networks and dispersal of manpower also led to airpower not being as effective as MacArthur had expected, accentuated by his new enemy's lack of a motorized supply system to target.

Finally, the PVA attack came as a great shock to the UN forces. Part of this was due to the Chinese military's march discipline of moving at night while remaining well camouflaged during the day to avoid aerial reconnaissance. Still, this surprise represents a historically remarkable failure of military intelligence. After all, the PRC had warned several times that it would intervene in Korea, the PVA had already attacked in force in late October, and prisoners had been taken who identified themselves as members of several distinct Chinese armies. MacArthur and his staff believed that the best time for the Chinese to intervene had passed and that therefore they simply could not do so. The statements emanating from government officials in Beijing were believed to be nothing more than bluster, and the fighting of the First Phase Offensive was somehow imagined to be only a rearguard action by a small number of Communist volunteers from the north. MacArthur ignored these warning signs at great cost.

In a final analysis, the Chinese Second Phase Offensive is one of the remarkable victories of military history. As such, while rarely discussed in America, the retreat from the Yalu is arguably the most embarrassing defeat the United States has ever suffered on the battlefield. A larger, post–World War II mechanized force equipped with jet fighters, modern tanks, heavy artillery, and strategic bombers was roundly defeated by a smaller army of foot soldiers that was poorly equipped, poorly supplied and, man for man, had less firepower than a similarly sized force fighting on the western front in 1918. The rout could have been much worse but for American trucks and jeeps. The motorized UN force retreated faster than the PVA could keep up on foot, and soon the two forces were no longer in contact.

CHAPTER 14

Stalemate

Douglas MacArthur reported to the Joint Chiefs of Staff (JCS) that he was vastly outnumbered and requested authorization to expand the war by sending the USAF to bomb military targets in China. He also wanted the U.S. Navy to blockade Chinese ports, ship 33,000 KMT troops to Korea, and land additional units of Chiang Kai-shek's army on the Chinese coast. These requests were all turned down. He also asked that atomic weapons be shipped to his command and placed under his tactical control. He intended to make PVA supply routes unusable with radioactive fallout. When Washington turned him down in these requests and President Truman decided against using atomic weapons, MacArthur wrote that his superiors had lost the will to win and had embraced "defeatism."[1]

Truman wanted to contain the war to Korea, even if victory could not be achieved. In contrast, MacArthur was willing to fight a global nuclear war against China and the Soviet Union if that was what it took to achieve victory. Correct or not in his policy, the president made his case quite clear in his memoirs:

> I have never been able to make myself believe that MacArthur, seasoned soldier that he was, did not realize that the "introduction of Chinese Nationalist forces into South China" would be an act of war; or that he, who had had a front-row seat at world events for thirty-five years, did not realize that the Chinese people would react to the bombing of their cities in exactly the same manner as the people of the United States reacted to the bombing of Pearl Harbor; or that, with his knowledge of the east, he could have overlooked the fact that after he had bombed the cities of China there would still be vast flows of materials from Russia so that, if he wanted to be consistent, his next step would have to be the bombardment of Vladivostok and the Trans-Siberian Railroad. But because I was sure that MacArthur could not possibly have overlooked these considerations, I was left with just one simple conclusion: General MacArthur was ready to risk general war. I was not.[2]

Truman accepted, and MacArthur did not, that in a world where both the United States and the USSR had atomic weapons, a third world war must be avoided, and through a policy of limited confrontation and overall containment, the Western democracies could eventually achieve victory over communism with limited bloodshed. World War II was a conflict where the United States demanded "unconditional surrender" from its enemies, and MacArthur believed this was how wars should be fought—until complete victory was achieved. However, the United States had often fought limited wars for limited aims, such as in the American Revolution, the War of 1812, the Mexican-American War, and the Spanish-American War. Even in the Civil War, the U.S. government offered generous terms to the defeated Confederates. Before 1941, only in the wars of genocidal extermination against the American Indians did the United States fight with no quarter given until final and complete victory was achieved.

The new atomic age was not one that MacArthur was able to easily accept. The United States possessed weapons that could ensure victory on the battlefield, but they were not used. He later wrote about fighting the Chinese, "The American tradition had always been that once our troops are committed to battle, the full power and means of the nation would be mobilized and dedicated to fight for victory—not for stalemate or compromise. And I set out to chart the strategic course which would make that victory possible. Not by the wildest stretch of imagination did I dream that this tradition might be broken."[3]

At this dark moment the UN forces in Korea received some tragic luck. General Walker was killed in a jeep crash on December 3. MacArthur's skill in picking field commanders was once more in evidence, as he had chosen Gen. Ridgway to take over if anything happened to Walker. Despite a few previous postings in the Far East, Ridgway was no expert on the "Oriental mind." However, he was a leader who knew how to get men to fight. As commander of the 82nd Airborne Division, he jumped with his troops behind enemy lines before D-Day and led that lightly equipped unit for more than a month of combat in which it took 45 percent casualties. He rose to command of a corps and was wounded by a German grenade in combat. He held several posts in the early years of the Cold War, and his intellect was such that he was able to adapt from leading airborne offensives in Europe to attritional defensive fighting on the Asian mainland in a conflict of limited political aims.

When Walker died, the UN forces in Korea were everywhere in retreat and MacArthur was informing the JCS of the likely need to evacuate from Korea. Nevertheless, when Ridgway arrived in Tokyo, he asked if he could use

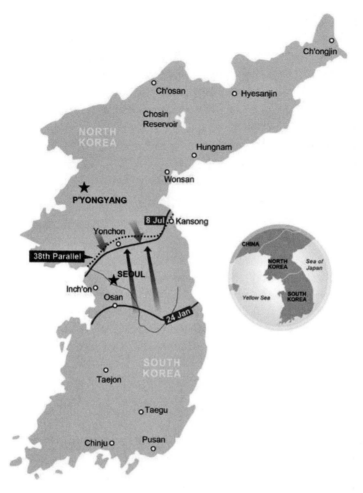

Ridgway's counterattack drives back the Chinese.

SOURCE: COURTESY OF THE U.S. SPECIAL OPERATIONS FORCES.

his forces to go over to the offensive. MacArthur replied, "The 8th Army is yours, Matt. Do what you think best."[4] Upon arriving in Korea, Ridgway's first task was to shore up the line as the Chinese launched their Third Phase Offensive at the very end of 1950. Over a week of fighting, the PVA focused their attacks on ROK units, and UN forces slowly gave ground. This led once more to the fall of Seoul. However, the PVA was exhausted at the end of the battle and suffered dramatically higher losses.

Ridgway was not happy with much of what he found in his forces in Korea. He sent many ineffective officers home and immediately instituted new procedures, including more aggressive patrolling, better night defensive preparations, and a mandate that unit commanders spend more time along the frontlines rather than in command posts to the rear. Nevertheless, the new 8th Army commander reported to the JCS that, contrary to MacArthur's cries for immediate reinforcement, he had sufficient means to hold his ground. On January 3, 1951, he wrote to General Collins, "We shall be in for some difficult days but I am completely confident of the ability of the 8th Army to accomplish every mission assigned."[5] A week later he cabled Washington, "The power is here. The strength and the means we have—short perhaps of Soviet military intervention."[6]

The new UN commander quickly determined the general tactics that would allow his more heavily armed troops to beat the Chinese and their KPA allies:

> I knew well enough that our forces were too thin to man a solid line across the peninsula, yet I saw no reason why these could not be mutually supporting, division-to-division and corps-to-corps. Our howitzers had a range of several miles, so that in many cases each unit could support the next to a considerable extent, and the units on the flanks, particularly, could tie in together well enough to offer each other some artillery support when it was needed. . . . [O]ur armor was far superior now and we had control of the air. We lacked the manpower to halt the night attacks. But by buttoning up tight, unit by unit, at night and counterattacking strongly, with armor and infantry teams, during the day, we had an excellent opportunity to deal out severe punishment to the hostile forces that had advanced through the gaps in our line.[7]

Ridgway's optimism contradicted MacArthur, who cabled Washington on January 10 that the morale of his "small" force was poor and added, "As I have pointed out before, under the extraordinary limitations and conditions imposed upon the command in Korea, its military position in Korea is untenable."[8] This report concerned the JCS, which sent Generals Collins and Vandenberg back to visit Tokyo and Korea from January 15 to 19. Their conclusions were the opposite of MacArthur's. Collins reported to Gen. Bradley that it was the Chinese whose morale was faltering, that Ridgway was responsible for the improved mind-set of the 8th Army, and that if there was a lack of American confidence, it was at the headquarters in Tokyo.[9]

Mao believed that the UN force in Korea was exhausted after the fall of Seoul, just as his was. He ordered the PVA to take the remainder of the winter to rest and refit and prepare for a spring offensive. The Chinese were surprised when on January 15 Ridgway launched the first of his offensives, code-named Operation Wolfhound. While limited in scope, it was effective at gaining ground and imposing higher costs on the Chinese than the attacking U.S. troops. This was followed on January 25 by the larger Operation

Thunderbolt in which the 8th Army advanced back to the Han River and the gates of Seoul. Further east, X Corps and the newly created ROK III Corps then launched Operation Roundup on February 5. This limited offensive was also effective at taking ground and fixing and pounding enemy positions with U.S. artillery. The overextended PVA attempted to regain the initiative with the Fourth Phase Offensive, but the Chinese vanguard was smashed at the battle of Chipyongni and the Third Battle of Wonju in mid-February.

Ridgway pushed his advantage with Operation Killer (February 20–March 6) and Operation Ripper (March 7–April 4), which were measured offensives designed to advance from one defendable line to the next and led to the UN retaking Seoul while imposing much higher casualties on the PVA. The battle lines now were almost back to where they had been prior to the war along the 38th parallel, and Mao's hopes of expelling U.S. forces from Korea were dashed. T. R. Fehrenbach concluded that the PVA "would try again, and again, but now a new pattern had been set. 8th Army had risen from its own bitter ashes. It would not fall again."[10] However, while the UN force had recovered and could hold ground, it did not have the strength to expel the Chinese from North Korea. The conflict slowly degenerated into a war of attrition with both sides dug into fortified lines that snaked across the peninsula and the opponents engaging in attacks with only limited territorial goals.

MacArthur's negative pronouncements were undermined by Ridgway's success on the battlefield. General Collins later observed that this precipitated the fall of the Far Eastern commander, and "as the general's estimation of Chinese intentions and capabilities proved to be wrong, he became more sensitive to criticisms that began to appear in the domestic and foreign press and began to yield to the temptation to defend himself in the public forum."[11] When the Chinese attacked, MacArthur expressed his views to the press that he should be allowed to bomb Manchuria. Truman admitted in his memoirs that once again he should have fired MacArthur for the infraction of questioning official U.S. policy. Again, he did not and instead issued an order to government employees and military commanders forbidding them from making statements regarding U.S. foreign policy until clearing such statements with the State Department.[12] Once more, MacArthur's prestige and political standing with the American public saved him from losing his job.

MacArthur was unwilling to accept that the war in Korea had become a stalemate. In his mind, it was important that the war be expanded to make China pay for robbing him of victory. A deadlock on the battlefield was not an acceptable outcome; it would impugn both America's honor and his own. He had repeatedly stated that if the United States showed weakness toward the Communist nations, they would push for even greater conquests in both Asia and Europe. When he was informed that peace might break out, MacArthur ratcheted up his campaign of behavior that blatantly attempted to undermine the president's policy. Truman was left with no choice but to fire his Far Eastern commander.

First, in the middle of March, Truman was provided with intercepts of messages from Tokyo-based diplomats of the fascist regimes of Spain and Portugal headed by the two dictators Francisco Franco and Antonio Salazar, respectively. "The messages were going in code, and the United States was decoding the messages. So, the U.S. Government knew what MacArthur was telling Franco and Salazar and that he was not telling Truman. He was telling Franco and Salazar that he was going to see to it that the U.S. got into a general war against China."[13] The president was livid that the General was attempting to undermine his policy, but the program of listening in on friendly nations' diplomatic communications was secret, and it was important that this information not be divulged.

More importantly for Truman, there seemed to be a window opening to end the war as

> officials of the Departments of State and Defense believed that Ridgway's recent successes might have convinced the Chinese and North Koreans that they could not win a military victory and, if this was the case, that they might agree to negotiate an end to hostilities. On the advice of these officials, President Truman planned to make a public statement suggesting the United Nations' willingness to end the fighting. The statement was carefully worded to avoid a threatening tone and so to encourage a favorable reply.[14]

On March 20, 1951, the JCS informed MacArthur of Truman's planned peace proposal. It was to be released after its wording was ironed out with other UN members that had supplied troops to fight in Korea. The war had clearly reached a delicate phase, and the president had ordered that no major military actions were to take place without previous authorization from Washington that might upset the diplomatic environment. Rather than follow these orders, the General decided to do what he could to scuttle the president's attempt to end the war with a draw.

On March 24, MacArthur issued a statement to the commander of the PVA offering to engage in his own cease-fire talks. However, the announcement was written in a way that denigrated the enemy's military and economic abilities and implied that the United States would soon attack China's coast and its heartland. The most inflammatory passage was as follows:

> Of even greater significance than our tactical successes has been the clear revelation that this new enemy, Red China, of such exaggerated and vaunted military power, lacks the industrial capacity to provide adequately many

critical items necessary to the conduct of modern war. . . . These military weaknesses have been clearly and definitely revealed since Red China entered upon its undeclared war in Korea. Even under the inhibitions which now restrict the activity of the United Nations forces and the corresponding military advantages which accrue to Red China, it has been shown its complete inability to accomplish by force of arms the conquest of Korea. The enemy therefore must by now be painfully aware that a decision of the United Nations to depart from its tolerant effort to contain the war to the area of Korea, through an expansion of our military operations to its coast area and interior bases, would doom Red China to the risk of imminent military collapse.[15]

Of course, after reading MacArthur's statement, U.S. allies contacted the White House to find why there had been a change in Truman's policy. After all, they had been engaged with the State Department in the final wordsmithing of a declaration designed to coax the Chinese to the negotiating table. The belittling and belligerent tone of MacArthur's cease-fire offer was immediately rejected by Mao and wrecked any chance of peace talks. However, instead of a wider war against China, MacArthur merely accomplished an extension of the fighting in Korea for an additional two years until the summer of 1953. The General took no responsibility for his actions and claimed in his memoirs that his communiqué of March 24 was "routine" in nature and that he never had any interest in expanding the war into China.[16]

The president was incensed. Truman later wrote of MacArthur's action, "This was a most extraordinary statement for a military commander of the United Nations to issue on his own responsibility. It was an act totally disregarding all directives to abstain from any declarations on foreign policy. It was in open defiance of my orders as President and as Commander in Chief. This was a challenge to the authority of the President under the Constitution. . . . By this act MacArthur left me no choice—I could no longer tolerate his insubordination."[17] But before Truman could act, Congressman Joseph Martin, the Republican minority leader, rose in the well of the Capitol Building on April 5 to read a letter he had written to MacArthur and the General's reply.

Martin's letter argued for a more forceful policy to confront the PRC and for using KMT troops in Korea. MacArthur's reply of March 20 included the following:

My views and recommendations with respect to the situation created by Red China's entry into war against us in Korea have been submitted to Washington in most complete detail. Generally these views are well known and clearly understood, as they follow the conventional pattern of meeting force with maximum counter force as we have never failed to in the past. Your view with respect to the utilization of the Chinese forces on Formosa is in conflict with neither logic nor this tradition. It seems strangely difficult for some to realize that here in Asia is where the Communist conspirators have elected to make their play for global conquest, and that we have joined the issue thus raised on the battlefield; that here we fight Europe's war with arms while the diplomats there still fight it with words; that if we lose the war to communism in Asia the fall of Europe is inevitable, win it and Europe most probably would avoid war and yet preserve freedom. As you point out, we must win. There is no substitute for victory.[18]

MacArthur's sharp criticism of administration policy was salt in the wound coming so soon after the General's intentional undermining of the president's hopes to negotiate an end to the war. Truman later said, "I was ready to kick him into the North China Sea, I was never so put out in my life."[19] Of the correspondence with Congressman Martin, General Collins concluded, "This letter clearly revealed the extent to which MacArthur's frustration over the limitations placed on his operations had gotten the better of his judgment. His reversion to his World War II pique at the priority given the European theater over the Pacific broke out again in the non-sequitur comparison of the Korean war with the situation in Europe. This was as untimely and unseemly as it was illogical."[20]

While Truman claims in his memoirs that he had already made up his mind, he convened his cabinet and the JCS and asked for opinions as to whether MacArthur should be relieved of command. While a president should be able to remove a military subordinate for any reason at any time, there were still reservations about firing such an august figure. After lengthy discussions, the cabinet and the Joint Chiefs agreed that MacArthur should be relieved but not officially due to insubordination or any other specific charge, as MacArthur could then have demanded a trial to prove his innocence. Rather Truman gave as his reason that his Far Eastern commander was "unable to give his whole-hearted support to the policies of the United States Government and of the United Nations in matters pertaining to his official duties. . . . Full and vigorous debate on matters of national policy is a vital element in the constitutional system of our free democracy. It is fundamental, however, that military commanders must be governed by the policies and directives issued to them in the manner provided by our laws and Constitution."[21]

U.S. Secretary of the Army Frank Pace was in the Far East touring the frontlines in Korea and was assigned the job of personally delivering the bad news to MacArthur in Tokyo. Unfortunately, instructions to Pace were delayed, and the story leaked to the press. While this was unfortunate and unintentional, MacArthur and his supporters were gravely insulted and focused on how he was fired rather than why. In the final analysis, MacArthur had entered into a calculated gamble: through his efforts he might shape U.S. foreign policy and spark a larger war with China and perhaps the USSR from which America could emerge triumphant. In his opinion, the risk of nuclear war and a Soviet invasion of western Europe was outweighed by the negatives of the fighting in Korea ending in a stalemate. After all, there is no substitute for victory. MacArthur was playing a weak hand, but the odds of success were still clearly better than the 5,000 to 1 that he claimed he wagered at Inchon. But here, up against the president of the United States, he lost.

Ridgway was elevated to overall command in the Far East and claimed his departing former boss was quite calm when they met in Tokyo. This is not surprising as MacArthur must have known he was likely to be fired due to the release of his "routine' communiqué" of condescension toward the Chinese, which threatened that nation with fiery attack from the sky and the sea. Ridgway's summary of MacArthur's character, while couched in kind language, is damning nonetheless:

> Accordingly I came to understand some traits of his complex character not generally recognized: the hunger for praise that led him on some occasions to claim or accept credit for deeds he had not performed, or to disclaim responsibility for mistakes that were clearly his own; the love of the limelight that continually prompted him to pose before the public as the actual commander on the spot at every landing and at the launching of every major attack in which his ground troops took part; his tendency to cultivate the isolation that genius seems to require, until it becomes a sort of insulation (there was no telephone in his personal office in Tokyo) that deprived him of the critical comment and objective appraisals a commander needs from his principal subordinates.[22]

LAST BATTLE

As MacArthur's plane took off from Tokyo to fly back to the United States, his boast that his Home by Christmas Offensive had saved the lives of so many of his men had become that much more tragically ironic. For as he departed the scene, rather than coming to an early end, the war was destined to continue primarily due to his efforts to scuttle any chance for peace. More than 13,000 Americans died fighting in Korea from the day MacArthur left the Far East until the guns finally fell silent two years later in the middle of 1953.[23] The same fate awaited thousands of fighting men from many other UN nations who served in Korea. Of course, the hardest burden fell on the South Koreans themselves, who had to suffer through month after month of additional attritional fighting until they were finally able to return to peace and rebuild their nation. It is true that the costliest days of the war were over by the time the *Bataan* flew off from Tokyo for the last time, but many bloody battles still had to be fought before the two sides were ready to accept the draw that could have been achieved so much earlier. The killing from MacArthur's departure

in July 1951 to the cease-fire in July 1953 was brutal, undecisive, and ultimately unnecessary. Little land traded hands, and the fighting increasingly
took on similarities to that of World War I, where the objective of an offensive was to seize or hold just one single strategically unimportant geographic
feature, such as in the battles of Bloody Ridge, Heartbreak Ridge, Triangle
Hill, and Pork Chop Hill.

MacArthur still had one last battle to fight. This one would be waged with
the General's favorite weapon: words. It was fought on the floor of the U.S.
Senate and in the national press, and at stake was what MacArthur held most
dear: his honor and his legacy. Arrayed on his side were his admirers; the GOP,
which wished to weaken the Democrats' hold on the White House; and those
who wished for a more muscular American foreign policy even if it threatened
to trigger World War III. Against him stood those MacArthur always believed
had tried to hold him back: foolish lightweight politicians like Truman, desk-
bound military leaders at the Pentagon, and the craven who cowered in the
face of totalitarian foes.

The General received a rapturous public welcome from his supporters as
he traveled from San Francisco to New York. His interviews with the press decried U.S. foreign policy as "defeatist" and "appeasement." Truman's approval
rating plunged to well below 50 percent, and thousands wrote to their con-
gressmen and senators calling for his impeachment. MacArthur basked in the
adulation, which hit its peak on April 19, 1951, when, finally attired in his
full-dress uniform, he gave a farewell address to Congress. Forever known for
its closing lines, in which he declared, "Old soldiers never die, they just fade
away," it was a remarkable example of rousing rhetoric. The contents of the
speech reiterated his recent statements and were very much in keeping with his
relation to the truth over the years.

Of course, there were several inaccuracies in the address designed to present MacArthur's position in the best possible light.[24] For example, he stated
that the PVA forces far outnumbered those of the UN coalition in Korea. He
exaggerated that the Nationalist Chinese had 600,000 trained military men in
Formosa who could be deployed to Korea and stated that Mao's government
was fighting with the maximum power it could commit. Again, he argued that
the loss of Formosa would likely push the U.S. frontier back to America's West
Coast, while claiming that practically all U.S. military leaders, including the
Joint Chiefs, agreed with the necessity of expanding the war against China.

MacArthur argued that continuing Truman's policies represented appeasement against Red China and could only lead to a "sham peace." He demanded
that the U.S. Navy blockade the enemy's coast, the U.S. Air Force begin flights
over China proper, and that Washington provide "logistical support" to the
Nationalist Chinese, who should be transported to the mainland to take action

against Mao's forces. Only through such measures could the United States win in Korea, and of course, "there is no substitute for victory."

Truman had rebutted MacArthur's position with a speech given from the White House just a few days earlier. He argued that his policy of fighting a limited war was designed to restore peace in Korea and oppose aggression while not expanding the conflict. Bombing China and assisting KMT forces to land on the mainland would only result in a much larger general war, which was not in America's interest. Truman asked, "What would suit the ambitions of the Kremlin better than for our military forces to be committed to a full-scale war with Red China?"[25] Due to MacArthur's reputation as a military leader, however, many Americans believed that the president must be incorrect.

The debate then moved to the Senate, where Republicans had called for hearings on the General's relief. There, MacArthur spent multiple days promoting his support for an expanded war and accusing the Truman administration of appeasement.[26] In a key moment of the proceedings, he was asked how he would propose to defend the United States if his plan to bomb and blockade China triggered a world war. The General replied,

> That doesn't happen to be my responsibility, Senator. My responsibilities were in the Pacific, and the Joint Chiefs of Staff and the various agencies of this Government are working day and night for an over-all solution to the global problem. Now I am not familiar with their studies. I haven't gone into it. I have been desperately occupied over on the other side of the world, and to discuss in detail things that I haven't even superficially touched doesn't contribute in any way, shape, or manner to the information of this committee or anybody else.[27]

After MacArthur finished his testimony, his position was overwhelmed in a direct attack by the Joint Chiefs and the Secretary of Defense. One senior military leader of the United States after another testified that he did not agree with a policy to expand the war with China, that MacArthur was unable to understand the global political situation as a mere theater commander, and that he had acted in an insubordinate manner. As was his want, Secretary of Defense George Marshall was most thorough and in prepared testimony under the heading "Question of Judgement" pointed out,

> General MacArthur, on the other hand, would have us, on our own initiative, carry the conflict beyond Korea against the mainland of Communist China, both from the sea and from the air. He would have us accept the risk of involvement not only in an extension of the war with Red China, but in an all-out war with the Soviet Union. He would have us do this even at the expense of losing our allies and wrecking the coalition of free peoples throughout the

world. He would have us do this even though the effect of such action might expose Western Europe to attack by the millions of Soviet troops poised in the Middle East and Eastern Europe. The fundamental divergence is one of judgement as to the proper course of action to be followed by the United States. The divergence arises from the inherent difference between the position of a field commander, whose mission is limited to a particular area and a particular antagonist and the position of the Joint Chiefs of Staff, the Secretary of Defense, and President who are responsible for the total security of the United States, and who, to achieve and maintain this security must weigh our interests and objectives in one part of the globe with those in other areas of the world so as to attain the best overall balance.[28]

Marshall went on to conclude,

What is new and what brought about the necessity for General MacArthur's removal is the wholly unprecedented situation of a local Theater Commander publicly expressing his displeasure at, and his disagreement with, the foreign policy of the United States. It became apparent that General MacArthur had grown so far out of sympathy with the established policies of the United States that there was grave doubt as to whether he could any longer be permitted to exercise the authority in making decisions that normal command functions would assign to a theater commander. In this situation, there was no other recourse but to relieve him.[29]

USAF General Vandenberg then made it clear in his testimony that MacArthur's plan to blockade China and bomb Manchuria to erode its capability to wage war in Korea was not realistic. This was because the United States simply did not have enough planes to face down the USSR in Europe and also engage in major aerial operations over China. The latter campaign would lead to a significant loss of aircraft. "The attrition that would inevitably be brought upon us by bombing north of the Yalu would leave us, in my opinion, naked for several years to come, and therefore I did not advocate it."[30]

The most famous statement from the hearings was in the testimony of General Bradley with his pronouncement, "Red China is not the powerful nation seeking to dominate the world. Frankly, in the opinion of the Joint Chiefs of Staff, this strategy would involve us in the wrong war at the wrong place at the wrong time, and with the wrong enemy."[31] He also made quite clear that MacArthur's insubordination was incompatible with our nation's constitutional form of government: "General MacArthur's actions were continuing to jeopardize the civilian control over military authorities."[32] These rebuttals presented on Capitol Hill were exceedingly damaging to MacArthur. They may not have resurrected President Truman in the minds of many Americans, but few were willing to disagree with the reasoned statements of so many of the U.S. military's most senior commanders—especially heroes of World War II such as Marshall and Bradley.

MacArthur also tarnished his reputation somewhat among many Americans and Japanese when in front of a separate Senate committee he testified as follows: "If the Anglo-Saxon was say 45 years of age in his development, in the sciences, the arts, divinity, culture, the Germans were quite as mature. The Japanese, however, in spite of their antiquity measured by time, were in a very tuitionary condition. Measured by the standards of modern civilization, they would be like a boy of 12 as compared with our development of 45 years."[33] As historian John Dower put it, "The bluntness of the metaphor embarrassed the general's Japanese admirers . . . and—in one of history's smaller losses— prompted some of them to abandon plans for a Statue of Liberty–size statue of the general in Tokyo Bay."[34]

Years later MacArthur made clear how far he was willing to go to win the Korean War and unify the peninsula. He disclosed that plans were prepared to drop thirty to fifty atomic bombs on Chinese military bases in Manchuria. Planeloads of radioactive cobalt would then have been scattered across the border region. The goal was to create a zone of deadly, long-lasting radioactivity hundreds of miles long, which would have been fatal to any human caught in the area.[35] Perhaps even the Romans might have blanched at such a plan. After all, they sowed the ground of Carthage with salt, not cobalt-60.

MacArthur's willingness to utilize such a plan makes one question if he truly was, as he claimed, "a friend of the Far East." If yes, imagine what an enemy of the region might do. As prevailing winds blow out of the west from Korea over the Pacific for much of the year, radioactive fallout resulting from MacArthur's "no substitute for victory" plan would have undoubtedly drifted over Japan. The North Korean border with China is due east of the Kanto Plain, so this radiation could have settled across Tokyo and the most densely populated part of the nation that had come to love their American shogun with such fervor. President Truman chose not to proceed with such a plan. For better or worse, while the inhabitants of North Korea still toil under the yoke of authoritarianism, those of the Republic of Korea have lived in general peace under an increasingly democratic government providing for rising standards of living for the last seventy years.

Of course MacArthur clearly did not wish to "fade away" after his return from the Far East. In fact, he hoped to become the Republican nominee for the presidency in 1952. Instead, the GOP chose the more moderate and less controversial Dwight D. Eisenhower, who easily won the election. Already stung by being eclipsed by his former aide, MacArthur went to visit the president-elect on December 17, 1952, to pass along his "simple and workable" plan for ending the Cold War. After listening to the proposal (which has never been disclosed), Eisenhower politely turned down the advice from his former commander. MacArthur concluded that Eisenhower was "naive" and took his leave stating, "You won't have to worry about me, once you're in the White House. I want nothing. I don't propose to take any part in public debates or attempt to push legislation of policies. Goodbye. God bless you."[36]

On his seventy-fourth birthday in 1954, MacArthur discussed the cobalt radiation plan and the final meeting with Eisenhower in interviews he gave to Bob Considine of Hearst Headline Service and Jim Lucas of the Scripps-Howard Newspapers. These only came to light after MacArthur's death a decade later. Considine concluded that being passed over by the GOP and ignored by Eisenhower left MacArthur quite bitter: "The two great setbacks in the sunset of his life far outweighed whatever disappointment General MacArthur felt over his own blighted political career. Indeed, they seemed to have transcended all the satisfaction he might have gained from his long and notable military career and his remarkable stewardship of defeated Japan. Douglas MacArthur died feeling his greatest works were left undone."[37]

While it was not actually his plan, MacArthur kept his promise to the U.S. Congress and indeed faded away.

CONCLUSION

General Douglas MacArthur remains one of the most famous and respected military leaders in our nation's history—this despite the fact that his wartime leadership began and ended with massive defeats. Yet, for many, his sterling reputation endures. Perhaps this is due to his victories in New Guinea, the Philippines, and at Inchon. While he certainly could, and did, take great credit for these triumphs, this book points out that his leadership in such periods was often lacking even when he commanded forces that outnumbered the enemy in both quantitative and qualitative measures. A conclusion can be drawn that his active public relations effort, along with a failure by his superiors to act appropriately, allowed the General to overstate his successes and dump his failures on others in the minds of the American public. Years of such behavior led this nation to the edge of a third world war and sparked a constitutional crisis.

What makes a good military leader? An ability to successfully prepare and motivate a force for combat, and then to take the necessary risks that lead to victory on the battlefield is paramount. This requires an ability to select, nurture, and promote competent field and staff officers who will attend to all the details that result in success over the enemy. Additionally, in the United States, a military officer's willingness to follow lawful orders from his superiors, especially the elected civilian president, is of great importance. Finally, the populace of this nation also believes that those in control of our military should only put its members in a position where they might have to make the ultimate sacrifice in honorable missions in which they are well equipped and where there is a high chance of success.

Against that set of criteria, what can be said of MacArthur's best traits as a wartime commander? First, we can commend his unmatched self-confidence, which allowed him to take great risks on the offensive when he had his enemy on the defensive. This led to lopsided victories such as those at Los Negros, Hollandia, Mindoro, and Inchon. That the odds may not have always been in his favor in these battles does not diminish the fact that he often knew when to rely on luck, and a lucky commander is often a successful one. However, MacArthur's self-confidence was a double-edged sword as it led to tragic overextensions, as with his discarding of the "defeatist" War Plan Orange in the Philippines in 1941, the "arrogant display of strength" that led to the decimation of the 24th Infantry Division in 1950, and the "Home by Christmas" race to the Yalu at the end of that year. His self-confidence could also crumble when he was forced onto the defensive, and he could become as defeatist as he accused others of being. Along Lingayen Gulf in late 1941, he missed an excellent opportunity to defeat a Japanese landing force and instead chose to retreat. In Bataan, while commanding a much larger force, he ignored the opportunity to counterattack in early 1942 after the Japanese significantly reduced the force besieging his own. Finally, in 1950 he refused to acknowledge all warning signs that the Chinese were intervening in Korea until it was too late and then convinced himself that his UN command could not hold the line despite its multifaceted advantages on the battlefield.

MacArthur was an excellent judge of who would perform well as a frontline commander. His choices of Robert Eichelberger, Walter Krueger, George Kenney, and Matthew Ridgway were excellent. He also knew how to work well with aggressive, competent leaders assigned to his command, such as Thomas Kinkaid, Walton Walker, William Halsey, Thomas Blamey, and James Doyle. On the other hand, his repeated need to elevate loyalty over competence in his command staff was a major negative. His initial selection of Richard Sutherland, Charles Willoughby, Edward Almond, and Cortney Whitney for high positions was bad enough, but that he kept them on long after they had proved themselves to be incompetent and a source of friction in the drive to victory is difficult to defend. That these men were all of questionable morality is of concern. When a leader consistently chooses to surround himself with subordinates with such characteristics, one can only come to conclude that perhaps the leader shares these traits.

The General was a consummate master of shaping public opinion about his persona. In a period when the power of mass propaganda rose to new heights, the United States needed leaders who understood how to utilize the press to transmit a message to the nation's public. However, any such positives

were certainly blemished by the pomposity of the General's public pronouncements. Statements such as, "I will return," "This is the voice of freedom speaking," "General MacArthur is in personal command at the front and landed
with his assault troops," and many others show questionable judgement. Even
worse were the transparent lies that he promulgated throughout his career.
Claiming that the defense of Bataan slowed the Japanese onslaught at a critical
time, when in fact it had allowed the enemy to accelerate its plans; telling the
American public that their men were engaged in the relative peace of Christmas Day prayer, when in fact they were involved in brutal fighting and under
air attack; and announcing the end of the battle of Manila, when the destruction of the city and the killing of its residents had barely begun, are only a few
of the outrageous departures from the truth the General promoted during his
many years of wartime command.

Next, we come to the relationship between MacArthur and the common
men who served under him. While he certainly bragged about his ability to
protect their lives in wartime, the historical record is more nuanced. Douglas
MacArthur simply was not that interested in the details. Sadly, he failed to prepare his men for combat in the peacetime period immediately before the U.S.
entry into both World War II and the Korean conflict. If a military command is
not properly trained and exhibits poor readiness, it is not ready to fight and win
on the battlefield. A commander who does not do everything he can to ensure his men are ready to fight leaves himself open to the charge of dereliction
of duty if they are subsequently defeated and thrown into retreat by a smaller
enemy force. The lackadaisical training regimen of the Philippine garrison and
Philippine Army before the attack on Pearl Harbor and that of the 8th Army
in Japan prior to the invasion of South Korea cannot be dismissed as a primary
reason for why these two commands exhibited poor performance on the battlefield when they were called into action.

Similarly, a successful commander makes sure that his forces are properly
supplied and equipped to win when they are sent to fight. MacArthur certainly failed in this mission when he ordered a retreat to Bataan. He had more
than enough time to prepare and sufficient supplies available to provide for
his men but failed to take action to ensure that they would not starve over
a long siege. Even worse, he then raged when these emaciated, diseased men
chose to surrender after he had been evacuated to safety in Australia. Similarly,
MacArthur failed to ensure that the U.S. 32nd Infantry Division was properly
trained and supplied when he sent it into battle in Papua New Guinea. That
the American unit was green was not his fault, but that they were sent into the
jungle without the basic equipment to be successful was his responsibility. He

compounded this error when he repeatedly ordered the men of the division to advance to victory or die in the attempt from his safe command post far from the frontlines.

This ignoring of details and potential enemy abilities emerged again and again over MacArthur's wartime career and cost many American lives. He believed Leyte to be poorly defended and geographically the right island to invade in the Philippines. This led him to ignore repeated sound warnings that the local climate and terrain made it a terrible place to fight a major battle and establish air bases. Thus, when the Japanese shipped in heavy reinforcements, the Southwest Pacific Area (SWPA) forces were unable to maximize the rapidly growing qualitative and quantitative advantages the United States had in air power. In Korea, the 24th Division was wantonly thrust forward into battle before adequate supplies, artillery, and armor arrived, and the formation paid a terrible price. Had one of a thousand things gone wrong at Inchon and the landing turned into a bloodbath, MacArthur would have been pilloried for ignoring a long list of details and his willful belief that he would beat the odds. Later that year, the 8th Army was pushed to advance to the Yalu with extremely low levels of fuel and ammunition and a lack of winter clothing. It paid dearly for these critical supply shortages when the Chinese, despite MacArthur's assurances to the contrary, intervened and shattered the UN lines.

Finally, MacArthur's repeated proclivity to exceed his orders and the related charge of insubordination need to be addressed. The General was always a terribly egotistical man and believed his brilliance was such that he should have the latitude to make American foreign policy himself. He also clearly took the position that he had no true superior and should be able to ignore orders when they did not conform with his opinion of what needed to be done. On these charges he was repeatedly guilty, but much blame should be placed on his superiors. When MacArthur blatantly ignored Secretary of War Patrick Hurley and President Herbert Hoover's orders not to cross the Anacostia River to clear out the Bonus Army encampments, he should have been relieved of duty. That he was not set a terrible precedent.

Soon after, MacArthur quarreled with President Franklin Roosevelt over reducing the army's budget, yelling "that when we lost the next war, and an American boy, lying in the mud with an enemy bayonet through his belly and an enemy foot on his dying throat, spat out his last curse, I wanted the name not to be MacArthur but Roosevelt."[1] The General immediately realized his error and offered his resignation. That FDR chose to forgive his army chief of staff was an error in a nation that believes the military should be appropriately deferential to civilian elected leaders. Emboldened, MacArthur repeatedly attempted to undermine enunciated U.S. foreign policy and gave orders for which he had no authority, from mounting a military campaign to conquer the southern Philippines to authorizing the bombing of North Korea. He also intentionally disregarded orders such as when he violated a JCS directive to only utilize South Korean forces in the region immediately south of the Yalu River in late 1950. It was only after repeated provocation that the buck stopped at the desk of President Harry Truman, who finally found the courage to fire MacArthur.

So, in conclusion, the balance swings hard against any accounting of Gen. Douglas MacArthur as an effective wartime commander. He is not worthy of the fame he still garners to this day. He was by no means the worst military leader in American history, but he was far, far from the best. He also proved himself to be one of the most dangerous due to his manipulation of a system that allowed a terribly vain man to be promoted too quickly and remain in command too long and that failed to impose limits on his actions in word and deed. The unwillingness of multiple presidents and several members of the JCS to properly perform their roles as MacArthur's superiors led to his eventual confrontation with the Constitution's mandate of civilian control over the military. Luckily, he lost that battle, as he lost several others due to a lack of preparation, an unwillingness to understand the competence of his adversaries, and an incorrect reading of the situation. MacArthur's defeat on the Potomac was an important victory for our nation. Ever since, America's military has made a great effort to maintain itself above politics whenever possible. Active military leaders shy away from partisan activities, and those few who have publicly disagreed with national policy have been swiftly removed from their posts.

Readers who previously had a poor opinion of MacArthur have likely found much to agree with and strengthen such a mind-set in this book. Many who had no strong opinion may have been convinced by the arguments in these pages that MacArthur was in most respects a poor wartime commander. While he may have blamed others for every defeat and trumpeted his own brilliance for every victory, the facts of his wartime years yield a record that no amount of positive spin can truly hide.

Finally, those who began this volume holding MacArthur's military feats in reverence may not have been sufficiently persuaded that his faults far outweighed his strengths. However, to continue to honestly believe that MacArthur was a great wartime commander, one has to find ways to explain away these ten errors of leadership during his career:

1. MacArthur's command was quickly defeated by a smaller Japanese invasion force in the Philippines. Neither the U.S. garrison nor the Philippine Army was properly prepared to fight, and both were ineffectively used when the enemy arrived. The defenders' most powerful

and mobile units were not committed to attacking the enemy beachheads even though rough seas delayed the landing of Japanese heavy equipment.

2. America's commander in the Philippines failed to properly supply Bataan despite years of planning to hold that point as a citadel through as long a siege as possible while maximizing the number of Japanese tied down in the effort. The events of December 7 and 8, 1941, fatally undermined MacArthur's strategy to defend all of the Philippines; yet in the next three weeks, no sufficient attempt was made to stockpile the peninsula appropriately. Americans starved as a result, and the garrison surrendered much sooner than it otherwise would have.

3. After Australia's communication links to Hawaii were secured, MacArthur's demand for a muscular and fully equipped offensive from SWPA to retake the Philippines weakened the competing central Pacific drive of Adm. Chester Nimitz. This resulted in the conquest of thousands of miles of malarial New Guinea jungle of questionable strategic value rather than a more vigorous effort to capture the Marianas at the earliest possible date. Thus, the bombing of the Japanese Home Islands and mining of its ports was delayed. The result was an enemy economy and military that was stronger and more difficult to defeat.

4. It was the Japanese who committed the war crimes that devastated Manila and its population. However, that such an atrocity would take place if the United States attempted to retake Luzon was highly likely and should have been anticipated. MacArthur's insistence that all of the Philippines be recaptured for political and personal reasons directly precipitated the destruction that took place in Manila.

5. MacArthur insisted that Operation Downfall take place and discounted intelligence that Kyushu was being reinforced by hundreds of thousands of Japanese soldiers and thousands of kamikaze craft. Had the dropping of the atomic bomb and Soviet entry into the war not happened, a great bloodbath likely would have unfolded if the American forces stormed ashore.

6. The 8th Army was poorly trained and underprepared to fight when the Korean War broke out. As in the Philippines in 1941, MacArthur took little interest in maximizing his army's preparedness and spent almost all of his time in a downtown office building and a personal residence rather than paying visits to subordinate commanders and units in the field.

7. When the fighting in Korea began, MacArthur decided that rushing multiple piecemeal elements of the 24th Infantry Division to the front

could better hold back the Communist invasion than having them form up as a combined whole along a prepared defensive river line with a larger complement of artillery, antitank weapons, and armor. The result was a string of humiliating defeats, large American casualties, and a North Korean advance that was not necessarily slowed.

8. MacArthur declared that the Chinese could not effectively intervene in Korea prior to several of its divisions suddenly appearing and handily defeating South Korean and U.S. formations north of the Chongchon River in late October and early November 1950. After the People's Volunteer Army units melted back northward into the mountains, he declared that the Chinese were no longer a threat and would not intervene in the war. MacArthur chose to press his attack to the Yalu in a manner that dispersed his formations into multiple unsupported advances in brutal winter conditions for which his men were not prepared. The UN command was subsequently ambushed, with several of its divisions surrounded and defeated in detail by a smaller attacking force in one of the most shocking defeats in military history.

9. Douglas MacArthur regularly made a habit of exceeding orders, expecting that he would suffer no consequences for his actions. While at the tactical level the U.S. Army encourages flexibility and initiative in its officers, MacArthur's choices in this regard were often more strategic in nature, such as ordering multiple divisions to invade several Philippine islands without authorization or personally authorizing the initiation of air attacks on the military bases of a nation with which the United States was not officially at war. In an era of rapid radio communication, there was no reason an American military leader should have believed it proper to order such actions without prior approval.

10. Lastly, we come to the behavior that led to MacArthur's dismissal at the end of his career: direct and willful insubordination against the explicit orders of the president of the United States. This was not confined to 1951 but rather was part of an ongoing pattern of inappropriate behavior that reached back decades. The General's insubordination finally came to a head when Mao Zedong sent his armies south of the Yalu and the UN forces were thrown back in disarray. Unwilling to accept anything less than a complete victory, MacArthur actively worked to undermine President Truman's clear policy that the Korean conflict be confined to that peninsula and general war with China be avoided. This led to the General intentionally and fatally undermining a planned peace overture with an insulting and provocative

challenge issued to the commander of China's military force, which, of course, was ultimately Mao Zedong himself. Those who continue to uphold MacArthur as a paragon of wartime leadership should confront the following question: If such a pattern of insubordination by a senior military leader of the United States is acceptable behavior, what exactly would they consider to be unacceptable conduct?

So, in conclusion, who was Gen. Douglas MacArthur? He was a gifted, intelligent man who dedicated his life to his nation and the institution of the U.S. Army. He was also a man with an overinflated belief in his own infallibility and a massive ego requiring constant reassurance from others that he was brilliant and honorable. These desires were satisfied through his holding senior positions in the U.S. military for more than thirty years. Sadly, his tenure overlapped with two great conflicts. Many lives were lost due to his wartime leadership, which revealed manifest deficiencies that could only be partially obscured through his use of adroit public relations and outright falsehoods. Still, being a compulsive liar and a poor military leader were not MacArthur's worst traits. Even his unseemly proclivity to take great risks and gamble with his men's lives in the furtherance of his own glory and fame is eclipsed by his unwillingness to submit to a chain of command. He was never in truth an American Caesar, never commander in chief of America's military forces. His refusal to accept this fact and his raging against it eventually almost unhinged our constitutional system and triggered World War III.

While he would have wished otherwise, MacArthur's greatest legacy is a military that has repudiated his style and methods. Today its leaders are rarely flashy in oratory or appearance, and they studiously attempt to distance themselves from partisan politics. They dedicate themselves to following the orders of the duly elected president, who is the head of America's armed forces. In contrast to the soft garrison life in the Philippines in 1941 and Japan in 1950, the men and women of our nation's far-flung legions train strenuously so that they are ready to fight and win on short notice. Today the concept of an American general or admiral actively and publicly attempting to undermine the enunciated policy of a sitting president is anathema to the military establishment. So too would be the idea of an active senior officer announcing an intention to accept the nomination of a major political party for the office of president while remaining on active duty.

The American public has also moved away from MacArthur's burning drive for victory at any cost. Over the last seventy-five years we have come to embrace the concept of limited war for limited aims. Nuclear weapons have not been used to stave off wartime defeat, and we have walked away from conflicts that we could not win but could afford to lose. MacArthur would be apoplectic that we have fought, lost, and retreated in a great arc across Eurasia, which stretches from North Korea to Vietnam, Afghanistan, Iraq, Syria, and Lebanon. Despite failing to secure victories in these wars, the Pax America has endured across much of the world, with commensurate increases in living standards, life expectancy, and free trade.

Our nation must remain vigilant against the rise of another MacArthur. We have no need for strutting military commanders who ignore the details of the job, embrace the spotlight of fame, and shy away from owning their mistakes. In this extremely partisan era, America can ill afford a general or an admiral who undermines the president and inflames and divides the population. The final conclusion of this book is that the United States does not need another MacArthur: One General Douglas MacArthur was more than enough.

NOTES

INTRODUCTION

1. Ovidiu Popa, "President Truman Talks about General MacArthur: A Cheater and a Bighead," War History Online, May 12, 2015, www.warhistoryonline.com/articles /president-truman-talks-general-macarthur-cheater-bighead.html (accessed December 2, 2021).
2. Stephen Ambrose, *Eisenhower: Soldier and President* (New York: Simon & Schuster, 1990), 45.
3. Carlo D'Este, *Eisenhower: A Soldier's Life* (New York: Henry Hold & Co., 2002), 224.

FIRST RETREAT: THE FALL OF THE PHILIPPINES

1. James Scott, *Rampage: MacArthur, Yamashita, and the Battle of Manila* (New York: W. W. Norton & Co., 2018), 15.

CHAPTER 1: AN APPOINTMENT WITH DESTINY

1. Data from Amazon.com sales ranking accessed November 14, 2021. *American Caesar* ranked 65,595 of all books sold on the site. *Reminiscences* was ranked 182,730 in books; *Douglas MacArthur: What Greater Honor* ranked 357,467. These specific numbers do change often, but the point remains that books on MacArthur read by the general public depict him in a positive light.
2. Scott, *Rampage*, 17.
3. Scott, *Rampage*, 15.
4. D. Clayton James, *Refighting the Last War: Command and Crisis in Korea, 1950–1953* (New York: Free Press, 1993), 41.
5. Richard Connaughton, *MacArthur and Defeat in the Philippines* (Woodstock, NY: Overlook Press, 2001), 40.

6. Paul Dickson, "The Bonus Army," Bill of Rights Institute, https://billofrightsinsti tute.org/essays/the-bonus-army (accessed November 26, 2021).
7. Mark Perry, "Four-Star Egos," *Foreign Policy Magazine*, November 13, 2012, https:// foreignpolicy.com/2012/11/13/four-star-egos (accessed February 2, 2022).
8. Connaughton, *MacArthur and Defeat in the Philippines*, 41.
9. Connaughton, *MacArthur and Defeat in the Philippines*, 38.
10. Douglas MacArthur, *Reminiscences* (New York: McGraw-Hill Book Co., 1964), 101.
11. "Formosa" will be used in this book as the island was generally referred to by that name by both the United States and Japan in the first half of the twentieth century.
12. Brian McAllister Linn, *Guardians of Empire* (Chapel Hill: University of North Carolina Press, 1997), 80–88.
13. Edward Miller, *War Plan Orange* (Annapolis, MD: Naval Institute Press, 1991), 331–332.
14. Miller, *War Plan Orange*, 58.
15. Linn, *Guardians of Empire*, 170.
16. Linn, *Guardians of Empire*, 171.
17. Benjamin Runkle, *Generals in the Making: How Marshall, Eisenhower, Patton, and Their Peers Became the Commanders Who Won World War II* (Lanham, MD: Stackpole Books, 2019), 228–229.
18. See Philip Jowett, *The Japanese Army 1931–45* (Oxford, UK: Osprey Publishing, 2002).
19. Eric Larrabee, *Commander in Chief: Franklin Delano Roosevelt, His Lieutenants and Their War* (New York: Harper & Row, 1987), 312.
20. Linn, *Guardians of Empire*, 236.

CHAPTER 2: THE SOUTHERN ROAD TO WAR

1. Ulrich Mohr, *Ship 16: The Story of the Secret German Raider Atlantis* (New York: John Day Company, 1956), 153–155.
2. Ernest King, *Fleet Admiral King* (New York: W. W. Norton & Co, 1952), 400.
3. Maurice Matloff and Edwin Snell, *Strategic Planning for Coalition Warfare, 1941–1942* (Washington, DC: United States Army, 1990), 32, 45.
4. D. Clayton James, *The Years of MacArthur* (New York: Houghton Mifflin, 1970), 1:378–379.
5. Miller, *War Plan Orange*, 61–62.
6. James, *Years of MacArthur*, 1:583.
7. William Manchester, *American Caesar* (New York: Little, Brown & Co., 1978), 188.
8. James, *Years of MacArthur*, 1:613.
9. James, *Years of MacArthur*, 1:613.
10. James, *Years of MacArthur*, 1:611.
11. James, *Years of MacArthur*, 1:614. Note: In the USAAF, a group consisted of two or more squadrons or aircraft.
12. Alan Schom, *The Eagle and the Rising Sun* (New York: W. W. Norton & Co., 2004), 202.
13. Schom, *The Eagle and the Rising Sun*, 205.

14. Herbert Bix, *Hirohito and the Making of Modern Japan* (New York: Harper, 2000), 399.

15. Connaughton, *MacArthur and Defeat in the Philippines*, 68.

16. Eri Hotta, *Japan, 1941: Countdown to Infamy* (New York: Knopf, 2013), 192.

17. Hotta, *Japan, 1941*, 135.

18. Hotta, *Japan, 1941*, 164.

19. Michael Ray, "Pearl Harbor in Context," *Encyclopedia Britannica*, https://britannica.com/story/pearl-harbor-in-context (accessed December 16, 2021).

20. "Sayre Depicts U.S. at the Brink of War," *New York Times*, October 17, 1941, https://timesmachine.nytimes.com/timesmachine/1941/10/17/105164529.html?pageNumber=10 (accessed December 6, 2021).

21. Thomas Fleming, "The Big Leak," *American Heritage*, December 1987, https://americanheritage.com/big-leak.

22. See James, *Years of MacArthur*, 1:595; Manchester, *American Caesar*, 194.

23. Louis Morton, *The Fall of the Philippines* (Washington DC: Center of Military History United States Army, 1953), 25–30.

24. Linn, *Guardians of Empire*, 245.

25. Manchester, *American Caesar*, 194.

26. D. Clayton James, *The Years of MacArthur* (Boston: Houghton Mifflin, 1970), 2:28.

27. Percy Greaves Jr., *Pearl Harbor: The Seeds and Fruits of Infamy* (Auburn, AL: Ludwig von Mises Institute, 2010), 165–166.

28. David DuBois, "Admiral Thomas C. Hart and the Demise of the Asiatic Fleet, 1941–1942," East Tennessee State University, School of Graduate Studies, May 2014, p. 27, https://dc.etsu.edu/cgi/viewcontent.cgi?article=3686&context=etd (accessed May 16, 2022).

29. James, *Years of MacArthur*, 615.

30. Steve Twomey, *Countdown to Pearl Harbor* (New York: Simon & Schuster, 2016), 84.

31. Kent G. Budge, "Hart, Thomas Charles (1877–1971)," Pacific War Online Encyclopedia, http://pwencycl.kgbudge.com/H/a/Hart_Thomas_C.htm (accessed May 16, 2022).

32. DuBois, "Admiral Thomas C. Hart and the Demise of the Asiatic Fleet, 1941–1942," 27.

33. Manchester, *American Caesar* (New York: Dell, 1978), 215.

34. Robert MacDougall, *Leaders in Dangerous Times: Douglas MacArthur and Dwight D. Eisenhower* (Bloomington, IN: Trafford Publishing, 2013), 61.

35. William Bartsch, *December 8, 1941: MacArthur's Pearl Harbor* (College Station: Texas A&M University Press, 2003), 153–155, 173–175.

36. Manchester, *American Caesar*, 198.

37. MacArthur, *Reminiscences*, 109, 111, 114.

38. Richard Frank, *MacArthur: A Biography* (New York: Palgrave MacMillan, 2007), 3.

39. Supreme Commander for the Allied Powers (SCAP) and Douglas MacArthur, *Reports of General MacArthur: The Campaigns of MacArthur in the Pacific* (Washington, DC: United States Army, 1966), 1:3.

CHAPTER 3: AIR RAID ON PEARL HARBOR:
THIS IS NOT A DRILL

1. *Pearl Harbor Attack: Hearings before the Joint Committee of the Pearl Harbor Attack* (U.S. Washington, DC: Government Printing Office, 1946), 1329.
2. MacArthur, *Reminiscences*, 113.
3. Manchester, *American Caesar*, 206.
4. Bartsch, *December 8, 1941*, 412.
5. John Correll, "Disaster in the Philippines," *Air Force Magazine*, November 1, 2019, www.airforcemag.com/article/disaster-in-the-philippines (accessed November 23, 2021).
6. Lewis Brereton, *The Brereton Diaries* (New York: De Capo Press, 1946); see Part I, "Philippines Phase," 7–47.
7. "M'Arthur Denies Brereton Report," *New York Times*, September 28, 1946, https://timesmachine.nytimes.com/timesmachine/1946/09/28/93155277.html?pageNumber=6 (accessed January 1, 2022).
8. Bartsch, *December 8, 1941*, 412.
9. Manchester, *American Caesar*, 207.
10. Schom, *The Eagle and the Rising Sun*, 148.
11. MacArthur, *Reminiscences*, 119–120.
12. Donald Caldwell, *Thunder on Bataan* (Lantham, MD: Stackpole Books, 2019), 70; Patrick Masell,"The P-40 Warhawk and the A6M Zero," Naval, Aviation and Military History, www.chuckhawks.com/p-40_vs_zero.htm (accessed November 16, 2021).
13. "M'Arthur Denies Brereton Report."
14. "M'Arthur Denies Brereton Report."
15. MacArthur, *Reminiscences*, 120; see also SCAP and MacArthur, *Reports of General MacArthur*, 1:6n13.
16. Wally Hoffman, "We Got Our Feet Wet," Preservation Foundation, www.storyhouse.org/wally6.html (accessed November 22, 2021).
17. Louis Morton, *Strategy and Command: The First Two Years* (Washington, DC: Center of Military History, United States Army, 1971), 100.
18. MacArthur, *Reminiscences*, 121.
19. Richard Frank, *Tower of Skulls*, Kindle ed. (New York: W. W. Norton & Co., 2020), location 8588.
20. John Sharkey, "The MacArthur Mutiny," *Washington Post*," December 5, 1993, www.washingtonpost.com/archive/opinions/1993/12/05/the-macarthur-mutiny/6e05abdb-ece1-46a4-b672-523c56ca5f4f (accessed October 18, 2021).
21. Forrest Pogue, *George C. Marshall: Ordeal and Hope, 1939–1942* (New York: Viking Adult, 1966), 234.
22. Correll, "Disaster in the Philippines."
23. Stephen Budansky, *Battle of Wits: The Complete Story of Codebreaking in World War II* (New York: Simon & Schuster, 2000), 10.
24. Michael Schaller, *Douglas MacArthur: The Far Eastern General* (Oxford: Oxford University Press, 1989), 64–65.

25. See MacArthur, *Reminiscences*, 121.
26. Morton, *The Fall of the Philippines*, 67–70.
27. Morton, *The Fall of the Philippines*, 69–70.
28. Lt. Col. Jeffrey Furbank, "A Critical Analysis of the Generalship of General Douglas MacArthur as Theater Commander in the Pacific during World War II," Air War College Research Report, Bataan Legacy Historical Society, February 1990, www.bataanlegacy.org/uploads/3/4/7/6/34760003/critique_of_macarthurs_leadership-air_war_college.pdf) (accessed October 29, 2021).
29. Manchester, *American Caesar*, 215.
30. MacArthur, *Reminiscences*, 121.
31. MacArthur, *Reminiscences*, 121.
32. Manchester, *American Caesar*, 213.
33. MacArthur, *Reminiscences*, 121.
34. Morton, *The Fall of the Philippines*, 125, 162.
35. Morton, *The Fall of the Philippines*, 162.
36. Morton, *The Fall of the Philippines*, 125, 162–163; also see Schom, *The Eagle and the Rising Sun*, 217, 219.
37. Morton, *The Fall of the Philippines*, 162.
38. MacArthur, *Reminiscences*, 123.
39. See the Japanese Mutumi Troop Encyclopedia at https://web.archive.org/web/20100516180653/http://homepage1.nifty.com/kitabatake/rikukaiguntop.html (accessed November 15, 2021). Also see "List of Japanese Imperial Infantry Divisions," Wikiwand, www.wikiwand.com/en/List_of_Japanese_Infantry_divisions (accessed November 15, 2021); Morton, *The Fall of the Philippines*, 262.
40. Morton, *The Fall of the Philippines*, 125.
41. US War Department, *Handbook on Japanese Military Forces* (1944; rpt. Baton Rouge: Louisiana State University Press, 1995), 16, 18.
42. Connaughton, *MacArthur and Defeat in the Philippines*, 205.
43. Connaughton, *MacArthur and Defeat in the Philippines*, 205.
44. Morton, *The Fall of the Philippines*, 163.
45. Manchester, *American Caesar*, 217.
46. Morton, *The Fall of the Philippines*, 144.
47. Morton, *The Fall of the Philippines*, 162.
48. Manchester, *American Caesar*, 217.
49. MacArthur, *Reminiscences*, 126.
50. Morton, *The Fall of the Philippines*, 259.

CHAPTER 4: BATAAN

1. MacArthur, *Reminiscences*, 126–127.
2. SCAP and MacArthur, *Reports of General MacArthur*, 2:104.
3. Morton, *The Fall of the Philippines*, 261; Manchester, *American Caesar*, 237.
4. Schom, *The Eagle and the Rising Sun*, 235.
5. Manchester, *American Caesar*, 237–238.

6. MacArthur, *Reminiscences*, 136.

7. MacArthur, *Reminiscences*, 121.

8. Manchester, *American Caesar*, 230.

9. Manchester, *American Caesar*, 330.

10. Morton, *The Fall of the Philippines*, 273–274.

11. SCAP and MacArthur, *Reports of General MacArthur*, 1:18.

12. SCAP and MacArthur, *Reports of General MacArthur*, 1:18.

13. SCAP and MacArthur, *Reports of General MacArthur*, 2:110.

14. SCAP and MacArthur, *Reports of General MacArthur*, 1n33, Volume 1, 18.

15. Morton, *The Fall of the Philippines*, 258.

16. Morton, *The Fall of the Philippines*, 405.

17. Morton, *The Fall of the Philippines*, 412–413.

18. Manchester, *American Caesar*, 237.

19. Dwight D. Eisenhower, *Crusade in Europe* (Baltimore: John Hopkins University Press, 1997), 21–22.

20. Eisenhower, *Crusade in Europe*, 21.

21. Matloff and Snell, *Strategic Planning for Coalition Warfare, 1941–1942*, 157.

22. Hampton Sides, *Ghost Soldiers* (New York: Knopf Doubleday, 2002), 43.

23. William Stevens, "Eisenhower Diary Said to Assail MacArthur and Adm. King in '42," *New York Times*, September 19, 1979, https://timesmachine.nytimes.com/times machine/1979/09/19/111062219.html?pageNumber=16 (accessed January 15, 2021).

24. For American average home prices in 1940, see "Historical Census of Housing Tables—Home Values," Economic Analysis Division, State of Wyoming, Department of Administration and Information, U.S. Census, www2.census.gov/programs.sur veys/decennial/tables/time-series/???-values/values-unadj.txt.

25. Radio Marshall to Wainwright, March 26, 1942, quoted from Morton, *The Fall of the Philippines*, 401.

FIRST ADVANCE: THE HARD WAY BACK

1. John Histon, ed., *American Airpower Comes of Age: General Henry H. "Hap" Arnold's World War II Diaries* (Maxwell Air Force Base, AL: Air University Press, 2002), 1:394.

CHAPTER 5: I SHALL RETURN

1. Edward Imparato, ed., *General MacArthur: Speeches and Reports, 1908–1964* (Nashville: Turner Publishing Company, 2000), 124.

2. Imparato, *General MacArthur: Speeches and Reports*, 124.

3. SCAP and MacArthur, *Reports of General MacArthur*, 29.

4. MacArthur's February 4, 1941, radio message to Marshall, George C. Marshall Foundation, www.marshallfoundation.org/library/digital-archive/to-general-doug las-macarthur-radio-no-1024 (accessed November 7, 2021).

5. Schom, *The Eagle and the Rising Sun*, 210.

6. Mark Perry, *The Most Dangerous Man in America* (New York: Basic Books, 2015), 182.

7. Richard Rovere and Arthur Schlesinger Jr., *General MacArthur and President Truman: The Struggle for Control of American Foreign Policy* (New Brunswick, NJ: Transaction Publishers, 1992), 23.

8. Jeffrey Grey, *A Military History of Australia*, 3rd ed. (Cambridge: Cambridge University Press, 2008), 176.

9. Henry Frei, *Japan's Southward Advance and Australia: From the Sixteenth Century to World War II* (Honolulu: University of Hawaii Press, 1991), 172–173.

10. "Admiral Ernest J. King—Chief of Naval Operations, 1942," Naval Heritage and Heritage Command, www.history.navy.mil/about-us/leadership/director/directors-corner/h-grams/h-gram-008/h-008-5.html (accessed December 14, 2021).

11. "Admiral Ernest J. King—Chief of Naval Operations, 1942."

12. "Admiral Ernest J. King—Chief of Naval Operations, 1942."

13. Stevens, "Eisenhower Diary Said to Assail MacArthur and Adm. King in '42."

14. King, *Fleet Admiral King*, 412.

15. King, *Fleet Admiral King*, 413.

16. King, *Fleet Admiral King*, 442.

17. King, *Fleet Admiral King*, 393.

18. Robert Eichelberger, *Our Jungle Road to Tokyo* (Mount Pleasant, SC: Arcadia Press, 1950), 17.

19. King, *Fleet Admiral King*, 533.

20. John Curtin, "The Task Ahead," John Curtin Prime Ministerial Library, December 27, 1941, http://john.curtin.edu.au/pmportal/text/00468.html (accessed December 16, 2021).

21. Grey, *A Military History of Australia*, 178.

22. Grey, *A Military History of Australia*, 187.

23. Grey, *A Military History of Australia*, 177.

24. Edward Drea, *MacArthur's Ultra: Codebreaking and the War against Japan, 1942–1945* (Lawrence: University of Kansas Press, 1992), 23.

25. Drea, *MacArthur's Ultra*, 59.

26. Drea, *MacArthur's Ultra*, 59.

27. Kent G. Budge, "Parafrag Bombs," Pacific War Online Encyclopedia, http://pwencycl.kgbudge.com/P/a/Parafrag_Bombs.htm (accessed November 8, 2021).

28. Stephan Wilkinson, "How the B-25 Became the Ultimate Strafer of World War II," HistoryNet, www.historynet.com/the-mighty-mitchell-how-b-25s-became-one-of-the-most-essential-aircraft-in-wwii.htm (accessed November 8, 2021).

29. Waldo Heinrichs and Marc Gallicchio, *Implacable Foes* (Oxford: Oxford University Press, 2017), 47.

30. George Kenney, *General Kenney Reports* (Washington, DC: Office of the Air Force History, U.S. Air Force, 1949), 26.

31. Herman Wolk, "The Genius of George Kenney," *Air Force Magazine*," April 1, 2002, www.airforcemag.com/article/0402kenney (accessed December 26, 2021).

32. Robert Eichelberger, *Dear Miss Em: General Eichelberger's War in the Pacific, 1942–1945* (Westport, CT: Greenwood Press, Inc., 1972), 29.

33. Drea, *MacArthur's Ultra*, 33.
34. Schom, *The Eagle and the Rising Sun*, 211.
35. Manchester, *American Caesar*, 379.
36. "Maj. General Courtney Whitney, 71, Advisor to MacArthur, Is Dead," *New York Times*, March 22, 1969, https://timesmachine.nytimes.com/timesmachine /1969/03/22/90073413.html?pageNumber=33 (accessed March 7, 2022).
37. Manchester, *American Caesar*, 530.
38. Manchester, *American Caesar*, 404, 530.
39. Frank, *MacArthur*, 108.
40. Drea, *MacArthur's Ultra*, 59.

CHAPTER 6: THE OFFENSIVE-DEFENSIVE

1. SCAP and MacArthur, *Reports of General MacArthur*, 35.
2. MacArthur, *Reminiscences*, 152.
3. MacArthur, *Reminiscences*, 159.
4. John Prados, "Security and Leaks: When the U.S. Government Prosecuted the Chicago Tribune," National Security Archive, October 25, 2017, https://nsarchive .gwu.edu/briefing-book/intelligence/2017-10-25/secrecy-leaks-when-us-government -prosecuted-chicago-tribune (accessed September 27, 2021).
5. John Miller, *Guadalcanal: The First Offensive* (Washington, DC: Center of Military History, United States Army, 1995), 2.
6. Frank, *MacArthur*, 61–62.
7. David Horner, "High Command and the Kokoda Campaign," Australian War Memorial, www.awm.gov.au/visit/events/conference/remembering-1942/horner (accessed January 13, 2022).
8. Larrabee, *Commander in Chief*, 324–325.
9. G.H.Q. South West Pacific Area Communique No. 140, August 31, 1942.
10. Histon, *American Airpower Comes of Age*, 1:392–393.
11. Histon, *American Airpower Comes of Age*, 1:394.
12. SCAP and MacArthur, *Reports of General MacArthur*, 1:81–82.
13. Manchester, *American Caesar*, 284.
14. "Guadalcanal Naval Battles," National Museum of the U.S. Navy, www.history .navy.mil/content/history/museums/nmusn/explore/photography/wwii/wwii-pacific /wwii-pacific-guadalancanal/naval-battles.html (accessed January 6, 2022).
15. Eichelberger, *Our Jungle Road to Tokyo*, 62.
16. Grey, *A Military History of Australia*, 181.
17. Eichelberger, *Our Jungle Road to Tokyo*, 62.
18. Manchester, *American Caesar*, 326.
19. Frank, *MacArthur*, 65.
20. Eichelberger, *Our Jungle Road to Tokyo*, 66.
21. Eichelberger, *Our Jungle Road to Tokyo*, 100.
22. GHQ SWPA Communique number 258, December 26, 1942.
23. Eichelberger, *Our Jungle Road to Tokyo*, 108–110.

24. GHQ SWPA Communique number 291, January 28, 1943.

25. Manchester, *American Caesar*, 327.

26. William O'Neil, *A Democracy at War: America's Fight at Home and Abroad in World War II* (Cambridge, MA: Harvard University Press, 1993), 281.

27. See, for example, GHQ Communiques 264, January 1, 1932, and 286, January 23, 1943.

28. Eichelberger, *Our Jungle Road to Tokyo*, 130.

29. Eichelberger, *Our Jungle Road to Tokyo*, 348–349.

30. Eichelberger, *Our Jungle Road to Tokyo*, 207.

31. Manchester, *American Caesar*, 327.

32. James Glusman, *Conduct under Fire: Four American Doctors and Their Fight for Life as Prisoners of the Japanese, 1941–1945* (New York: Penguin Books, 2005), 133; Schaller, *Douglas MacArthur*, 73.

33. Manchester, *American Caesar*, 339.

CHAPTER 7: THE ADVANCE ACCELERATES

1. William Halsey and Joseph Bryan, *Admiral Halsey's Story* (New York: Whittlesey House, 1947), 161.

2. See King, *Fleet Admiral King*, 434; Manchester, *American Caesar*, 337–338.

3. Manchester, *American Caesar*, 337.

4. MacArthur, *Reminiscences*, 169.

5. Frank, *MacArthur*, 3.

6. Manchester, *American Caesar*, 337.

7. SCAP and MacArthur, *Reports of General MacArthur*, 1:100.

8. "The Solomon Islands Campaign: Guadalcanal," *National WWII Museum*, www.nationalww2museum.org/war/articles/solomon-islands-campaign-guadalcanal, *(accessed October 20, 2021)*.

9. Derrick Wright, *Tarawa 1943: The Turning of the Tide* (Oxford, UK: Osprey Publishing, 2000), Appendix 3.

10. Gordon Rottman, *The Marshall Islands 1944: Operation Flintlock, the Capture of Kwajalein and Eniwetok* (Oxford, UK: Osprey Publishing, 2004), 88.

11. Rottman, *The Marshall Islands 1944*, 87.

12. SCAP and MacArthur, *Reports of General MacArthur*, plate 134, 1:463.

13. Richard Frank, "The MacArthur No One Knew," HistoryNet, August 13, 2018, www.historynet.com/macarthur-no-one-knew.

14. SCAP and MacArthur, *Reports of General MacArthur*, 1:134.

15. Phillips Payson O'Brien, *How the War Was Won* (Cambridge: Cambridge University Press, 2015), 398.

16. O'Brien, *How the War Was Won*, 400–401.

17. Walter Krueger, *From Down Under to Japan* (Lawrence, KS: Zegner, 1953), 48–49.

18. SCAP and MacArthur, *Reports of General MacArthur*, 1:140.

19. See GHQ SWPA Communique No. 691, March 1, 1944.

20. Manchester, *American Caesar* (Dell ed.), 397.

21. John McManus, *Island Infernos* (New York: Calibur, 2021), 445.

22. King, *Fleet Admiral King*, 485.

23. See, for example, Manchester, *American Caesar* (Dell ed.), 410–414.

24. John Miller, *Cartwheel: The Reduction of Rabaul* (Washington, DC: Center of Military History, United States Army, 1959), 222.

25. Brian Eno, "The Whipsaw at Work: US Mastery in Sequential and Cumulative Operations in the Pacific War," Naval War College, May 4, 2018, https://apps.dtic.mil/sti/citations/AD1061990 (accessed January 21, 2022).

26. Drea, *MacArthur's Ultra*, 106.

27. SCAP and MacArthur, *Reports of General MacArthur*, 2:273.

28. Robert Ross Smith, *The Approach to the Philippines* (Washington, DC: Center for Military History, United States Army, 1953), 233.

29. GHQ SWPA Communique, May 28, 1944.

30. Eichelberger, *Our Jungle Road to Tokyo*, 293.

SECOND ADVANCE: HONOLULU TO TOKYO

1. MacArthur Memorial, "MacArthur's 'I Have Returned Speech,'" YouTube, October 9, 2018, www.youtube.com/watch?v=ptVKbN27_4g (accessed January 28, 2022).

CHAPTER 8: LEYTE

1. King, *Fleet Admiral King*, 538.

2. King, *Fleet Admiral King*, 567.

3. Halsey and Bryan, *Admiral Halsey's Story*, 195.

4. Robert Ross Smith, *Triumph in the Philippines* (Washington, DC: Center of Military History, United States Army, 1993), 8–10.

5. Howard G. Bruenn, "Clinical Notes on the Illness and Death of President Franklin D. Roosevelt," *Annals of Internal Medicine* 72 (1970): 579–559.

6. Stephen Ambrose, *Americans at War* (Jackson: University Press of Mississippi, 1997), 118.

7. Manchester, *American Caesar*, 369.

8. O'Brien, *How the War Was Won*, 401.

9. Richard B. Frank, *Downfall: The End of the Imperial Japanese Empire* (New York: Penguin, 2011), 276.

10. See SCAP and MacArthur, *Reports of General MacArthur*, 1:358, 365.

11. John Adams, *If Mahan Ran the Great Pacific War: An Analysis of World War II Naval Strategy* (Bloomington: Indiana University Press, 2008), 312.

12. King, *Fleet Admiral King*, 566.

13. SCAP and MacArthur, *Reports of General MacArthur*, 1:192.

14. SCAP and MacArthur, *Reports of General MacArthur*, 1:191.

15. Peter Dean, ed., *Australia 1944–45: Victory in the Pacific* (Cambridge: Cambridge University Press, 2015), 9–27.

16. Joseph Connor, "Shore Party: The Truth behind the Famous MacArthur Photo," HistoryNet, www.historynet.com/shore-party-macarthur-photo.htm (accessed November 1, 2021).

17. MacArthur Memorial, "MacArthur's 'I Have Returned Speech.'"
18. Evan Thomas, *Sea of Thunder: Four Commanders and the Last Great Naval Campaign, 1941–1945* (New York: Simon & Schuster, 2006), 244–245.
19. See the discussion of radio communications during the battle in "Calmness, Courage and Efficiency," Naval History and Heritage Command, www.history.navy.mil /browse-by-topic/wars-conflicts-and-operations/world-war-ii/1944/battle-of-leyte -gulf/calmness-courage-and-efficiency.html (accessed January 9, 2021).
20. SCAP and MacArthur, *Reports of General MacArthur*, 1:216, 217.
21. MacArthur, *Reminiscences*, 230.
22. Kenneth Friedman, *Afternoon of the Rising Sun: The Battle of Leyte Gulf* (Novato, CA: Presidio Press, 2001), 263.
23. Samuel Eliot Morison, *History of the United States Naval Operations in World War II, Volume XII*. Boston: Little Brown and Company, 1975, 309.
24. Friedman, *Afternoon of the Rising Sun*, 263.
25. SCAP and MacArthur, *Reports of General MacArthur*, 1:218, 220.
26. Morison, *History of United States Naval Operations in World War II, Volume XII*, 295.
27. Morison, *History of the United States Naval Operations in World War II, Volume XII*, 211–23.
28. Manchester, *American Caesar* (Dell ed.), 459.
29. King, *Fleet Admiral King*, 580.
30. Max Hastings, *Retribution* (New York: Alfred A. Knopf, 2008), 187, 188, 191.
31. McManus, *Island Infernos*, 503.
32. Drea, *MacArthur's Ultra*, 176–178.
33. Eichelberger, *Our Jungle Road to Tokyo*, 340.
34. Manchester, *American Caesar*, 405.
35. GHQ SWPA communique December 26, 1944.
36. McManus, *Island Infernos*, 540–541.
37. Hastings, *Retribution*, 189.

CHAPTER 9: REDEMPTION AND DESTRUCTION

1. Drea, *MacArthur's Ultra*, 186.
2. MacArthur, *Reminiscences*, 126–127.
3. SWPA HQ communique, January 10, 2025.
4. Drea, *MacArthur's Ultra*, 194.
5. Scott, *Rampage*, 133.
6. "Luzon 1944–1945," U.S. Army Center of Military History, p. 11, https://history .army.mil/brochures/luzon/72-28.htm (accessed August 1, 2022).
7. See CriticalPast, "General Douglas MacArthur Visits Santo Tomas University after Liberation by the U.HD Stock Footage," YouTube, June 16, 2014. https://youtube .com/watch?v=R7ypV_wrMBw. (accessed February 1, 2022).
8. GHQ SWPA communique no 1035, 6 February 1945.
9. Eichelberger, *Our Jungle Road to Tokyo*, 369.
10. GHQ SWPA communique no 1039, February 10, 1945.
11. GHQ SWPA communique no 1040, February 11, 1945.
12. GHQ SWPA communique no 1050, February 21, 1945.

13. GHQ SWPA communique no 1051, February 22, 1945.

14. 37th Infantry Division "After Action Report: The Luzon Campaign (M-1 Operation) Part II, 1945," 35, in Caleb Ling, "The Smart City: Achieving Positions of Relative Advantage during Urban Large-Scale Combat Operations" (thesis presented to U.S. Army Command and General Staff College, Fort Leavenworth, Kansas, 2019), https://apps.dtic.mil/sti/pdfs/AD1085100.pdf (accessed August 1, 2022).

15. Scott, *Rampage*, 316.

16. Hastings, *Retribution*, 237.

17. Manchester, *American Caesar*, 414.

18. Hastings, *Retribution*, 239.

19. Stephen Lofgren, *Southern Philippines: The U.S. Army Campaigns of World War II* (Washington, DC: Center of Military History, US Army, 1966), 22.

20. Manchester, *American Caesar*, 428–429.

21. Samuel Eliot Morrison, *The Liberation of the Philippines, Luzon, Mindanao, the Visayas, 1944–1945* (Urbana: University of Illinois Press, 1959), 214.

22. SCAP and MacArthur, *Reports of General MacArthur*, 1:327.

23. Lida Mayo, *The Ordnance Department: On Beachhead and Battlefront* (Washington DC: Center of Military History, United States Army, 1991), 492.

24. Smith, *Triumph in the Philippines*, 692, Appendix H-1.

25. Smith, *Triumph in the Philippines*, 498.

26. SWPA HQ Communique, June 28, 1945.

27. US Chiefs of Staff, "Operations for the Defeat of Japan," in *Argonaut Conference, January–February 1945: Papers and Minutes of Meetings*, ed. Combined Chiefs of Staff (Washington, DC: Combined Chiefs of Staff, 1945), 12, www.JCS.mil/Portals/36/Documents/History/WWII/Argonaut3.pdf (accessed October 1, 2021).

28. King, *Fleet Admiral King*, 575.

29. CINCAFPAC Radio No. C-14442 to WARCOS, April 20, 1945, C/S GHQ, WD No. 982 (TS), as cited in SCAP and MacArthur, *Reports of General MacArthur*, 1:398.

30. Popa, "President Truman Talks about General MacArthur."

31. Frank, *Downfall*, 117–118.

32. Frank, *Downfall*, 276.

33. "Harry S Truman's Decision to Use the Atomic Bomb," National Park Service, www.nps.gov/articles/trumanatomicbomb.htm (accessed February 16, 2022).

34. "Minutes of Meeting Held at the White House on Monday, 18 June 1945," Foreign Relations of the United States: Diplomatic Papers, the Conference of Berlin (the Potsdam Conference), 1945, Volume I, Office of the Historian, U.S. Department of State, https://history.state.gov/historicaldocuments/frus1945Berlinv01/d598 (accessed October 1, 2021).

35. Drea, *MacArthur's Ultra*, 210.

36. D. M. Giangreco, *Hell to Pay: Operation Downfall and the Invasion of Japan, 1945–1947* (Annapolis, MD: Naval Institute Press, 2017), 1.

37. Giangreco, *Hell to Pay*, 107.

38. Frank, *Downfall*, 275.

39. Frank, *Downfall*, 276.
40. MacArthur, *Reminiscences*, 269.
41. Frank, *Downfall*, 276.
42. MacArthur, *Reminiscences*, 270.
43. Eichelberger, *Our Jungle Road to Tokyo*, 488–490.
44. Eichelberger, *Our Jungle Road to Tokyo*, 491.

SECOND RETREAT: SEOUL TO THE NAKTONG

1. Robert Coram, *Brute: The Life of Victor Krulak, U.S. Marine* (New York: Little Brown and Co., 2010), 216.

CHAPTER 10: A NEW WAR

1. Schaller, *Douglas MacArthur*, 123.
2. Note that the U.S. Army Air Force became the U.S. Air Force in 1947.
3. Manchester, *American Caesar*, 555–556.
4. The War Department was renamed the Department of Defense in 1947.
5. Robert Smith, *MacArthur in Korea: The Naked Emperor* (New York: Simon & Schuster, 1982), 59.
6. "Report by the National Security Council to the President," Foreign Relations of the United States, 1949, the Far East and Australasia, Volume VII, Part 2, Office of the Historian, U.S. Department of State, March 22, 1949, https://history.state.gov/historicaldocuments/frus1949v07p2/d209 (accessed December 15, 2021).
7. Dean Acheson, *Present at the Creation: My Years in the State Department* (New York: W. W. Norton & Co., 1969), 357.
8. James Schnabel, *Policy and Direction: The First Year* (Washington, DC: Center of Military History, United States Army, 1992), 55.
9. "Truman Wrote of '48 Offer to Eisenhower," *New York Times*, July 11, 2003, www.nytimes.com/2003/07/11/us/truman-wrote-of-48-offer-to-eisenhower.html (accessed February 25, 2022).
10. Matthew Ridgway, *The Korean War* (New York: Doubleday, 1967), 14.
11. Manchester, *American Caesar*, 543.
12. Donggil Kim and William Stueck, "Did Stalin Lure the United States into the Korean War? New Evidence on the Origins of the Korean War," Wilson Center, August 27, 1950, https://digitalarchive.wilsoncenter.org/document/112225 (accessed February 28, 2022).
13. Manchester, *American Caesar*, 544.
14. Schnabel, *Policy and Direction*, 64.
15. Schnabel, *Policy and Direction*, 64.
16. Schnabel, *Policy and Direction*, 64.
17. Ridgway, *The Korean War*, 14.
18. MacArthur, *Reminiscences*, 330.
19. Manchester, *American Caesar*, 345.
20. Manchester, *American Caesar*, 548–549.
21. Schnabel, *Policy and Direction*, 66.

22. "Letter from Filipov (Stalin) to Soviet Ambassador in Prague, Conveying Message to CSSR Leader Klement Gottwald," Wilson Center, August 27, 1950, https://digitalarchive.wilsoncenter.org/document/112225 (accessed March 1, 2022).
23. Manchester, *American Caesar*, 554.
24. Schnabel, *Policy and Direction*, 77.
25. Schnabel, *Policy and Direction*, 78.
26. MacArthur, *Reminiscences*, 333.
27. T. R. Fehrenbach, *This Kind of War: The Classic Korean War History* (Washington, DC: Brassey's, 1994), 108.
28. Smith, *MacArthur in Korea*, 67.
29. Clay Brair, *The Forgotten War* (New York: Doubleday, 1987), 89; Roy Edgar Appleman, *South to the Naktong, North to the Yalu* (Washington, DC: Center of Military History, United States Army, 1961), 381.
30. MacArthur, *Reminiscences*, 335–336.
31. Smith, *MacArthur in Korea*, 66.
32. Smith, *MacArthur in Korea*, 67.
33. MacArthur, *Reminiscences*, 336.
34. Fehrenbach, *This Kind of War*, 75.
35. Fehrenbach, *This Kind of War*, 78.
36. Appleman, *South to the Naktong*, 179–180.
37. Appleman, *South to the Naktong*, 179–181.
38. Appleman, *South to the Naktong*, 180.
39. Fehrenbach, *This Kind of War*, 103.
40. Appleman, *South to the Naktong*, 383.
41. MacArthur, *Reminiscences*, 336.
42. Schnabel, *Policy and Direction*, 78.
43. "The Outbreak: Campaign," *The Korean War*, U.S. Army Center of Military History, https://history.army.mil/html/bookshelves/resmat/korea/part01/sec01.html#lg=1&slide=1.
44. Appleman, *South to the Naktong*, 190–192, 382–383; Brair, *The Forgotten War*, 172.
45. Appleman, *South to the Naktong*, 186.
46. Brair, *The Forgotten War*, 141.
47. Brair, *The Forgotten War*, 115.
48. Appleman, *South to the Naktong*, 208.
49. Appleman, *South to the Naktong*, 209.

LAST ADVANCE: INCHON TO THE YALU

1. Jussi Hanhimaki, ed., *The Routledge Handbook of Transatlantic Security* (London: Routledge Taylor & Francis Group, 2010), 31.

CHAPTER 11: INCHON

1. Ridgway, *The Korean War*, 38.
2. Bernard Duffy and Ronald Carpenter, *Douglas MacArthur: Warrior as Wordsmith* (Westport, CT: Greenwood Press, 1997), 85.

3. "Commandership at the Chosin Reservoir: A Triumph of Optimism and Resilience," Marine Corps University, November 2018, p. 30, www.usmcu.edu/Portals/218/LLI/MLD/Commandership%20at%20the%20Chosin%20Reservoir%20%2019%20Feb%2019.pdf?ver=2019-02-19-093922-057 (accessed April 18, 202022).

4. D. Clayton James, "General John H. Chiles Oral History Interview," Harry S Truman Library, https://trumanlibrary.gov/library/oral-histories/chilesj (accessed May 22, 2022).

5. Brair, *The Forgotten War*, 32.

6. Coram, *Brute*, 199.

7. Schnabel, *Policy and Direction*, 216.

8. Joseph Lawton Collins, *War in Peacetime: The History and Lessons of Korea* (Boston: Houghton Mifflin, 1969), 115.

9. Manchester, *American Caesar* (Dell ed.), 686.

10. Samuel Wells, "The Korean War," in Hanhimaki, *The Routledge Handbook of Transatlantic Security*, 27.

11. John Toland, *In Mortal Combat* (New York: Morrow, 1991), 179.

12. Appleman, *South to the Naktong*, 494–495.

13. MacArthur, *Reminiscences*, 351.

14. MacArthur Memorial, "Outgoing message GHQ Far East Command, September 8, 1950." https://macarthurmemorial.org/DocumentCenter/View/561 (accessed April 13, 2022).

15. Coram, *Brute*, 207.

16. MacArthur, *Reminiscences*, 376.

17. Harry S Truman, *Memoirs by Harry S Truman*, vol. 2: *Years of Trial and Hope* (New York: Doubleday & Co., 1956), 348.

18. "Biographies: Douglas Macarthur," Wilson Center Digital Archive, https://digitalarchive.wilsoncenter.org/resource/cold-war-history/douglas-macarthur (accessed October 13, 2021).

19. "Extracts of a Memorandum of Conversations, by Mr. W. Averell Harriman, Special Assistant to the President, with General MacArthur in Tokyo on August 6 and 8," Foreign Relations of the United States, 1950, East Asia and the Pacific, Volume VI, Office of the Historian, U.S. Department of State, 1950, https://history.state.gov/historicaldocuments/frus1950v06/d253 (accessed October 13, 2021).

20. Truman, *Years of Trial and Hope*, 351.

21. Chen Jian, *China's Road to the Korean War* (New York: Columbia University Press, 1996), 136.

22. Chen, *China's Road to the Korean War*, 138.

23. Chen, *China's Road to the Korean War*, 139.

24. Chen, *China's Road to the Korean War*, 144–145.

25. Chen, *China's Road to the Korean War*, 146.

26. "The Secretary of State to Certain Diplomatic Offices," Foreign Relations of the United States, 1950, East Asia and the Pacific, Volume VI, Office of the Historian, U.S. Department of State, August 26, 1950, https://history.state.gov/historicaldocuments/frus1950v06/d266 (accessed October 13, 2021).

27. Truman, *Years of Trial and Hope*, 355–356.
28. "MacArthur 'Directed' to Withdraw Message on Formosa to V.F.W.," *New York Times*, August 28, 1950, https://timesmachine.nytimes.com/timesmachine/1950/08/28/91633716.html?pageNumber=1) (accessed October 13, 2021).
29. Harvey Stockwin, "MacArthur's Audacious Landing at Inchon Astounded Everyone—except Mao," *Japan Times*, September 21, 2000, www.japantimes.co.jp/opinion/2000/09/21/commentary/world-commentary/macarthurs-audacious-landing-at-inchon-astounded-everyone-except-mao (accessed November 4, 2021).
30. Manchester, *American Caesar*, 580.
31. Ridgway, *The Korean War*, 31.
32. Joseph H. Alexander, "Battle of the Barricades: U.S. Marines in the Recapture of Seoul," Marines in the Korean War Commemorative Series, Marines: Official U.S. Marine Corps Website, 2000, p. 32, www.marines.mil/Portals/59/Publications/BATTLE%20OF%20THE%20BARRICADES%20U.S.%20Marines%20in%20the%20Recapture%20of%20Seoul%20%20PCN%2019000315200_1.pdf?ver=2012-10-11-164225-087 (accessed April 22, 2022).
33. Appleman, *South to the Naktong*, 606.
34. Appleman, *South to the Naktong*, 605–606.

CHAPTER 12: TO DESTROY THE ENEMY

1. Collins, *War in Peacetime*, 82–83.
2. Francis Sempa, "George Kennan's Other Long Telegram—About the Far East," *The Diplomat*, December 5, 2017, https://thediplomat.com/2017/12/george-kennans-other-long-telegram-about-the-far-east (accessed November 4, 2021).
3. "The Acting Secretary of State to the United States Mission at the United Nations," Office of the Historian, U.S. Department of State, September 26, 1950, https://history.state.gov/historicaldocuments/frus1950v07/d543 (accessed April 23, 2022).
4. MacArthur, *Reminiscences*, 358.
5. Chen, *China's Road to the Korean War*, 164.
6. Appleman, *South to the Naktong*, 608.
7. Chen, *China's Road to the Korean War*, 169.
8. MacArthur, *Reminiscences*, 359.
9. Appleman, *South to the Naktong*, 610. Also see "H-055-1: Wonsan: October–November 1950," Naval History and Heritage Command, www.history.navy.mil/about-us/leadership/director/directors-corner/h-grams/h-gram-055/h-055-1.html (accessed April 23, 2022).
10. See "Korean Peninsula 1950 Road and City Map," Battle Archives, https://battlearchives.com/collections/korea (accessed April 23, 2022).
11. See "The Korean War Chronology," US Army Center of Military History, https://history.army.mil/reference/korea/kw-chrono.htm (accessed April 25, 2022).
12. Truman, *Years of Trial and Hope*, 362–363.
13. Michael David Pearlman, *Truman and MacArthur: Policy, Politics, and the Hunger for Honor and Renown* (Bloomington: Indiana University Press, 2008), 112–113.

14. "Substance of Statements Made at Wake Island Conference Compiled by General of the Army Omar N. Bradley, Chairman, J.C.S."; Appleman, *South to the Naktong*, 760.

15. Spencer Tucker, ed., *The Encyclopedia of the Korean War* (Santa Barbara, CA: ABC-CLIO, 2010), 1:979.

16. Hanhimaki, *The Routledge Handbook of Transatlantic Security*, 31.

17. Chen, *China's Road to the Korean War*, 206–208.

18. Appleman, *South to the Naktong*, 670.

19. Ridgway, *The Korean War*, 61.

20. Ridgway, *The Korean War*, 62.

21. David Halberstam, "MacArthur's Grant Delusion," *Vanity Fair*, September 24, 2007, www.vanityfair.com/news/2007/10/halberstam200710 (accessed May 2, 2022).

22. Brair, *The Forgotten War*, 384.

23. Richard Stewart, "The Chinese Intervention," Korean War Commemorative Brochure Series, U.S. Army Center of Military History, p. 14, https://history.army.mil /brochures/kw-chinter/chinter.htm (accessed May 11, 2022); also see, Appleman, *South to the Naktong*, 707–708.

24. MacArthur, *Reminiscences*, 365.

25. Truman, *Years of Trial and Hope*, 373.

26. Schnabel, *Policy and Direction*, 243.

27. "The Joint Chiefs of Staff to the Commander in Chief, Far East (MacArthur)," Foreign Relations of the United States, 1950, Korea, Volume VII, Office of the Historian, US Department of State, November 6, 1950, https://history.state.gov /historicaldocuments/frus1950v07/d758.

28. Edward Daily, *MacArthur's X Corps in Korea: Inchon to the Yalu, 1950* (Paducah, KY: Turner Publishing Company, 1999), 57.

29. MacArthur, *Reminiscences*, 368.

30. MacArthur, *Reminiscences*, 371, 373.

31. "The Commander in Chief, Far East (MacArthur) to the Joint Chiefs of Staff," Office of the Historian, U.S. Department of State, Foreign Relations of the United States, 1950, Korea, Volume VII, November 9, 1950, https://history.state.gov/his toricaldocuments/frus1950v07/d792 (accessed May 1, 2022).

32. Schnabel, *Policy and Direction*, 259.

33. Ridgway, *The Korean War*, 60.

34. Roy Appleman, *Disaster in Korea: The Chinese Confront MacArthur* (College Station: Texas A&M University Press, 1989), 57.

35. Ridgway, *The Korean War*, 60.

36. Appleman, *South to the Naktong*, 752.

37. MacArthur, *Reminiscences*, 366.

38. Appleman, *South to the Naktong*, 767–769.

39. Toland, *In Mortal Combat*, 279.

40. Schnabel, *Policy and Direction*, 257.

41. Ridgway, *The Korean War*, 63.

LAST RETREAT: FROM THE YALU TO THE POTOMAC

1. Merle Miller, *Plain Speaking: An Oral Biography of Harry S Truman* (New York: Berkley Publishing Corp., 1974), 327.

CHAPTER 13: THERE IS NO SUBSTITUTE FOR VICTORY!

1. Toland, *In Mortal Combat*, 282.

2. Daily, *MacArthur's X Corps in Korea*, 83.

3. Shen Zhihua, "Revisiting Stalin's and Mao's Motivations in the Korean War," Wilson Center, June 22, 2020, www.wilsoncenter.org/blog-post/revisiting-stalins -and-maos-motivations-korean-war (accessed November 4, 2021); also see Chen, *China's Road to the Korean War*, 204.

4. Toland, *In Mortal Combat*, 272.

5. MacArthur, *Reminiscences*, 374.

6. Billy Mossman, *Ebb and Flow* (Washington, DC: Center of Military History, United States Army, 1990), 65–73.

7. Appleman, *Disaster in Korea*, 213.

8. "The Joint Chiefs of Staff to the Commander in Chief, Far East (MacArthur)," Foreign Relations of the United States, 1950, Korea, Volume VII, Office of the Historian, US Department of State, November 29, 1950, https://history.state.gov /historicaldocuments/frus1950v07/d898 (accessed May 5, 2022).

9. "The Commander in Chief, United Nations Command (MacArthur) to the Joint Chiefs of Staff," Foreign Relations of the United States, 1950, Korea, Volume VII, Office of the Historian, US Department of State, November 30, 1950, https://his tory.state.gov/historicaldocuments/frus1950v07/d906 (accessed May 5, 2022).

10. "The Commander in Chief, United Nations Command (MacArthur) to the Joint Chiefs of Staff," Foreign Relations of the United States, 1950, Korea, Volume VII, Office of the Historian, US Department of State, December 3, 1950, https://history .state.gov/historicaldocuments/frus1950v07/d947 (accessed May 8, 2022).

11. Toland, *In Mortal Combat*, 310.

12. MacArthur, *Reminiscences*, 374.

13. Manchester, *American Caesar* (Dell ed.), 729.

14. Richard Echker, *Korean Battle Chronology: Unit-by-Unit United States Casualty Figures and Medal of Honor Citations* (Jefferson, NC: McFarland & Co., 2004), 62.

15. "The Commander in Chief, United Nations Command (MacArthur) to the Joint Chiefs of Staff," December 3, 1950.

16. Richard Ruetten, "The Rationalization of a Defeat in Korea," *Pacific Historical Review* 36, no. 1 (February 1967): 79–93.

17. MacArthur, *Reminiscences*, 377.

18. Mossman, *Ebb and Flow*, 23.

19. Mossman, *Ebb and Flow*, 53–55.

20. Edwin Simmons, *Frozen Chosin: U.S. Marines at the Changjin Reservoir* (New York: St. John's Press, 2018), 48.

CHAPTER 14: STALEMATE

1. MacArthur, *Reminiscences*, 378.
2. Truman, *Years of Trial and Hope*, 415–416.
3. MacArthur, *Reminiscences*, 334–335.
4. Ridgway, *The Korean War*, 83.
5. Collins, *War in Peacetime*, 249.
6. Collins, *War in Peacetime*, 252.
7. Ridgway, *The Korean War*, 89.
8. Collins, *War in Peacetime*, 249.
9. Collins, *War in Peacetime*, 251–255.
10. Fehrenbach, *This Kind of War*, 266.
11. Collins, *War in Peacetime*, 279.
12. Truman, *Years of Trial and Hope*, 381–384.
13. Neil Johnson, "Charles Burton Marshall Oral History Interview," Harry S Truman Library, June 21, 23, 1989, trumanlibrary.gov/library/oral-histories/marshall (accessed May 9, 2022).
14. Mossman, *Ebb and Flow*, 344.
15. "The Secretary of State to Certain Diplomatic Offices," Foreign Relations of the United States, 1950, Korea, Volume VII, Part 1, Office of the Historian, US Department of State, March 24, 1951, https://history.state.gov/historicaldocuments/frus1951v07p1/d184 (accessed October 14, 2021).
16. MacArthur, *Reminiscences*, 387–389.
17. Truman, *Years of Trial and Hope*, 441–442.
18. Copy of letter from Gen. Douglas MacArthur to Rep. Joseph William Martin Jr. of Massachusetts, March 20, 1951, U.S. Capital Visitor Center, www.visitthecapitol.gov/exhibitions/artifact/copy-letter-general-douglas-macarthur-representative-joseph-william-martin-jr (accessed October 14, 2021).
19. Peter Grier, "Three Military Commanders before General McChrystal Who Got the Ax," *Christian Science Monitor*, June 23, 2010, www.csmonitor.com/USA/Politics/2010/0623/Three-military-commanders-before-General-McChrystal-who-got-the-ax (accessed May 9, 2020).
20. Collins, *War in Peacetime*, 281.
21. "Statement and Order by the President on Relieving General MacArthur of His Commands," Truman Library, April 11, 1951, www.trumanlibrary.gov/library/public-papers/77/statement-and-order-president-relieving-general-macarthur-his-commands (accessed May 10, 2022).
22. Ridgway, *The Korean War*, 142.
23. See the Korean War fatality extract data file at the National Archives, https://aad.archives.gov/aad/display-partial-records.jsp?s=4552&dt=2512&tf=F&bc=%2Csl%2Cfd&q=1951&btnSearch=Search&as_alq=&as_anq=&as_epq=&as_woq= (Accessed May 10, 2022); also see daily combat fatalities by year at the Korean War Project, www.koreanwar.org/chart/2014-kccf1-line-chart.html?ch_id=22&svc_cook=ALL (accessed May 10, 2022).

24. Full text and video of MacArthur's address to Congress can be found at "General Douglas MacArthur: Farewell Address to Congress," American Rhetoric, www .americanrhetoric.com/speeches/douglasmacarthurfarewelladdress.htm (accessed May 12, 2022).

25. "Report to the American People on Korea," Miller Center at the University of Virginia, April 11, 1951, https://millercenter.org/the-presidency/presidential-speeches /april-11-1951-report-american-people-korea.

26. "Constitutional Crisis Averted," United States Senate, May 3, 1951, www.senate .gov/artandhistory/history/minute/Constitutional_Crisis_Averted.htm (accessed May 20, 2022).

27. "Senate Hearings on Korea," American Experience, www.pbs.org/wgbh/ameri canexperience/features/macarthur-senate-hearings-korea.

28. Congressional Record Vol. 97, pt. 4, April 26, 1951–May 24, 1951 (Washington, DC: U.S. Government Printing Office, 1951), 5043.

29. Congressional Record Vol. 97, pt. 4, 5044.

30. Collins, War in Peacetime, 291.

31. Military Situation in the Far East: Hearings before the Committee on Armed Services and the Committee on Foreign Relations, United States Senate (Washington, DC: U.S. Government Printing Office, 1951), 732.

32. "Senate Hearings on Korea," American Experience, www.pbs.org/wgbh/americanex perience/features/macarthur-senate-hearings-korea (accessed May 20, 2022).

33. Military Situation in the Far East, 312.

34. John Dower, War without Mercy: Race and Power in the Pacific War (New York: Parthenon Books, 1986), 303–304.

35. "Pentagon Weighed Plan to Use Cobalt in Korea," New York Times, April 9, 1964.

36. "Text of Accounts by Lucas and Considine on Interviews with MacArthur in 1954," New York Times, April 9, 1964.

37. "Text of Accounts by Lucas and Considine on Interviews with MacArthur in 1954."

CONCLUSION

1. MacArthur, Reminiscences, 101.

SELECTED BIBLIOGRAPHY

Acheson, Dean. *Present at the Creation: My Years in the State Department*. New York: W. W. Norton & Company, 1969.

Adams, John A. *If Mahan Ran the Great Pacific War: An Analysis of World War II Naval Strategy*. Bloomington: Indiana University Press, 2008.

Alexander, Joseph. "Battle of the Barricades U.S. Marines in the Recapture of Seoul PCN 19000315200_1." *Marines in the Korean War Commemorative Journal*, n.d. Accessed April 22, 2022.

Ambrose, Stephen E. *Americans at War*. Jackson: University Press of Mississippi, 1997.

———. *Eisenhower: Soldier and President*. New York: Simon & Schuster, 1990.

Appleman, Roy E. *Disaster in Korea: The Chinese Confront MacArthur*. College Station: Texas A&M University Press, 1989.

Appleman, Roy Edgar. *South to the Naktong, North to the Yalu: June–November 1950*. Washington, DC: Center of Military History, U.S. Army, 1961.

"April 11, 1951: Report to the American People on Korea." Miller Center at the University of Virginia. October 20, 2016. https://millercenter.org/the-presidency/presidential-speeches/april-11-1951-report-american-people-korea.

Archive, Wilson Center Digital. "Wilson Center Digital Archive." Wilson Center. Accessed February 28, 2022. https://digitalarchive.wilsoncenter.org/document/112225.

Bartsch, William H. *December 8, 1941: MacArthur's Pearl Harbor*. College Station: Texas A&M University Press, 2012.

Bix, Herbert P. *Hirohito and the Making of Modern Japan*. New York: Harper Collins, 2009.

Blair, Clay. *The Forgotten War: America in Korea, 1950–1953*. New York: Doubleday, 1987.

Brereton, Lewis Hyde. *The Brereton Diaries: The War in the Air in the Pacific, Middle East and Europe, 3 October 1941–8 May 1945*. New York: De Capo Press, 1946.

Bruenn, Howard. "Clinical Notes on the Illness and Death of President Franklin D. Roosevelt." *Annals of Internal Medicine* 72, no. 4 (April 1, 1970): 579. https://doi.org/10.7326/0003-4819-72-4-579.

Bryan, J., and William F. Halsey. *Admiral Halsey's Story*. New York: Whittlesey House, 1947.

Budge, Kent G. "Parafrag Bombs." Pacific War Online Encyclopedia. http://pwencycl.kgbudge.com/P/a/Parafrag_Bombs.htm (accessed November 8, 2021).

Budiansky, Stephen. *Battle of Wits: The Complete Story of Codebreaking in World War II*. New York: Simon & Schuster, 2000.

Caldwell, Donald L. *Thunder on Bataan: The First American Tank Battles of World War II*. Lanham, MD: Stackpole, 2019.

"'Calmness, Courage, and Efficiency': Remembering the Battle of Leyte Gulf." Naval History and Heritage Command. https://history.navy.mil/browse-by-topic/wars-conflicts-and-operations/world-war-ii/1944/battle-of-leyte-gulf/calmness-courage-and-efficiency.html (accessed August 29, 2022).

Collins, Joseph Lawton. *War in Peacetime: The History and Lessons of Korea*. Boston: Houghton Mifflin, 1969.

"Congressional Record." In *Congress A to Z*. Washington, DC: CQ Press, 2008. http://dx.doi.org/10.4135/9781483300498.n91.

Connaughton, Richard. *MacArthur and Defeat in the Philippines*. New York: Overlook Press, 2001.

Connor, Joseph. "Shore Party: The Truth behind the Famous MacArthur Photo." HistoryNet. December 14, 2016. www.historynet.com/shore-party-macarthur-photo.htm.

"Copy of Letter from General Douglas MacArthur to Representative Joseph William Martin Jr. of Massachusetts, March 20, 1951." U.S. Capitol Visitor Center. March 5, 1951. https://visitthecapitol.gov/exhibitions/artifact/copy-letter-general-douglas-macarthur-representative-joseph-william-martin-jr.

Coram, Robert. *Brute: The Life of Victor Krulak, U.S. Marine*. New York: Little Brown & Co., 2010.

Correll, John. "Disaster in the Philippines." *Air Force Magazine*. November 1, 2019. www.airforcemag.com/article/disaster-in-the-philippines.

CriticalPast. "General Douglas MacArthur Visits Santo Tomas University after Liberation by the UHD Stock Footage." Video. YouTube. June 16, 2014. www.youtube.com/watch?v=R7ypV_wrMBw.

D'Este, Carlo. *Eisenhower: A Soldier's Life*. New York: Holt Paperbacks, 2002.

Daily, Edward. *MacArthur's X Corps in Korea: Inchon to the Yalu, 1950*. Paducah, KY: Turner Publishing Company, 1999.

Dean, Peter J. *Australia 1944–45: Victory in the Pacific*. Cambridge: Cambridge University Press, 2015.

Dickson, Paul. "The Bonus Army." Bill of Rights Institute. https://billofrightsinstitute.org/essays/the-bonus-army (accessed November 26, 2021).

Dower, John. *War without Mercy: Race and Power in the Pacific War*. New York: Pantheon, 1986.

Drea, Edward J. *MacArthur's Ultra: Codebreaking and the War against Japan, 1942–1945*. Lawrence: University of Kansas Press, 1992.

DuBois, David. "Admiral Thomas C. Hart and the Demise of the Asiatic Fleet 1941–1942." Paper 2331. Electronic Theses and Dissertations. May 2014. https://dc.etsu.edu/etd/2331.

Duffy, Bernard K., and Ronald H. Carpenter. *Douglas MacArthur: Warrior as Wordsmith*. Westport, CT: Greenwood Publishing Group, 1997.

Ecker, Richard E. *Korean Battle Chronology: Unit-by-Unit United States Casualty Figures and Medal of Honor Citations*. Jefferson, NC: McFarland, 2004.

Eichelberger, Robert L. *Dear Miss Em: General Eichelberger's War in the Pacific, 1942–1945*. Westport, CT: Greenwood Press, 1972.

———. *Our Jungle Road to Tokyo*. Mount Pleasant, SC: Arcadia Press, 1950.

Eisenhower, Dwight David. *Crusade in Europe*. Baltimore: Johns Hopkins University Press, 1997.

"Eisenhower Diary Said to Assail MacArthur and Adm. King in '42; Earlier Excerpts in Book." *New York Times*. September 19, 1979. https://timesmachine.nytimes.com/timesmachine/1979/09/19/111062219.html?pageNumber=16.

Eno, Brian. "The Whipsaw at Work: U.S. Mastery in Sequential and Cumulative Operations in the Pacific War." Defense Technical Information Center. May 4, 2018. https://apps.dtic.mil/sti/citations/AD1061990.

Fehrenbach, T. R. *This Kind of War: The Classic Korean War History*. Washington, DC: Brassey's, 1994.

Fleming, Thomas. "The Big Leak." *American Heritage*. December 1987. https://americanheritage.com/big-leak.

"Foreign Relations of the United States: Diplomatic Papers, the Conference of Berlin (The Potsdam Conference), 1945, Volume I." Office of the Historian, Department of State. https://history.state.gov/historicaldocuments/frus1945Berlinv01/d598 (accessed October 1, 2021).

Frank, Richard B. *MacArthur: A Biography*. New York: Palgrave MacMillan, 2007.

———. "The MacArthur No One Knew." HistoryNet. August 13, 2018. www.historynet.com/macarthur-no-one-knew.

Frank, Richard. *Tower of Skulls: A History of the Asia-Pacific War.* Vol. 1: *July 1937–May 1942.* New York: W. W. Norton, 2020.

Frei, Henry P. *Japan's Southward Advance and Australia: From the Sixteenth Century to World War II.* Honolulu: University of Hawaii Press, 1991.

Friedman, Kenneth I. *Afternoon of the Rising Sun: The Battle of Leyte Gulf.* Novato, CA: Presidio Press, 2001.

"General Douglas MacArthur—Farewell Address to Congress." American Rhetoric. www.americanrhetoric.com/speeches/douglasmacarthurfarewelladdress.htm (accessed May 12, 2022).

Giangreco, D. M. *Hell to Pay: Operation DOWNFALL and the Invasion of Japan, 1945–1947.* Annapolis, MD: Naval Institute Press, 2017.

Glusman, John A. *Conduct under Fire: Four American Doctors and Their Fight for Life as Prisoners of the Japanese, 1941–1945.* New York: Penguin, 2005.

Greaves, Percy L., Jr. *Pearl Harbor: The Seeds and Fruits of Infamy.* Auburn, AL: Ludwig von Mises Institute, 2010.

Grey, Jeffrey. *A Military History of Australia.* Cambridge: Cambridge University Press, 2008.

Grier, Peter. "Three Military Commanders before General McChrystal Who Got the Ax." *Christian Science Monitor.* June 23, 2010. https://csmonitor.com/USA/Politics/2010/0623/Three-military-commanders-before-General-McChrystal-who-got-the-ax.

"Guadalcanal: Naval Battles." Naval History and Heritage Command. www.history.navy.mil/content/history/museums/nmusn/explore/photography/wwii/wwii-pacific/wwii-pacific-guadalancanal/naval-battles.html (accessed January 17, 2022).

"H-008-5 Admiral Ernest J. King." Naval History and Heritage Command. www.history.navy.mil/about-us/leadership/director/directors-corner/h-grams/h-gram-008/h-008-5.html (accessed December 14, 2021).

Halberstam, David. "MacArthur's Grand Delusion." *Vanity Fair.* September 24, 2007. www.vanityfair.com/news/2007/10/halberstam200710.

Hanhimäki, Jussi, Georges-Henri Soutou, and Basil Germond. *The Routledge Handbook of Transatlantic Security.* London: Routledge, 2010.

"Harry S Truman's Decision to Use the Atomic Bomb (U.S. National Park Service)." National Park Service. https://nps.gov/articles/trumanatomic-bomb.htm (accessed February 16, 2022).

Hastings, Max. *Retribution: The Battle for Japan, 1944–45.* New York: Alfred A. Knopf Inc., 2008.

Heinrichs, Waldo, and Marc Gallicchio. *Implacable Foes: War in the Pacific, 1944–1945.* Oxford: Oxford University Press, 2017.

Histon, John, ed. *American Airpower Comes of Age: General Henry H. "Hap" Arnold's World War II Diaries*. Vol. 1. Maxwell Air Force Base, AL: Air University Press, 2002.

Hoffman, Wally. "We Get Our Feet Wet." Preservation Foundation. http://storyhouse.org/wally6.html (accessed November 22, 2021).

Homer, David. "High Command and the Kokoda Campaign." Australian War Memorial. Last updated November 1, 2019. www.awm.gov.au/visit/events/conference/remembering-1942/horner.

Hotta, Eri. *Japan 1941: Countdown to Infamy*. New York: Vintage, 2013.

Imparato, Ed. *General MacArthur: Speeches and Reports, 1908–1964*. Nashville: Turner Publishing Company, 2000.

James, D. Clayton. "General John H. Chiles Oral History Interview." Harry S Truman Library. https://trumanlibrary.gov/library/oral-histories/chilesj (accessed May 22, 2022).

James, Dorris Clayton. *The Years of MacArthur: 1880–1941*. New York: Houghton Mifflin, 1970.

Jian, Chen. *China's Road to the Korean War: The Making of the Sino-American Confrontation*. New York: Columbia University Press, 1996.

Jowett, Philip. *The Japanese Army 1931–45*. Vol. 2: *1942–45*. Oxford, UK: Osprey Publishing, 2002.

Kenney, George. *General Kenney Reports: A Personal History of the Pacific War*. Washington, DC: Office of the Air Force History, 1949.

King, Ernest Joseph, and Walter Muir Whitehill. *Fleet Admiral King: A Naval Record*. New York: W. W. Norton & Co., 1952.

"The Korean War: The Chinese Intervention." U.S. Army Center for Military History. https://history.army.mil/brochures/kw-chinter/chinter.htm (accessed May 11, 2022).

"Korean War Casualty Chart." Korean War Project. www.koreanwar.org/chart/2014-kccf1-line-chart.html (accessed August 29, 2022).

Krueger, Gen. Walter. *From Down Under to Nippon: The Story of the 6th Army in World War II*. Lawrence, KS: Zegner, 1953.

Larrabee, Eric. *Commander in Chief: Franklin Delano Roosevelt, His Lieutenants and Their War*. New York: Harper & Row, 2019.

Linn, Brian McAllister. *Guardians of Empire: The U.S. Army and the Pacific, 1902–1940*. Chapel Hill: University of North Carolina Press, 1997.

Lofgren, Stephen. *Southern Philippines: The U.S. Army Campaigns of World War II*. Washington, DC: Center of Military History, United States Army, 1966.

"Luzon 1944–1945." U.S. Army Center of Military History. https://history.army.mil/brochures/luzon/72-28.htm (accessed July 1, 2021).

"[Maj.] Gen. Courtney Whitney, 71, Adviser to MacArthur, Is Dead; Confidant during Occupation of Japan and in Korean War—Spokesman at Inquiry." *New York Times*. March 22, 1969. https://timesmachine.nytimes.com/timesmachine/1969/03/22/90073413.html?pageNumber=33.

"M'Arthur Denies Brereton Report; Says He Received No Request from Air Officer in 1941 to Bomb Foe on Formosa Defends Strategy at Time Declares His Assignment Was to Hold the Philippines, Not Attack Japanese." *New York Times*. September 28, 1946. https://timesmachine.nytimes.com/timesmachine/1946/09/28/93155277.html?pageNumber=6.

MacArthur Memorial, All SWPA HQ Daily Communiques quoted.

MacArthur Memorial. "MacArthur's 'I Have Returned' Speech." Video. YouTube. October 9, 2018. www.youtube.com/watch?v=ptVKbN27_4g.

MacArthur Memorial, "Outgoing message GHQ Far East Command, September 8, 1950." https://macarthurmemorial.org/DocumentCenter/View/561.

MacArthur, Douglas. *Reminiscences: General Douglas MacArthur*. New York: McGraw-Hill Books, 1964.

Macdougall, Robert. *Leaders in Dangerous Times: Douglas MacArthur and Dwight D. Eisenhower*. Bloomington, ID: Trafford Publishing, 2013.

Manchester, William. *American Caesar*. New York: Dell, 1981.

Matloff, Maurice, and Edwin Marion Snell. *Strategic Planning for Coalition Warfare, 1941–1942 [–1943–1944]*. Washington, DC: Office of the Chief of Military History, Department of the Army, 1953.

McManus, John C. *Island Infernos: The US Army's Pacific War Odyssey, 1944*. New York: Calibur, 2021.

Miller, Edward. *War Plan Orange: The U.S. Strategy to Defeat Japan, 1897–1945*. 1991. Reprint, Annapolis, MD: Naval Institute Press, 2013.

Miller, John. *Cartwheel: The Reduction of Rabaul*. Washington, DC: Center of Military History, United States Army, 1959.

———. *Guadalcanal: The First Offensive: The War in the Pacific*. Washington, DC: Center of Military History, United States Army, 1995.

Miller, Merle. *Plain Speaking: An Oral Biography of Harry S Truman*. New York: Berkley Publishing Corp., 1974.

Morison, Samuel Eliot. *History of United States Naval Operations in World War II, Volume XII, Leyte June 1944-January 1945*. New York: Little, Brown & Co, Boston, 1975.

———. *The Liberation of the Philippines, Luzon, Mindanao, the Visayas, 1944–1945*. Urbana: University of Illinois Press, 1959.

Morton, Louis. *The Fall of the Philippines*. Washington, DC: Center of Military History, United States Army, 1953.

Mossman, Billy C., and Center of Military History. *Ebb and Flow: November 1950–July 1951*. Washington, DC: Center of Military History, United States Army, 1990.

O'Brien, Phillips Payson. *How the War Was Won: Air-Sea Power and Allied Victory in World War II.* Cambridge: Cambridge University Press, 2015.

O'Neill, William L. *A Democracy at War: America's Fight at Home and Abroad in World War II.* Cambridge, MA: Harvard University Press, 1993.

"The Outbreak: Campaign—The Korean War Era." U.S. Army Center of Military History. https://history.army.mil/html/bookshelves/resmat/korea/part01/sec01.html#lg=1&slide=1 (accessed August 29, 2022).

Pearlman, Michael D. *Truman and MacArthur: Policy, Politics, and the Hunger for Honor and Renown.* Bloomington: Indiana University Press, 2008.

Perry, Mark. *The Most Dangerous Man in America: The Making of Douglas MacArthur.* New York: Basic Books, 2015.

Popa, Ovidiu. "President Truman Talks about General MacArthur: A Cheater and a Bighead." War History Online. May 12, 2015. www.warhistoryonline.com/articles/president-truman-talks-general-macarthur-cheater-bighead.html.

Prados, John. "Secrecy and Leaks: When the U.S. Government Prosecuted the Chicago Tribune." National Security Archive. October 25, 2017. https://nsarchive.gwu.edu/briefing-book/intelligence/2017-10-25/secrecy-leaks-when-us-government-prosecuted-chicago-tribune.

Ray, Michael. "Pearl Harbor in Context." *Encyclopedia Britannica.* https://britannica.com/story/pearl-harbor-in-context (accessed December 16, 2021).

Ridgway, Matthew B. *The Korean War.* New York: Doubleday, 1967.

Rottman, Gordon L. *The Marshall Islands 1944: Operation Flintlock, the Capture of Kwajalein and Eniwetok.* Oxford, UK: Osprey Publishing, 2004.

Rovere, Richard Halworth. *General MacArthur and President Truman: The Struggle for Control of American Foreign Policy.* New Brunswick, NJ: Transaction Publishers, 1992.

Ruetten, Richard T. "General Douglas MacArthur's 'Reconnaissance in Force': The Rationalization of a Defeat in Korea." *Pacific Historical Review* 36, no. 1 (February 1, 1967): 79–93. https://doi.org/10.2307/3637092.

Runkle, Benjamin. *Generals in the Making: How Marshall, Eisenhower, Patton, and Their Peers Became the Commanders Who Won World War II.* Lanham, MD: Stackpole Books, 2019.

Schaller, Michael. *Douglas MacArthur: The Far Eastern General.* New York: Oxford University Press, 1989.

Schnabel, James F. *Policy and Direction: The First Year.* Washington, DC: Center of Military History, United States Army, 1992.

Schom, Alan. *Eagle and the Rising Sun: The Japanese American War, 1941–1943, Pearl Harbor through Guadalcanal.* New York: W. W. Norton & Company, 2004.

Scott, James M. *Rampage: MacArthur, Yamashita, and the Battle of Manila*. New York: W. W. Norton & Company, 2018.

Sellwood, Arthur V., and Ulrich Mohr. *Ship 16: The Story of the Secret German Raider Atlantis*. New York: John Day Company, 1956.

Sempa, Francis. "George Kennan's Other Long Telegram—About the Far East." *The Diplomat*. December 5, 2017. https://thediplomat.com/2017/12/george-kennans-other-long-telegram-about-the-far-east.

"Senate Hearings on Korea." *American Experience*. July 9, 2018. https://pbs.org/wgbh/americanexperience/features/macarthur-senate-hearings-korea.

Sharkey, John. "The MacArthur Mutiny." *Washington Post*. December 5, 1993. www.washingtonpost.com/archive/opinions/1993/12/05/the-macarthur-mutiny/6e05abdb-ece1-46a4-b672-523c56ca5f4f.

Sides, Hampton. *Ghost Soldiers: The Epic Account of World War II's Greatest Rescue Mission*. New York: Knopf Doubleday, 2002.

Simmons, Edwin. *Frozen Chosin: U.S. Marines at the Changjin Reservoir*. New York: St. John's Press, 2018.

Smith, Robert Ross. *Triumph in the Philippines*. Washington, DC: Center of Military History, United States Army, 1993.

———. *The War in the Pacific: The Approach to the Philippines*. Washington, DC: Center of Military History, United States Army, 1953.

Smith, Robert. *MacArthur in Korea: The Naked Emperor*. New York: Simon & Schuster, 1982.

"The Solomon Islands Campaign: Guadalcanal." National World War II Museum. July 10, article on museum's website, https://nationalww2museum.org/war/articles/solomon-islands-campaign-guadalcanal.

Soutron LMS. "Search," February 4, 1941. www.marshallfoundation.org/library/digital-archive/to-general-douglas-macarthur-radio-no-1024.

Stockwin, Harvey. "MacArthur's Audacious Landing at Inchon Astounded Everyone—except Mao." *Japan Times*. September 21, 2000. www.japantimes.co.jp/opinion/2000/09/21/commentary/world-commentary/macarthurs-audacious-landing-at-inchon-astounded-everyone-except-mao.

Supreme Commander for the Allied Powers and Douglas MacArthur. *Reports of General MacArthur: The Campaigns of MacArthur in the Pacific*. Vol. 1. Washington, DC: United States Army, 1966.

Curtin, John. "The Task Ahead." John Curtin Prime Ministerial Library. December 27, 1941. http://john.curtin.edu.au/pmportal/text/00468.html.

Truman, Harry S. *Memoirs by Harry S Truman*. Vol. 2: *Years of Trial and Hope*. New York: Doubleday, 1956.

Tucker, Spencer C., and Paul G. Pierpaoli Jr. *The Encyclopedia of the Korean War: A Political, Social, and Military History*. 2nd ed. Santa Barbara, CA: ABC-CLIO, 2010.

"U.S. Senate: Constitutional Crisis Averted." U.S. Senate. www.senate.gov/artandhistory/history/minute/Constitutional_Crisis_Averted.htm (accessed May 20, 2022).

U.S. Senate Committee on Armed Services. *Military Situation in the Far East: Hearings before the Committee on Armed Services and the Committee on Foreign Relations, United States Senate, Eighty-Second Congress, First Session, to Conduct an Inquiry into the Military Situation in the Far East and the Facts Surrounding the Relief of General of the Army MacArthur from His Assignments in That Area.* Washington, DC: Government Printing Office, 1951.

U.S. War Department. *Handbook on Japanese Military Forces.* 1944. Reprint, Baton Rouge: Louisiana State University Press, 1995.

Wolk, Herman. "The Genius of George Kenney." *Air Force Magazine.* June 28, 2008. www.airforcemag.com/article/0402kenney.

Wright, Derrick. *Tarawa 1943: The Turning of the Tide.* Oxford, UK: Osprey Publishing, 2000.

Zhihua, Shen. "Revisiting Stalin's and Mao's Motivations in the Korean War." Wilson Center. June 22, 2022. www.wilsoncenter.org/blog-post/revisiting-stalins-and-maos-motivations-korean-war.

INDEX

ABOUT THE AUTHOR

James Ellman holds a bachelor's degree in history and economics from Tufts University and an MBA from Harvard. He is the author of several books, including *Hitler's Great Gamble: A New Look at German Strategy, Operation Barbarossa, and the Axis Defeat in World War II* (Stackpole, 2019). He lives in Hawaii.